Constraining Development

Anthem IGLP Rethinking Global Law and Policy Series

In today's world, poverty, conflict, injustice and inequality are also legal and institutional regimes. The Anthem IGLP Rethinking Global Law and Policy Series explores the ways in which they are reproduced and what might be done in response. The series seeks contributions mapping the levers of global political, economic and legal authority, and which bring new and critical perspectives to international legal research and policy. We aim to encourage innovative approaches to global policy in the face of a legal and institutional architecture manifestly ill-equipped to address our most urgent global challenges. The series is particularly interested in contributions which highlight voices from and issues of concern to the Global South. Proposals which cross disciplinary lines and draw upon heterodox intellectual and political traditions are encouraged.

This series is undertaken by Anthem in collaboration with Harvard's Institute for Global Law and Policy.

Series Editor
David Kennedy,
Harvard Law School, USA

Editorial Board
The editorial board is comprised of members of the Academic/Advisory Councils of IGLP.

Constraining Development

The Shrinking of Policy Space in the International Trade Regime

Rachel Denae Thrasher

ANTHEM PRESS

Anthem Press
An imprint of Wimbledon Publishing Company
www.anthempress.com

This edition first published in UK and USA 2026
by ANTHEM PRESS
75–76 Blackfriars Road, London SE1 8HA, UK
or PO Box 9779, London SW19 7ZG, UK
and
244 Madison Ave #116, New York, NY 10016, USA

First published in the UK and USA by Anthem Press in 2021

British Library Cataloguing-in-Publication Data
A catalogue record for this book is available from the British Library.

Library of Congress Control Number: 2025938726

ISBN-13: 978-1-83999-649-8 (Pbk)
ISBN-10: 1-83999-649-8 (Pbk)

Cover image: By Yavuz Sariyildiz/Shutterstock.com

This title is also available as an eBook.

CONTENTS

Acknowledgments   vii

List of Abbreviations   ix

1. Constraining Policy Space: How Global Trade Rules Conflict with National Development Goals   1

2. Modern Trade Agreements, Industrial Policy and Development Sovereignty   11

3. Trade-Related Aspects of Intellectual Property, Investment Rules and Access to Medicines   41

4. Land Grabs, Land Governance and International Investment Commitments   61

5. Capital Flow Regulation and Trade Agreements: An Empirical Investigation   83

6. The Emerging Role of International Investment Agreements in Sovereign Debt Restructuring   103

7. Trade and Investment Policy for Climate Change and the Energy Transition   125

8. Conclusion: A Way Forward   145

References   155

Index   179

ACKNOWLEDGMENTS

A debt of gratitude is owed to Kevin P. Gallagher, who provided years of oversight and encouragement for this research. And thank you Stephen, Mom, Dad, Marlee, Hazel and Lucy for your patience and support.

I also want to thank Jeronim Capaldo, Dario Bevilacqua, Sarah Sklar, and Kevin P. Gallagher, who coauthored earlier versions of the some of these ideas in the following journals and publications:

Thrasher, Rachel D., and Kevin Gallagher. "21st Century Trade Agreement: Implications for Development Sovereignty." *Denver Journal of International Law and Policy* 38, no. 2 (2010): 313–50.

Thrasher, Rachel, Dario Bevilaqua and Jeronim Capaldo. "Trade Agreements and the Land: Investment Agreements and Their Potential Impacts on Land Governance." Global Development and Environment Institute Background Paper, 2015.

Thrasher, Rachel D., and Kevin P. Gallagher. "Mission Creep: The Emerging Role of International Investment Agreements in Sovereign Debt Restructuring." *Journal of Globalization and Development* 6, no. 2 (2016): 257–85.

Gallagher, Kevin P., Sarah Sklar and Rachel D. Thrasher. "Quantifying the Policy Space for Regulating Capital Flows in Trade and Investment Treaties." A G-24 Working Paper, April 2019.

ABBREVIATIONS

AfCFTA	African Continental Free Trade Agreement
BIT	Bilateral Investment Treaty
CETA	Comprehensive Economic Trade Agreement (Canada–EU)
CPTPP	Comprehensive and Progressive Trans-Pacific Partnership
CRTA	WTO's Committee on Regional Trade Agreements
ECT	Energy Charter Treaty
EFTA	European Free Trade Association
FDI	foreign direct investment
FET	fair and equitable treatment
FIT	feed-in tariff
FTA	free trade agreement
GATS	General Agreement on Trade in Services
GATT	General Agreement on Tariffs and Trade
GDP	gross domestic product
ICSID	International Centre for the Settlement of Investment Disputes
IIA	international investment agreement
IMF	International Monetary Fund
IP	intellectual property
ISDS	investor–state dispute settlement
KORUS	Korea–United States Free Trade Agreement
LDC	least developed country
MERCOSUR	Common Market for the Southern Cone
MFN	most-favored nation
MNC	multi-national corporation
NAFTA	North American Free Trade Agreement
RCEP	Regional Comprehensive Economic Partnership
SADC	Southern African Development Community
SCM Agreement	Agreement on Subsidies and Countervailing Measures

SDR	sovereign debt restructuring
TRIMs Agreement	Agreement on Trade-Related Investment Measures
TRIPS Agreement	Agreement on Trade-Related Aspects of Intellectual Property Rights
USMCA	United States–Mexico–Canada Agreement
WTO	World Trade Organization

Chapter 1

CONSTRAINING POLICY SPACE: HOW GLOBAL TRADE RULES CONFLICT WITH NATIONAL DEVELOPMENT GOALS

President Biden has ambitious plans for the US economy. Biden's "Made in America" plan aims to pour public investment into manufacturing, as well as research and development, in order to respond to domestic concerns about unfair global competition and off-shoring US jobs. These policies, however, inasmuch as they prioritize US economic interests over competing interests in other countries, are likely to run afoul of international treaty commitments made over the past 25 years. In this, Biden will be in good company—joining a community of world leaders attempting to meet the needs of their domestic constituents within the constraints of the global trading system.

There is clearly an unresolved tension between the network of rules that make up the global trading system and the individual members of that system. The system of global trade is made up of one overarching set of multilateral trade agreements, more than 300 preferential free trade agreements and almost 3,000 bilateral investment treaties. The primary rationale for these trade and investment agreements is to establish a stable regulatory environment in which protectionist national interests are neutralized in favor of a more optimal distribution of global wealth.[1] They have the ostensibly unbiased role of paving the way for global commerce so that economic growth takes place as quickly and efficiently as possible. National governments, on the other hand, must constantly respond to changing circumstances through new laws and regulations. They aim at increasing economic diversification and development, maintaining financial stability and fiscal solvency, protecting vulnerable populations, providing affordable access to medicines, and responding quickly and agilely to domestic and global crises.

---

1 Rodrik, "What Do Trade Agreements Really Do?"

Troubling trends in treaty-making and international jurisprudence, however, suggest that global rules increasingly present obstacles to national governments pursuing these aims. While the original project of liberalizing international trade was focused on lowering tariffs and nontariff border measures among as many nations as possible, while allowing them to regulate as they like,[2] treaty texts since the mid-1990s have encroached more and more on domestic policymaking. As this volume highlights, this encroachment takes place in industrial and investment policy, capital flow management and debt policy, as well as health and climate policy.

Moreover a growing number of international legal cases have demonstrated that these treaties have teeth. Members of the World Trade Organization (WTO) have brought complaints against fellow members over a wide variety of public policy measures. The dispute settlement arm has even proven capable of striking down certain policies aimed at facilitating a transition to renewable energy.[3] Outside of the WTO, private investors have challenged countries attempting to address debt, public health and climate crises. Both Argentina and Greece faced investor suits after restructuring their unsustainable public debt burden.[4] Pharmaceutical giant, Eli Lilly, challenged Canada's constraints on patent protection and, though unsuccessful, laid the groundwork for future arbitration claims based on intellectual property law.[5] Canada's attempt to transition from fossil fuels to renewable energy has faced a complaint by Westmoreland, a coal company with corporate offices in the United States.[6]

The chapters in this volume demonstrate, over a wide variety of issues and themes, that entering into broader and deeper trade agreements is not the best way to pursue development. Modern trade and investment agreements keep national governments from making and maintaining the policies they need to promote economic growth, financial stability, debt sustainability, public health and environmental protection. In response to that reality, new trade and investment treaties should take a step back from their interference with domestic regulatory sovereignty, and focus on narrower, shallower economic integration at a global level.

---

2 Rodrik, *The Globalization Paradox*, 75.

3 *Canada—Certain Measures Affecting the Renewable Energy Generation Sector*, wto.org; *India— Certain Measure Relating to Solar Cells and Solar Modules*, wto.org; *United States—Certain Measures Relating to the Renewable Energy Sector*, wto.org.

4 Abaclat and others v. The Argentine Republic—Decision on Jurisdiction and Admissibility, www.italaw.com.

5 Baker and Geddes, "The Incredible Shrinking Victory."

6 Westmoreland Mining Holdings LLC v. Government of Canada—Canada's Statement of Defense, www.italaw.com.

The Promise and Limits of Free Trade

Twentieth-century economic theory laid the foundation for most free trade agreements in effect today. According to accepted models of comparative advantage and gains from trade, lowering barriers to international trade is the most effective engine for economic growth and, as a result, human development. In 1947, the parties to the General Agreement on Tariffs and Trade (GATT), acknowledged that trade and economic activity "should be conducted with a view to raising the standards of living, ensuring full employment and a large and steadily growing volume of real income and effective demand," among other goals.[7] As a result they agreed to contribute to these goals by reducing tariffs and nontariff barriers and eliminating "discriminatory treatment in international commerce."[8]

The GATT, as the name suggests, focused on achieving these goals through successive rounds of tariff negotiations, each of which involved more countries and more tariff lines of traded goods. Its primary institutional role was to provide a forum for negotiation, trade policy accountability and dispute settlement. Over 40 years of negotiations, the process increased in complexity due to a growing diversity among GATT parties and the sheer scope of tariff lines covered under the agreement. Nevertheless, each negotiating round helped countries to dip further in their bound tariff rates—the upper limits of the duties they imposed on imported goods—and by 1988 there was very little room to move in terms of decreasing tariffs. Contemporaneously, the volume of world trade boomed, while the percentage of people living in poverty and certain measures of inequality had substantially decreased.[9] Of course not all of those outcomes can be attributed only to the new global trade rules, but by most measures, the global trade integration made possible by the GATT was a huge success.

In 1988, the historic Uruguay Round began, with an aggressive agenda to expand international trade rules into new trade-related areas. In addition to removing the remainder of tariffs and quotas on goods, developed countries sought an agreement that would expand market access in the fastest growing areas of the global economy: services and foreign investment. It went further as well, establishing new disciplines in technical, sanitary and phytosanitary regulations and intellectual property standards. In the end, newly baptized WTO members (a change from the GATT Contracting Parties) agreed to

---

7 "General Agreement on Tariffs and Trade (GATT)," preamble.
8 "General Agreement on Tariffs and Trade (GATT)," preamble.
9 Trebilcock, Howse and Eliason, *The Regulation of International Trade*; Harrison, McLaren, and McMillan, *Recent Perspectives on Trade and Inequality*; Kremer and Maskin, "Globalization and Inequality."

a single undertaking that would oversee all these areas and provide a more enforceable dispute settlement system to boot. Unlike the established argument in defense of free trade, as it has been narrowly construed—lowering tariff barriers and eliminating other border measures—these new rules had virtually no foundation in economic theory.[10] As some economists have pointed out, if the original trade rules were aimed at undermining the perverse incentives created by domestic protectionist interests, it seems that this new integration traded one set of private interests for another.[11]

In the midst of the Uruguay Round negotiations, the world's first two modern free trade agreements were born. Beginning with the Canada–United States Free Trade Agreement in 1988 and culminating in the North American Free Trade Agreement (NAFTA), the United States put in place a sort of first draft of US foreign trade policy going forward. These treaties became the template that was drafted, re-drafted and adopted in various forms all over the world in the following two and a half decades. Like many of its successors, NAFTA ratcheted up commitments in trade in services, investment and intellectual property. It put greater barriers in place to government procurement practices and generally demanded deeper regulatory integration between treaty parties.

This is, in one way, necessary. Under Article XXIV of the GATT (incorporated into the WTO), countries are narrowly permitted to engage in bilateral and regional (economic) integration so long as the result is to "substantially liberalize all trade."[12] Only treaties that go *further* than the multilateral commitments to liberalize trade comply with those rules. The drafters of the GATT envisioned Article XXIV as a way to facilitate further removal of tariff barriers worldwide. As such, the NAFTA represented a new kind of agreement—one with extensive commitments in all services sectors (article 1201), including telecommunications (article 1301) and financial services (article 1401), protection for foreign investments in all sectors (article 1101), and strict protection for intellectual property rights (article 1701). The fundamental WTO standards of nondiscriminatory treatment in trade were incorporated and expanded such that treaty parties committed to abstain from many of the investment measures they historically had deployed for domestic industrial development.

NAFTA and other modern treaties pay homage to the "truths" of market freedom—that the economic system does best on its own, without the intervention of government policymakers and that expanded trade is a good proxy for economic development. And this approach seemed to work fine for

---

10 Rodrik, "The Global Governance of Trade as If Development Really Mattered."
11 Rodrik, "What Do Trade Agreements Really Do?"
12 "General Agreement on Tariffs and Trade (GATT)," XXIV.

a time. There were wild successes in East Asia where neoliberal champions pointed to the rapid development of Taiwan and South Korea as an indicator of the success of the free market. Chile and Argentina were the poster children for trade liberalization in South America, and Mexico registered rapid industrial growth (at least in certain sectors) on the heels of NAFTA.

Today, however, those stories ring hollow.

Scholars have pointed out that the emerging economies in East Asia, far from employing a hands-off approach to governance, actively selected industries as winners in the new economy.[13] Chile was likewise careful in its liberalization, retaining a tax on short-term capital inflows and protecting the country when the financial crisis of 2008 began to spread in East Asia.[14] Argentina, by the late 1990s, began to suffer financial instability, rapid inflation, an inability to service public debt and soaring unemployment. By contrast, the Chinese economy, long criticized for its central government planning, began to take off during the 1980s. Chinese economic growth in the 1990s and early 2000s reached unprecedented levels, and that growth, along with targeted reforms, contributed to decreasing the number of people in poverty from 250 million to 29 million.[15]

Furthermore, deep trade integration has coincided with rapid increases in global inequality.[16] The entrenched protectionist interests that existed at the end of World War II and during the drafting of the GATT have given way to the interests of multinational corporations (MNCs). MNCs especially benefit from strict investor and intellectual property protection, fewer regulations and the free flow of capital. The 2008 financial crisis also exposed economic vulnerability to fluctuations in global capital flows. Although that crash could have offered insight into the fragility of the financial system and led to innovative regulatory mechanisms to keep inequality in check, instead MNCs have continued their upward movement toward holding an increasing percentage of the global wealth.[17] As these giant proponents of broad and deep globalization exert influence on their home governments, trade agreements begin to reflect their interests.[18]

---

13 Kumar and Gallagher, "Relevance of 'Policy Space' for Development: Implications for Multilateral Trade Negotiations."

14 Stiglitz, *Globalization and Its Discontents*.

15 Fan, Zhang and Zhang, "Reforms, Investment, and Poverty in Rural China."

16 Zucman, "Global Wealth Inequality"; Harrison, McLaren and McMillan, *Recent Perspectives on Trade and Inequality*; Kremer and Maskin, "Globalization and Inequality."

17 Gallagher and Kozul-Wright, "A New Multilateralism for Shared Prosperity: Geneva Principles for a Global Green New Deal."

18 Sell, "TRIPs Was Never Enough"; Devereaux, Lawrence and Watkins, *Case Studies in US Trade Negotiation, Volume 1*.

These interests are reflected in strict rules constraining industrial policy—especially policies aimed at building up new domestic industries, transferring state-of-the-art technology and creating backward and forward linkages into the economy. They are reflected in expansive protections for foreign investors and their capital flows, prohibiting capital flow management measures, preserving their rights to set up shop wherever they like and giving them a private right of action against states for interfering with the value of their investment. They are reflected in the extended patent terms, data exclusivity and stringent enforcement of their intellectual property rights.

Even in new areas of near global consensus, treaty rules continue to reflect the interests of MNCs through the solutions to collective problems. Newer treaties have begun to acknowledge the real, immediate and long-term impacts of our changing climate, for example. But they have focused on liberalizing and expanding trade in a "green" economy instead of allowing countries to forge long-term solutions in climate change adaptation and mitigation.

As international trade and investment rules reflect more and more the interests of the global private sector, however, there is an increasingly palpable tension between the global rules and domestic policymaking goals. Moreover, just as happens whenever economic livelihoods are threatened, governments, urged on by their (non-MNC) constituents, often turn inward, preferring to protect domestic interests at all costs. This has manifested in various concrete ways in the recent past. Countries have demonstrated a reluctance to engage in international fora, including investor–state dispute settlement institutions, bilateral investment treaties and even the WTO.[19] Some even attribute the United Kingdom's referendum to withdraw from the European Union, the United States' trade war with China, and nationalist movements worldwide to voters' willingness to hunker down and protect their own interests, whatever the (international) costs.

Where domestic concerns bump up against international ones, history suggests that domestic priorities will prevail in the long-run.[20] And the current framework on international trade and investment rules does not mesh well with the international political climate. So how do we respond? The following chapters make the case that perhaps the best way forward is to take a step back.

Dani Rodrik, who articulated the "trilemma" of global integration, points out the tension between three key features of the global economy: hyperglobalization (fully free trade in goods and services, free flow of capital, etc.), national sovereignty and democracy. The nature of the trilemma is that you can pick two, but not have all three at once.[21] We can give up

---

19 Tucker, *Judge Knot*; Tucker, "RIP, World Trade Organization?"
20 Rodrik, *Straight Talk on Trade*; Rodrik, *The Globalization Paradox*.
21 Rodrik, *The Globalization Paradox*.

national sovereignty in favor of a global democratic government. We can give up on democratic representation in favor of nation states in a hyperglobalized society. Or we can give up hyperglobalization in favor of democratic national governments. Since people tend to associate more strongly with their national identity than even their local or familial ties, and since global democracy would likely be overwhelmed with efficiency and efficacy challenges, the third option is the most pragmatic and appealing. While there are certainly some issues that require global cooperation and concurrence—a global pandemic or climate crisis, for example—global governance mechanisms may not be the most effective way to address those issues.

Instead, I argue that the tension between global rules and national policies can be resolved through narrower and shallower integration. New agreements can be forged but should take place at the multilateral level. Disputes should remain firmly in the domain of domestic courts or state-to-state fora. And challenges requiring collective action should focus on capacity building to face those challenges in the short and long terms.

Many scholars have studied and written on the importance of policy space—the flexibility a government retains to put in place laws and regulations that benefit its constituents.[22] There exists a corresponding weight of literature that discusses how trade rules constrain that policy space.[23] This volume brings together much of that literature in one place to highlight the scope of the challenges facing national governments today.

Going Forward

In the following pages, I begin by examining the extent to which the emerging world trade regime leaves nations the policy space to deploy effective industrial policy for long-run diversification and development, and the extent to which

---

22 Gallagher, "Globalization and the Nation-State: Reasserting Policy Autonomy of Development"; Stiglitz, "Development Policies in a World of Globalization"; Lall, "Rethinking Industrial Strategy: The Role of the State in the Face of Globalization"; Wade, "What Strategies Are Viable for Developing Countries Today? The World Trade Organization and the Shrinking of 'Development Space.'"

23 Thrasher and Gallagher, "21st Century Trade Agreements"; Thrasher and Gallagher, "Defending Development Sovereignty: The Case for Industrial Policy and Financial Regulation in the Trading Regime"; Thrasher and Gallagher, "Mission Creep: The Emerging Role of International Investment Agreements in Sovereign Debt Restructuring"; Gallagher, Sklar and Thrasher, "Quantifying the Policy Space for Regulating Capital Flows in Trade and Investment Treaties: A G24 Working Paper"; Thrasher, "Policy Space for Jobs and Clean Energy: Trade, Investment Rules and Local Content Requirements in Renewable Energy Policies."

there is a convergence of such policy space under global and regional trade regimes (Chapter 2). Chapter 2 compares and contrasts rules under the WTO, recent trade agreements negotiated by the European Union and the United States, and trade agreements between and among developing countries (South–South agreements). In particular, it highlights the depth of existing integration in current trade and investment agreements, and demonstrates how these commitments, especially in US and EU agreements, constrain the industrial policy toolkit for development.

In addition to constraining industrial policies, today's trade and investment commitments also have impacts on intellectual property policies (Chapter 3). The COVID-19 pandemic has made it painfully obvious that global cooperation is needed to make diagnostic and protective equipment, treatment and vaccines more readily available. Beyond simple trade in those goods, however, global cooperation should stretch into the area of sharing of essential knowledge. Chapter 3 explores the nexus between intellectual property commitments and how they impact access to medicines. The evidence shows that, just as in other contexts, the trend in these treaties is to limit the kinds of policies that countries can put in place to protect and increase medicine access. Furthermore, it points to the importance of preserving policy space in drafting treaties through fewer binding commitments in intellectual property rules and more deference to national institutions in crafting these laws.

Chapter 4 highlights the particular role that international investment commitments have played in land ownership policies and land governance practices, especially in countries that have historically specialized in agriculture and extractive industries. A common phenomenon impacting land governance occurs when state-owned corporations and private investors have purchased or (where land is not sale-able) acquired long-term leases on large swathes of foreign land for food and biofuel production. Chapter 4 examines the extent to which investment treaties have facilitated large-scale land purchases, undermining policy space for health and environmental protection, as well as social and labor rights. It highlights both the importance of policy flexibility for host countries in their land governance, and deference to host state institutions in resolving conflicts over its own land.

In addition to land governance, public health and industrial development policies, two decades of tandem financial crises have unveiled the importance of regulating volatile capital flows to prevent financial instability (Chapter 5). Many scholars, including researchers at the International Monetary Fund (IMF), have noted that modern trade and investment treaties restrict the ability of nations to respond adequately to those concerns. Chapter 5 quantifies the variation across almost 300 trade and investment treaties with respect to their level of policy space for capital flow management measures.

It then demonstrates that trends in preferential trade agreements exacerbate the challenges that countries face in a financial crisis, lending credence to the proposal to push back toward narrower and shallower trade agreements. It also reveals yet another context in which global cooperation to build capacity, rather than punitive trade remedies, for low-income countries would provide financial stability at a global level.

Chapter 6 dives deeper into some of the outcomes related to financial instability. One common outcome to afflict low- and middle-income countries is an overwhelming increase in their public debt burdens. When this debt burden becomes too large, countries seek to restructure that debt by negotiating with their creditors to extend the maturity on their debt or decrease the value of the debt by some percentage. Currently, there is no global regime for sovereign debt restructuring. However, in the wake of the 2008 financial crisis, international investment agreements have begun to expand their reach into the realm of public debt. In so doing, these treaties have enabled private investors to attempt to recoup the full value of their sovereign debt in order to circumvent the debt restructurings in Argentina and Greece. Chapter 6 argues that existing legal norms governing sovereign debt should leave room for policy experimentation. Furthermore, it proposes that international investment agreements (IIAs) step back from the realm of overseeing sovereign debt management, keeping both oversight and dispute settlement at the national level.

Climate change arguably poses the greatest global challenge we have ever faced. In order to save lives in both the short and long terms, we need large-scale collective action and cooperation (Chapter 7). Nevertheless, in the face of such an insurmountable challenge, countries must still respond to needs in their domestic communities—jobs, economic growth, health care, education and more. To address this challenge, countries have returned to the use of certain industrial policies to meet both the short-term (jobs) and the long-term (climate change mitigation) needs of their constituents. In particular, countries have used various green industrial policies to link foreign capital to the development of domestic renewable energy sectors. These policies can create backward and forward linkages in their economies and build up infant industries for economic diversification. However, as Chapter 7 demonstrates, trade and investment treaties and international disputes have made it more difficult for countries to address climate change. Instead, future treaties should, once more, make space for policy experimentation and provide avenues for capacity building as we collectively address the climate crisis.

In the final section, I argue that we need a new approach to trade and investment treaty-making worldwide. While liberalizing international trade has been the most effective engine for economic growth in the twentieth century, various areas of human development have suffered, and troubling trends in global political economy suggests that we need to change our strategy. To address these shortcomings, we must take a step back from the regime's foray into domestic regulatory sovereignty. Instead of attempting to micromanage each potential policy that might get in the way of international commerce, new treaties should be narrower and shallower—playing the more restrained role of smoothing out the bumps in international commerce, while allowing countries to regulate in their own interests. This strategy has three essential components: reviving multilateralism, eliminating private investor–state disputes, and global cooperation through capacity building. Through these mechanisms, trade and investment treaties can stop constraining development and begin to live into their stated goals of improved standards of living, economic growth and sustainability.

Chapter 2

MODERN TRADE AGREEMENTS, INDUSTRIAL POLICY AND DEVELOPMENT SOVEREIGNTY

The United States renegotiated its accord with Mexico and Canada, redubbed the United States–Mexico–Canada Agreement (USMCA) in December 2019. Dissatisfied with the trade adjustment resulting from competition in tradeable sectors worldwide, the United States Trade Representative demanded new protections for regional automotive and other industrial manufacturers, including stricter rules of origin and labor protection rules. The ultimate goal was to rebuild the United States' manufacturing sector and protect its vulnerable people from the repeated ravages of trade liberalization. The agreement offers similar protections to small and medium enterprises, as well as the agricultural industry. The message is clear: the United States is interested in protecting its manufacturing sector, and is taking steps to make it so that treaties play a role in protecting and supporting those sectors.

Interest in these kinds of economic-restructuring policies is rising all over the world and is not new. As evidenced by the rhetoric surrounding US trade relations, and the demand in the United Kingdom to exit from the European Union, even developed countries are seeking ways to restructure their economies and meet the needs of those sectors that have lost out to global competition under neoliberalism. Although industrial policies, as they are commonly called, are usually associated with countries in earlier stages of development, overt attempts by highly industrialized nations offer yet more evidence that most countries are only interested in free trade inasmuch as it serves the interests of their voting constituents.[1]

Trade and industrial policy together are broadly defined as those measures that countries put in place to adjust the balance of trade (imports and exports) and/or the industrial structure of their economies. They vary widely, including

---

1 Even today, developed countries point to essentially mercantilist rationales to support certain levels of domestic protectionism. Keynes and Bown, "What's in the New EU-UK Trade Deal? Brexperts Explain."

measures that fund and support public education, subsidies supporting specific types of economic activity and taxes discouraging other types. They also include investment incentives offered in specific sectors, tariffs and export taxes, and even varying levels of protection for intellectual property rights. Ideally, the countries put in place these measures to increase welfare among their constituents. In most cases, countries are seeking the elusive idea of *development*.

Development is the long-run process of transforming an economy from concentrated assets based on primary products to a diverse set of assets based on knowledge.[2] Development provides not only a more diversified economy but also a deepening such that the economy develops backward and forward linkages and domestic firms increase in productivity.[3] It is often associated with higher incomes, better public health and education indicators, and even stronger democratic institutions.

Nevertheless, the deep economic integration, as embodied in current global trade and investment commitments, keeps countries from being able to pursue that development. The following pages will demonstrate that policy limitations under the shallower WTO rules, and the narrower integration present in many South–South trade agreements are far less constraining (though not nonexistent). Moreover, the trends in new trade and investment treaty commitments, especially those driven by the Unites States and the European Union have an increasingly constraining impact on development policy.

Neoclassical Trade Theory and Market Failures

Neoclassical trade theory demonstrates that liberalizing trade has the potential to promote this deep and diversified development. Beginning with David Ricardo, the theory shows that when each country produces and exports in those industries where it has a comparative advantage, the whole world benefits.[4] Moreover, countries should choose to focus on sectors that utilize their most abundant factors of production—land, labor or capital.[5] Businesses may also move across borders to gain access to local demand for goods and services. In so doing they may offer new employment and training opportunities, education and even the introduction of new technology from foreign firms.[6] Trade adjustment in some sectors will, of course, be necessary,

---

2 Thrasher and Gallagher, "21st Century Trade Agreements."
3 Krugman, *Development, Geography and Economic Theory*; Amsden, *The Rise of "The Rest."*
4 Ricardo, *On the Principles of Political Economy, and Taxation.*
5 Ohlin, *Interregional and International Trade.*
6 Jayaraman and Singh, "Foreign Direct Investment and Employment Creation in Pacific Island Countries."

but the gains from trade accruing to winning sectors freed to exploit their comparative advantages can compensate the so-called losers of trade liberalization. Moreover, if the net gains from trade are positive there are more funds available to stimulate growth and protect the environment. In an ideal world then, free trade could indeed promote development.

The theory, however, suffers from some shortcomings. It assumes perfect competition and constant, readily available technology, factors of production which move freely between industries and an unchanging mix of goods and services in global markets.[7] In other words, this model assumes static, rather than dynamic, economic growth, and that the market does not fail to efficiently distribute the world's goods and wealth.[8] Unfortunately, we live in a world in which economic gains are often elusive for those countries most in need of them.[9] Developing countries that only have a comparative advantage in a single commodity experience price volatility and long-run price declines relative to industrial goods. Static comparative advantages of this sort have exacerbated inequality and expanded into a growing technology gap between rich and poor countries.[10]

Moreover, the global economy is rife with so-called market failures.[11] Market failures refer to a myriad of situations in which markets fail to efficiently distribute wealth and resources around the globe. Economists commonly measure efficiency by whether there is an overall amount of wealth increase such that the winners can compensate the losers. For developing countries, dynamic growth and economic diversification—development by this definition—demands that they create whole new industries and establish backward and forward linkages to markets for inputs, labor, transportation and final products.[12] Yet markets on their own often fail to coordinate these efforts. In some cases, the market structure itself, defined by increasing returns to scale or the immobility of certain factors of production, creates barriers to new companies entering and competing with existing firms. Markets also fail to provide socially optimal amounts of information to producers and consumers. Without the right amount of information, producers and consumers will fail to invest in human capital formation, both in the form of public education and

7 Tucker, "Mind-Maps for Market Failure, Perfect Competition, and Government Failure."
8 Caves, Jones and Frankel, *World Trade and Payments.*
9 Ackerman and Gallagher, "The Shrinking Gains from Global Trade Liberalization in Computable General Equilibrium Models."
10 Lucas, "On the Mechanics of Economic Development"; Chang, *Bad Samaritans.*
11 Tucker, "Mind-Maps for Market Failure, Perfect Competition, and Government Failure."
12 Kumar and Gallagher, "Relevance of 'Policy Space' for Development: Implications for Multilateral Trade Negotiations."

workforce training. At the same time, they will overproduce and overconsume products that are socially or environmentally harmful.[13]

Fortunately, we have alternative models. Countries like South Korea and China, which deployed comprehensive industrial and trade policies resulted in high-tech, high-growth industrialization. All of the emerging markets, indeed even today's developed countries, have engaged in some strategic way with industrial policy to change their development trajectory (see Table 2.1).[14] Historically, countries engaged in large-scale industrial planning efforts and explicit infant industry protection. More recently, however, countries have attempted to improve market coordination by introducing support for domestic firms and regulation for foreign firms. These measures include requirements that foreign companies use local inputs in production or transfer technological advancements to local producers.[15] To produce dynamic growth trajectories, countries have encouraged (and sometimes required) foreign firms to form joint ventures with domestic companies, in addition to technology transfer rules. Industrial policies like these go hand in hand with education reform, public research and development and increased tariff protection to support domestic firms until they can compete at the global technological frontier.[16]

In sum, where markets do not produce a socially optimal amount of a particular good, governments have stepped in to provide incentives and support (toward positive externalities) and regulation or taxation (to mitigate negative ones).[17] Table 2.1 lays out an illustrative list of trade and industrial policies that countries have deployed, along with the market failure they aim to correct.

In identifying these potential policy tools, it is important to acknowledge that not all policy implementation is created equal. While there is a strong theoretical justification for proactive government policy to address market failures, successful countries had to combine these policy tools with effective political economy. Countries like South Korea, China and Taiwan experienced

---

13 Tucker, "Mind-Maps for Market Failure, Perfect Competition, and Government Failure"; Kumar and Gallagher, "Relevance of 'Policy Space' for Development: Implications for Multilateral Trade Negotiations."

14 Thrasher and Gallagher, "21st Century Trade Agreements"; Kumar and Gallagher, "Relevance of 'Policy Space' for Development: Implications for Multilateral Trade Negotiations"; Chang, *Bad Samaritans*.

15 Nikièma, "Performance Requirements in Investment Treaties"; Amsden, *The Rise of "The Rest."*

16 Murphy, Shleifer and Vishny, "Industrialization and the Big Push"; Weiss, "Export Growth and Industrial Policy: Lessons from the East Asian Miracle Experience."

17 Tucker, "Mind-Maps for Market Failure, Perfect Competition, and Government Failure."

Table 2.1. Tools for correcting market failures

Policy Instrument	Targeted Market Failure
Tariff sequencing Quantitative restrictions Selective liberalization	Static growth trajectory/Coordination failures: Industrial diversification
Export subsidies Technology transfer and local content requirements Joint venture requirements Patent protection Compulsory licensing	Coordination failures: Lack of new innovation support Industrial diversification
Tax breaks and/or industrial subsidies Subsidized credit for entrepreneurship Administrative and marketing support	Information asymmetry: Lack of new innovation support Industrial diversification
Local hiring and training requirements Public education reform Subsidized research and development	Information asymmetry: Lack of human capital formation Lack of new innovation support
Environmental regulations Labor protections	Information asymmetry: Over production/consumption in socially and environmentally harmful activities

Source: Tucker, "Mind-Maps for Market Failure, Perfect Competition, and Government Failure"; Kumar and Gallagher, "Relevance of 'Policy Space' for Development: Implications for Multilateral Trade Negotiations."

remarkable growth in the latter half of the 20th century, while Indonesia, Nigeria and Brazil lagged behind. Experts point out that effective industrial policy requires a state that is embedded in the private sector while maintaining autonomy from the elite interests seeking rents.[18] In order for these relationships to work, however, industrial policy has to be coupled with a good deal of discipline and accountability for both private actors and the state.[19]

Nevertheless, the failures of certain governments to successfully implement trade and industrial policies should not dictate whether countries are *able* to experiment with policies to promote development. Indeed the successes of the lucky few suggest we should encourage policy experimentation for the rest. At the same time, many trade and industrial policies arguably conflict with the international trade rules, and for that reason, we must understand what those conflicts are and how they impact government decision-making.

---

18 Evans, *Embedded Autonomy: States & Industrial Transformation*.
19 Thrasher and Gallagher, "21st Century Trade Agreements."

Testing for Policy Space in the WTO and Beyond

Since the signing of the GATT in 1947, parties to the agreement have attempted to establish a baseline of liberalization for global trade in goods. As discussed in detail in the previous chapter, the WTO's "single undertaking" expanded that vision to cover trade in services, investment, intellectual property, and a host of other sub-issues related to trade, while countries have also clamored to sign bilateral and regional accords with even broader and deeper commitments.[20]

The most-favored nation (MFN) clause, requiring that WTO members treat all other members as their most-favored trade partner,[21] would seem to make the parallel development of bilateral and regional agreements moot. However, Article XXIV of the GATT, as well as Article V of the General Agreement on Trade in Services (GATS) make room for these agreements so long as they liberalize "substantially all" trade in goods and services.[22] By fully liberalizing trade between partners, proponents of the multilateral trading system hope that the agreements will act as building blocks toward multilateral free trade. The 1979 GATT decision on "differential and more favorable treatment" (also called the Enabling Clause) makes more room for lesser-developed countries to sign bilateral accords without demanding reciprocity or liberalization of substantially all trade, as Article XXIV requires.[23]

WTO oversight has met with very limited success, however. Of the more than 300 agreements notified to the Committee on Regional Trade Agreements (CRTA), not one has ever been found by consensus to be inconsistent with the terms of GATT Article XXIV or GATS Article V.[24] The same Committee, tasked with receiving and reviewing trade agreement notifications, as well as implementation reports, has been unable to adequately provide oversight due largely to countries' failure to submit said reports.[25]

Despite minimal oversight, most bilateral and regional agreements do exceed the WTO in both breadth and depth, the details of which follow. General trends,

---

20 World Trade Organization, "WTO Legal Texts"; Carpenter, "A Historical Perspective on Regionalism."
21 "General Agreement on Tariffs and Trade (GATT)," pt. I.
22 "General Agreement on Tariffs and Trade (GATT)," XXIV; World Trade Organization, "General Agreement on Trade in Services (GATS)," V.
23 GATT, "Enabling Clause."
24 Trebilcock, Howse and Eliason, *The Regulation of International Trade.*
25 Each regional trade agreement has an implementation period, by which date the parties must bring their treaty into full compliance with GATT Article XXIV, GATS Article V or the Enabling Clause. As of March 2019, 92 percent of implementation reports that were due had not been submitted. Committee on Regional Trade Agreements, "Regional Trade Agreements Subject to Implementation Reports."

however, indicate that treaties where the United States is a party tend to be among the broadest and deepest. Treaties with the European Union run along roughly two tracks: one comprehensive model for developed country trade partners, and a more flexible option for developing country parties. Treaties between developing country members (South–South trade agreements) are much more difficult to categorize due to the diversity of countries in that category. Nevertheless, the overarching goal—to preserve extra policy space while selectively liberalizing trade—remains a theme. Even in relatively comprehensive South–South trade agreements, the depth of coverage can act as much to protect developing economy trade partners from the outside as to liberalize within.

Goods trade policies

The global trade rules were initially created for the context of trade in goods. With these rules, countries sought after the relatively humble goal of lowering trade barriers between countries so that products could move more easily from place to place. In this way, less of the world's wealth would be captured by government agencies and administrations and more would go to the individuals engaged in creating more wealth. This was the liberal goal.

At the same time, when governments crafted the multilateral rules of the GATT, most were not willing to hand over their sovereign rights of policymaking, taxation and regulation so that the early rules struck a delicate balance between liberalizing trade and letting each party continue to do what it liked.[26] Indeed, the delegates of the Bretton Woods meetings proposed a third institution—the International Trade Organization, which would have governed global trade alongside the rebuilding, restructuring and finance work of the World Bank and IMF. The United States, however, rejected that idea as too tight a control on its domestic policy goals. In that context, we have the relatively skeletal rules of the GATT, set upon three pillars: MFN treatment, national treatment and the progressive elimination of tariffs. The MFN standard requires that all GATT parties treat all other parties as their most-favored trading partner (so that there is no distinction) with respect to trade (tariffs) and domestic policy (taxes, regulations, etc.). Narrow exceptions, such as the carve-out for preferential agreements (mentioned above), made room for existing trading arrangements and historical circumstances.

The national treatment standard is a much more precarious balance. Countries committed through it to treat imports no less favorably than they

---

26 Rodrik, *One Economics, Many Recipes: Globalization, Institutions and Economic Growth*; Rodrik, *The Globalization Paradox*.

treat "like" competitive or substitutable goods produced domestically. This rule hits closer to home as all countries have some policies in place designed to promote, build up and sometimes protect local sectors and industries. Much of the historical jurisprudence centers around whether locally distilled alcohol[27] or locally built automobiles[28] are really "like" the foreign imports and therefore must be subject to the same treatment.

The third pillar sets the stage for many of the other rules in the GATT—that imports must not be subject to tariffs greater than those listed in their GATT schedules.[29] Those schedules were then progressively updated as GATT parties negotiated down their tariff levels over time. As a corollary to the progressive elimination of tariffs, countries agreed to remove nontariff barriers (such as quotas and import licenses) and to tightly circumscribe their reliance on subsidies. To allow countries to respond to balance of payments crises resulting from a sudden influx of imports (or shortages of essential goods due to the exports of those goods), the GATT permits temporary quantitative restrictions on imports or exports. The rules are carefully crafted, however, so that those restrictions do not remain in place longer than necessary to address the immediate crisis.[30] Subsidies were permitted as long as they were not conditioned on export and did not explicitly discriminate against imported goods or target specific companies and sectors.[31] General exceptions were available for measures necessary to protect human, animal and plant life and health, or public morals, and those related to the conservation of exhaustible natural resources.[32]

Moreover, there are unilateral remedies available in the case where a country suspects foreign firms of engaging in anticompetitive behavior,[33] a GATT party of subsidizing those firms,[34] or when imports simply overwhelm the domestic market in unexpected ways.[35] In each case, country-parties may increase tariffs on affected goods to the extent necessary to correct for these market disruptions.

These three pillars of trade liberalization in the GATT have made their way into almost every bilateral, regional and mega-regional trade treaty

---

27 *Chile—Taxes on Alcoholic Beverages*, World Trade Organization.
28 *Indonesia—Certain Measures Affecting the Automobile Industry*, World Trade Organization.
29 "General Agreement on Tariffs and Trade (GATT)," pt. II.
30 *India—Quantitative Restrictions on Imports of Agricultural, Textile and Industrial Products*, World Trade Organization.
31 "Agreement on Subsidies and Countervailing Measures."
32 "General Agreement on Tariffs and Trade (GATT)," pt. XX.
33 "General Agreement on Tariffs and Trade (GATT)," VI.
34 "General Agreement on Tariffs and Trade (GATT)," VI.
35 "General Agreement on Tariffs and Trade (GATT)," XIX.

in force today. As new treaties have formed, the MFN standard has taken on new life. MFN provisions allow older treaties to potentially incorporate improved standards of treatment (e.g., lower tariffs, fewer exceptions to the rules) introduced in newer treaties.[36] This has resulted in a large web of trade commitments beyond the existing multilateral rules, all relying on a strong nondiscrimination standard and a preference for tariffs over other trade barriers. Table 2.2 provides a brief overview of the goods trade policies traditionally deployed and their compatibility with the current web of international treaties.

Table 2.2. Goods checklist

Policy instrument	GATT	US treaties	EU treaties	S–S treaties
Tariffs rate flexibility	√	x	x	√
Non-tariff barriers (quotas & licensing)	x	x	x	x
Balance of payments and shortages safeguards	√	x	√	√
Special economic zones (subsidies for export and strategic sectors)	Actionable	Actionable	Actionable	√

Note: "x" indicates the policy is not available; "√" indicates that it is. Where the table says "Actionable," the policy is permitted but may be challenged under the treaty if it discriminates against foreign goods.

Tariffs

Tariffs have long been the preferred trade barrier under the GATT (and subsequently, the WTO) because they are easy to measure, transparent to apply and straightforward to liberalize progressively over time.[37] Employed carefully, countries can raise and lower tariffs to protect nascent industries until they are ready to face global competition.[38] This is called strategic tariff sequencing. Under the GATT, countries may deploy these measures if their bound tariff rate for a good is higher than their actual applied customs rate (also called the MFN applied rate), provided they apply the tariff rate change

---

36 This is not straightforward and the exact application of this idea is controversial. Many countries have changed the way they draft MFN language to avoid just such an outcome. For more on this idea, see Chapter 3.

37 Thrasher and Gallagher, "21st Century Trade Agreements."

38 Chang, *Bad Samaritans*.

to all trading partners. Average bound rates are much higher than applied rates, suggesting that most states retain the space at the WTO to move their tariffs up and down, even if they don't use it.

By contrast, tariffs in a vast majority of bilateral and regional free trade agreements are bound much lower.[39] Even where they are not, they often include a schedule for progressive elimination of tariffs over a transition period, ultimately resulting in zero percent tariff rates.[40] Table 2.3 provides an example, comparing WTO bound and applied rates for iron and nonalloy steel bars and rods, with commitments under other trade agreements. Although this particular tariff line was chosen somewhat arbitrarily, it does offer a glimpse of a product in the middle of the supply chain with a wide variety of bound tariff rates among the countries in this study.

Table 2.3. Illustrative tariff comparison: iron and non-alloy steel bars and rods (2012 HS06 721310)

Country/Agreement	WTO binding	Regional and bilateral tariff commitment	MFN applied rate (avg)
Chile (CPTPP, EU-Chile)	25	6→0 (8 years, immed.)	6
Mexico (USMCA)	35	0	15
Colombia (US-Col., EU-Col.)	35	15→0 (10 years, 11 years)	10
Ukraine (EU-Ukraine)	0	0	0
Georgia (China-Georgia)	0	0	0
China (China-Georgia)	3	3→0 (1 year)	3
Singapore (CPTPP, US-Singapore)	0	0	0
Mongolia (Japan-Mongolia)	20	0	5
Malaysia (CPTPP, Malaysia-Australia FTA)	unbound	0	5
Japan (EU-Japan, Japan-Mongolia)	0	0	0
Average	13.1	0	4.5

---

39 World Trade Organization, "International Trade and Tariff Data."

40 This occurs in part because of the power dynamics in smaller-scale trade negotiations, as well as the rules for preferential trade agreements under the GATT, which requires the liberalization of "substantially all trade". "General Agreement on Tariffs and Trade (GATT)."

This table reflects the broader trend of GATT bound rates far exceeding the applied rates and even further outstripping the ultimate commitments in bilateral and regional agreements. This is true even among developing countries, whose South–South tariff commitments are very low.

Maintaining bilateral or regional tariff commitments lower than bound or even applied rates at the WTO has two important impacts. First of all, those treaties do not permit countries to employ strategic tariff sequencing once the agreement enters into force, or at least to a much lesser degree—once tariffs are eliminated there is no way to re-introduce them (outside of temporary unilateral remedies mentioned above). Second, it offers some measure of protection for industries within those arrangements from competition outside.

In this way, *who* your trading partner is can be as important as *what* those trading commitments are. The European Union, for example, is involved in a process of updating its existing economic partnership agreements. The proposed European Union–Mexico tariff elimination schedule is quite detailed, in which it seems Mexico has negotiated six additional staging categories for tariff removal that do not involve a complete removal of tariffs for select goods.[41] In addition to EU treaties, regional trade agreements like the African Continental Free Trade Agreement (AfCFTA), the Southern Common Market (MERCOSUR) and the much older Andean Community offer ways for developing countries to cooperate in their development strategy by lowering barriers within and keeping external barriers relatively high.

This second outcome is not so helpful when the South–South bloc involves countries with very diverse levels of development. On-going negotiations for the Regional Comprehensive Economic Partnership (RCEP), for example, propose to lower trade barriers among East and South Asian trade partners, which may foster regional cooperation in trade policy, but will also reinforce the positions of dominant players in that region, like China and South Korea. As a result, it may improve economic indicators for the region as a whole, while exacerbating interregional inequalities.

South–South agreements have historically also permitted wholesale exceptions to tariff commitments—so-called sensitive lists—which keep products at the center of a country's industrializing strategy outside of the scope of these commitments. Parties to the AfCFTA have not yet settled their tariff schedules, but the agreement does include a "special and differential treatment" standard, acknowledging the different needs of parties at "different levels of development," which may result in just such an arrangement.[42]

---

41 EU-Mexico, "Modernisation of the Trade Part of the EU-Mexico Global Agreement."
42 African Union, "AfCFTA," 6.

It is important to point out that the current predominance of global supply chains impacts the potential benefits that a country may try to secure through tariff rate adjustments. Given that most manufactured products are part of a global supply chain, tariffs are not likely to produce the protectionist effect that they previously did. Indeed, introducing tariffs on an imported final good is likely to injure a country's intermediate good producers. Likewise, tariffs on intermediate goods may make it more difficult for domestic producers of the final good.[43] Nevertheless, while the complex impacts of tariffs in a globalized world may motivate countries to reduce tariff barriers on their own, it does not take away the desire many countries have to strategically lower and raise those barriers within their bound rates. Moreover, as we'll see in the following paragraphs, tariff barriers diminish in importance when the real barriers countries have sought to eliminate are behind the border measures and other domestic policies.

Special exceptions to the prohibition on quantitative restrictions

Almost all trade agreements contain some preference for tariff barriers over quantitative restrictions. The GATT, as well as treaties among developing countries and US and EU agreements, all call for a prohibition on such practices either by a multiyear phase out or immediately upon entry into force of the agreement.[44] At the same time, the GATT permits a few narrow exceptions that allow member states to rely on quantitative restrictions when facing crises. The first allows countries to implement export restrictions in the midst of critical food shortages or import restrictions in the case of a surplus of agricultural or fisheries products.[45] The second, mentioned above, allows temporary, limited import restrictions to deal with balance of payments crises.[46]

Quantitative restrictions during these crises are indeed quite useful tools. A country facing a critical food shortage may need to restrict food exports so that its constituents have access to at least the food produced domestically. On the other hand, a domestic surplus of agricultural or fisheries products could result in enormous food waste or price deflation in the absence of import restrictions. Moreover, in the midst of a balance of payments crisis, import restrictions offer a quick fix to the trade balance, allowing countries more time to respond with other policy measures to lend long-term stability.

---

43 Blanchard, Bown and Johnson, "Global Supply Chains and Trade Policy"; Handley, Kamal and Monarch, "Rising Import Tariffs, Falling Export Growth."
44 African Union, 9; "USMCA," 2.11; EU-Vietnam, "EU-Vietnam FTA," 2.14; EU-Singapore, "EU-Singapore FTA," 2.9.
45 "General Agreement on Tariffs and Trade (GATT)," pt. XI.
46 "General Agreement on Tariffs and Trade (GATT)," pt. XII.

The need for these exceptions is so well-accepted that almost all trade agreements retain them either by repeating the same words as the GATT or incorporating the relevant exceptions by reference.[47] Some treaties also permit transitional safeguards, which may be imposed solely to protect infant industry.[48]

Subsidies and incentives for export

An important area of trade and industrial policy that falls outside of traditional trade policy instruments is subsidies. Subsidies are generally defined as financial contributions by a government, which confer a benefit.[49] WTO disciplines on subsidies are fairly permissive as long as they are not linked to export performance or reliance on local inputs, or are not tied to specific individual firms or locations. Although the topic of subsidies is too broad to adequately examine here, there is one mechanism of subsidization that offers a peek at the impact of the rules of subsidies on industrial policy.

To improve and increase trade in goods, countries often create special economic zones to focus government support on the industries and geographical regions most capable of competing in the world marketplace. Although they are considered among the most important policy tools for developing countries, these zones have been used by countries all over the world at all levels of development.[50] The most universal aspect of special economic zones is preferential tariff treatment.[51] Firms located in those zones are able to import intermediate goods at reduced or zero tariffs, driving down their production costs. They also often include other preferential tax treatment, as well as the benefits of improved infrastructure and proximity to other firms up and down the supply chain. In return for all these benefits, countries often ask that those firms meet a certain threshold of local content in their production and export a certain proportion of the goods they produce.

---

47 African Union, "AfCFTA," 9; "USMCA," 2.11, 32.4.8; EU-Viet Nam, "EU-VietNam FTA," 2.14, 17.12; Dominican Republic-Central America-United States, "DR-CAFTA," 21.4; United States-Chile, "United States-Chile Free Trade Agreement," 23.4. A few US treaties omit the exception of import restrictions to safeguard the balance of payments. United States-Korea, "US-Korea FTA," 2.8; United States-Colombia, "US-Colombia FTA," 2.8.

48 EU-South Africa, "EU-S. Afr. Agreement on Trade, Development and Cooperation," 24; African Union, "AfCFTA," 24.

49 "Agreement on Subsidies and Countervailing Measures," 1.

50 Creskoff and Walkenhorst, "Implications of WTO Disciplines for Special Economic Zones in Developing Countries."

51 Grant, "Why Special Economic Zones?"

These policies were a major component of successful industrial policy in East Asia, and are linked to a 20 percent increase in gross domestic product (GDP) in China according to one study.[52] Outside of East Asia, the results of such policies have been mixed, but examples in Côte d'Ivoire[53] and India[54] demonstrate the diversity of contexts in which the policies have been tried with some measure of success—either by increasing industrialization or improving the welfare of citizens living and working in those zones.

For obvious reasons, most of the key components of special economic zones are inconsistent with the WTO subsidies rules. They almost always confer a benefit, at the expense of the government, to firms in a specific geographic area, contingent on either export performance or local sourcing of inputs, or both. Not all such zones are inconsistent with the agreement, however, and their consistency depends heavily on the specific circumstances surrounding government support.[55]

The clearest example of a WTO-compliant policy is called a duty drawback, where a firm receives a reimbursement of the tariffs it paid for intermediate goods that it imported. As long as the reimbursement does not exceed the amount initially paid, these incentives are widely considered to be legal under WTO rules.[56] On the other hand, if the firm must export a certain percentage of its products *in order to* secure a financial benefit as a part of the zone, this is a prohibited subsidy.[57] Some components of special economic zones may occupy a gray area between permitted and prohibited government support. Linking financial benefits only to the firms' geographic location makes the policy ripe for a challenge by affected trade partners only if they prove adverse effects as a result of the subsidy.[58]

---

52 Alder, Shao and Zilibotti, "Economic Reforms and Industrial Policy in a Panel of Chinese Cities."

53 Grover Goswami, Medvedev and Olafsen, *High-Growth Firms: Facts, Fiction, and Policy Options for Emerging Economies.*

54 Chaurey, "Location-Based Tax Incentives."

55 Creskoff and Walkenhorst, "Implications of WTO Disciplines for Special Economic Zones in Developing Countries."

56 The SCM Agreement contains an Interpretive Note Ad Article XVI, which states that "the exemption of an exported product from duties or taxes in amounts not in excess of those which have accrued, shall not be deemed to be a subsidy." "Agreement on Subsidies and Countervailing Measures."

57 Although many developing countries employed this tactic to improve their terms of trade and build up a competitive export sector, they have been forced to eliminate those programs on a progressive basis and the final deadline for that removal was December 31, 2015. Defever et al., "Does the Elimination of Export Requirements in Special Economic Zones Affect Export Performance?"

58 This is an economic calculation that must be proven before a panel of judges.

What is curious about the area of subsidies is how little direct treatment they receive under bilateral and regional trade agreements. The majority simply make a reference to the WTO rules or to the Agreement on Subsidies and Countervailing Measures (SCM Agreement) more specifically.[59] In some cases, they may even explicitly permit subsidies that are necessary to achieve a public policy objective and prohibit those that negatively affect or are likely to affect trade.[60] A small handful of treaties, most of which are among southern countries, stand out by either specifically mentioning duty drawbacks and special economic zones without any clear boundaries on them[61] or omitting any reference to either.[62]

Trade rules in traditional goods sectors are fairly similar across treaty regimes, with just a handful of textual distinctions making small differences in how countries may protect the goods they produce. As the first and oldest area of trade treaty coverage, it is no surprise that countries have settled ways of dealing with this. In recent years, however, trade in goods has changed dramatically. Rather than physical goods crossing borders, many goods are digitized and delivered via the internet. Moreover, the line between goods and services has blurred and disciplines in one sector often have impacts across others.

The global rules governing trade in services are, in many ways, much less comprehensive than those governing trade in goods—in part because of its relative novelty and in part because the rules potentially involve much more invasive interference in domestic policies and regulations. As we'll see, however, trade in services is quite harmonized across treaty regimes, with most of the differences revealed in negotiation modalities, domestic regulation standards and the overlap between services and investment.

Trade in services

Since the founding of the WTO in 1995 and the introduction of GATS disciplines, services have been among the most dynamic of all economic sectors.[63] Some of the fastest-growing industries, including computer-related, legal, advertising and technical services grew between 70 and 250 percent

---

59 EU-Mexico, "EU-Mexico Modernisation Agreement"; Japan-Mongolia, "Japan-Mongolia FTA."

60 EU-Mexico, "EU-Mexico Modernisation Agreement."

61 Brunei-Cambodia-Indonesia-Laos-Malaysia-Myanmar-Philippines-Singapore-Thailand-Vietnam, "ASEAN Trade in Goods Agreement"; African Union, "AfCFTA."

62 China-Georgia, "China-Georgia FTA."

63 Delimatsis, "Trade in Services and Regulatory Flexibility: 20 Years of GATS, 20 Years of Critique."

from 1994 to 2004.[64] Although services amounts to only about one-third of the value of goods trade as of 2019, trade in services[65] plays a pivotal role in global value chains by providing "transport, logistics, finance, communication and other business and professional" support.[66]

The GATS, at its adoption, was the product of a decade of negotiation and compromise. The European Commission and the United States, alongside other major services exporters, including emerging economies like Hong Kong and Singapore, had been pushing for a multilateral accord that would lower global barriers to their service suppliers.[67] At the same time, some governments in the Global South, such as Argentina, Brazil and India, were very reluctant to remove protections to their nascent service sectors.[68] The end result was the GATS, with its complex four-mode, positive list scheduling, paired with well-established nondiscrimination rules and standards.

This approach required countries to break each sector into four different modes of supply: (1) cross-border supply of services, (2) consumption of services abroad, (3) commercial presence of foreign services suppliers (also known as foreign direct investment in services), and (4) the presence of (foreign) natural persons supplying services (also known as immigration). Described as "hopelessly dysfunctional" for those desiring actual liberalization across service sectors, this allowed countries to tightly circumscribe their commitments, especially in so-called sensitive sectors.[69] Proponents of the agreement, however, pointed to the careful balance between securing domestic policy "in order to establish competition and market access in service sectors without curtailing the freedom of members to regulate so as to meet national policy objectives."[70]

---

64 Perera, "The Globalisation of Services and Its Implications for Sustainable Development: A Preliminary Discussion Document."

65 In fact, some argue that the so-called trade in services is not trade at all but simply another way for neoliberalism to reach deeper into the regulatory domain of states. Kelsey, "From GATS to TiSA: Pushing the Trade in Services Regime Beyond the Limits."

66 Trade Policy Review Body, "Report of the TPRB from the Director-General on Trade-Related Developments"; Voon, "Balancing Regulatory Autonomy with Liberalisation of Trade in Services: An Analytical Assessment of Australia's Obligations under Preferential Trade Agreements."

67 Kelsey, "From GATS to TiSA: Pushing the Trade in Services Regime beyond the Limits," Marchetti and Mavroidis, "The Genesis of the GATS (General Agreement on Trade in Services)."

68 Marchetti and Mavroidis, "The Genesis of the GATS (General Agreement on Trade in Services)."

69 Kelsey, "From GATS to TiSA: Pushing the Trade in Services Regime beyond the Limits."

70 Voon, "Balancing Regulatory Autonomy with Liberalisation of Trade in Services: An Analytical Assessment of Australia's Obligations under Preferential Trade Agreements," 2; Wouters and Coppens, "Gats and Domestic Regulation," 210.

There were two unforeseen negative impacts to this approach, however. The complexity of scheduling resulted in some countries making unintended commitments, which the WTO Dispute Settlement Body made very clear it would enforce.[71] Moreover, this approach allowed developed countries to push for liberalization in modes one, two and three while carefully preserving the right to keep immigration of low-skilled workers to a minimum. Nevertheless, the GATS has remained largely as it began, and free trade agreements have modeled their own scheduling after the four-mode approach.

As major service exporters began to grow more impatient with the limitations of the GATS, services commitments increased in bilateral and regional trade agreements. The United States and the European Union each attempted to craft new services rules with their interests in mind. When countries negotiate directly with either party, liberalizing their service sectors is linked with access to the largest global markets in the world. The inherent power imbalance has allowed the United States and the European Union to create templates of services schedules for their trading partners, which seek to overcome some of the obstacles to services supply chains while continuing to maintain protection over their most sensitive mode—immigration.[72] These templates acted to cluster commitments within key supply chains rather than allow trading partners to be selective about different modes of supply for the same service.

The results were treaties that differed from the GATS in both the general structure of negotiating commitments and specific areas of policy flexibility. By changing the ways that countries agree to services liberalization, expanded commitments in new treaties limit the ability of the parties to employ taxation and subsidies as "effective tools to achieve their regulatory goals".[73] They can also limit policies that would allow low- and middle-income countries to build up domestic financial and business services to support local manufacturing sectors.[74] Ultimately, these "GATS+" commitments act to undermine the policy flexibility that developing countries need to achieve a more diversified economy.

---

71 This occurred for the United States when Antigua and Barbuda sued the United States for restrictions on foreign supply of online gambling. *United States—Measures Affecting the Cross-Border Supply of Gambling and Betting Services*, www.wto.org.

72 Kelsey, "From GATS to TiSA: Pushing the Trade in Services Regime beyond the Limits."

73 Voon, "Balancing Regulatory Autonomy with Liberalisation of Trade in Services: An Analytical Assessment of Australia's Obligations under Preferential Trade Agreements," 6.

74 Aiginger and Rodrik, "Rebirth of Industrial Policy and an Agenda for the Twenty-First Century," 198.

Positive and negative list schedules

Perhaps the most significant overarching difference between the GATS and the new bilateral and regional agreements, however, is negative-list scheduling. The GATS has a negative-list approach to MFN treatment, but a positive-list approach to both market access and national treatment commitments.[75] Practically speaking, this means that WTO members *may not* discriminate between or among the service suppliers of diverse trading partners unless they list such treatment as an exemption. On the other hand, WTO members are free to treat national service suppliers better, and restrict market access to foreign service suppliers *unless* they commit that sector and mode of supply.

Most trade in services agreements negotiated after the formation of the WTO take the opposite approach so that national treatment and market access for foreign service suppliers is *assumed* unless carved out and placed on a list of exemptions. And this new approach has had a definite impact on the depth and breadth of services commitments. The new "negative-list" schedules in regional and bilateral treaties resulted in more assurances that foreign service suppliers could supply their services in the domestic market without limitations (market access commitments) and that they would be treated on par with domestic service suppliers (national treatment commitments). A look at the treaties signed in the first decade since the GATS entered into force shows that a much larger percentage (on average, more than double) of sectors are committed under bilateral and regional services schedules, and those already liberalized under the GATS had further constraints removed.[76] Moreover, they were often accompanied by specific commitments in audiovisual, telecommunications, transport and financial services.[77]

Beyond the differences in scheduling modalities and sector-specific commitments, there are also a handful of differences in the extent to which treaties put limits on domestic policymaking and manage the overlap between services and investment rules. Table 2.4 illustrates how different trade agreement approaches compare.[78] Exceptions exist, in part due to the flexibilities inherent in the GATS, which require developed countries to take into consideration the development level of their trading partners when negotiating new services

---

75 Voon, "Balancing Regulatory Autonomy with Liberalisation of Trade in Services: An Analytical Assessment of Australia's Obligations under Preferential Trade Agreements."

76 Roy, Marchetti and Lim, "Services Liberalization in the New Generation of Preferential Trade Agreements (PTAs): How Much Further than the GATS?"

77 Roy, Marchetti and Lim, "Services Liberalization in the New Generation of Preferential Trade Agreements (PTAs): How Much Further than the GATS?"

78 Exceptions exist in part due to flexibilities inherent in the GATS, which require developed countries to take into consideration the development level of their trading

Table 2.4. Services checklist

Policy instrument	GATS	US treaties	EU treaties	S–S treaties
Sequencing liberalization and control over sensitive sectors	√	x	mixed	√
Preserving commercial presence as services commitment	√	x	√	√
Impose duty of establishment	√	x	√	√
Introduction of new services regulations	√	x	mixed	√

commitments.[79] Treaties between developing countries tend to resemble the GATS in terms of policy flexibility as well as general text.

Domestic regulation, local presence and the right to regulate

Just like market access and national treatment commitments take the form of either a negative or positive list, rules on domestic regulation and establishing a local presence do the same. Domestic regulation provisions, as modeled in the GATS, generally set out to ensure that new regulations in scheduled sectors (positive list) are "administered in a reasonable, objective and impartial manner".[80] The GATS also proposes that the Council for Trade in Services establish clearer disciplines so that new measures are "based on objective and transparent criteria […] not more burdensome than necessary to ensure the quality of a service; [and] […] not in themselves a restriction on the supply of a service."[81] The Council has never come to an agreement on these guidelines, which has been an additional frustration for countries seeking more expansive global liberalization of services, not to mention a relief for those wanting to put the brakes on that liberalization.

The GATS, therefore, places no concrete constraints on the substance of the regulation—only on the *administration* of such. The preamble further asserts the rights of states to regulate in the public interest, and the agreement does indeed appear to protect that right, however vague it might be. Other treaties,

---

partners when negotiating new services commitments. World Trade Organization, "General Agreement on Trade in Services (GATS)," pt. V.3.

79 World Trade Organization, "General Agreement on Trade in Services (GATS)," V.3.
80 World Trade Organization, "General Agreement on Trade in Services (GATS)," VI.1.
81 World Trade Organization, "General Agreement on Trade in Services (GATS)," VI.4.

however, have put more substantive constraints on domestic regulation. Many of the newest treaties with the United States, Canada or Japan as a party adopt a negative-list approach to domestic regulation—as with national treatment and market access standards.[82] Moreover, in some cases, the substantive requirements for domestic regulation are immediately and directly enforceable against states.[83] The negative-list approach combined with self-enforcing provisions naturally broadens the reach of rules on administration, while adding additional obstacles to states crafting domestic regulation.

Newer treaties have also targeted one specific type of regulation—local presence rules. Both the USMCA and the Comprehensive and Progressive Trans-Pacific Partnership (CPTPP) explicitly proscribe rules that would require foreign service suppliers to establish a domestic residence in the service-importing country.[84] Of course, not all bilateral and regional agreements take this proactive stance to domestic regulation rules. Negotiations with the European Union tend to vary heavily depending on treaty partner, especially when the partner is a developing country.[85] South–South agreements differ even more widely, which is unsurprising given the diversity of the class of countries identified as developing. The agreement between China and Georgia, for instance, virtually copies the terms of the GATS verbatim,[86] while services commitments in the AfCFTA does not even reach to the level of the GATS disciplines on national treatment, market access and domestic regulation.[87]

Countries that count themselves "really good friends of services" have not yet given up gaining ground on multilateral services rules at the WTO.[88] A coalition of such countries has crafted a Joint Initiative in Services Domestic Regulation, which has a number of so-called improvements to the existing

---

82 Canada-Australia-Brunei-Chile-Japan-Malaysia-Mexico-New Zealand-Peru-Singapore-Viet Nam, "CPTPP," 10.8; "USMCA," 15.8; Japan-Mongolia, "Japan-Mongolia FTA," 7.8; EU-Japan, "EU-Japan EPA," 8.29.

83 "USMCA," 15.8. These requirements orbit around ideas of "objective and transparent criteria" "not more burdensome than necessary" and others. Japan-Mongolia, "Japan-Mongolia FTA," 7.8.

84 "USMCA,"   15.6;   Canada-Australia-Brunei-Chile-Japan-Malaysia-Mexico-New Zealand-Peru-Singapore-Viet Nam, "CPTPP," 10.6.

85 EU-Singapore employs a positive list approach to domestic regulation, which is self-enforcing for liberalized sectors. Meanwhile, EU-Viet Nam does not contain domestic regulation rules at all. EU-Singapore, "EU-Singapore FTA"; EU-Viet Nam, "EU-Viet Nam FTA."

86 China-Georgia, "China-Georgia FTA."

87 The AfCFTA parties are still in the process of negotiating both tariff and services scheduling. African Union, "AfCFTA."

88 European Commission, "Negotiations for a Plurilateral Agreement on Trade in Services."

GATS rules. The proposal assumes a negative-list scheduling mechanism, along with self-enforcing commitments to domestic regulation rules akin to the commitments in the strongest agreements with the United States and Japan. Some parties even proposed that new regulations would have to pass a "not more burdensome than necessary" test in order to comply with the new rules.[89]

Services and investment: Mode 3 commitments

A final important aspect of trade in services commitments relates to the overlap between services and investment liberalization commitments. Mode 3 under the GATS framework is effectively a way to liberalize foreign direct investment for service suppliers. Under the GATS, this makes sense, as the Agreement on Trade-Related Investment Measures (TRIMs Agreement) covers only (goods) trade-related measures and Mode 3 is a way to secure commitments in investment somewhat more broadly.

One result of keeping goods-related investment and services-related investment confined to separate silos and different types of governance, within the larger agreement, is similar to the dysfunctionality of four-mode services scheduling. It has a naturally slowing effect on global supply chains, allowing countries to treat different sectors differently. Since the GATS, however, bilateral and regional trade agreements have sought to eliminate those differences, and they go about it in roughly two ways. Some treaties have created parallel commitments for foreign direct investment and the other three modes of services supply.[90] These commitments include traditional services rules like national treatment and market access, as well as investment rules requiring free transfers. In general, these commitments are not as extensive as those found in full-fledged investment chapters, but they attempt to broaden the scope of previously narrow services commitments.

Other treaties double up on coverage for foreign direct investment in services. In both the CPTPP and the USMCA, the provisions on trade in services incorporate investment disciplines by reference such as fair and equitable treatment, expropriation and free transfers, and some even allow investor–state dispute enforcement of Mode 3 commitments.[91] For many reasons, measures affecting trade in services face a much narrower set of rules than those affecting investment. Nevertheless, as a result of the efforts by

89 "Communication on Disciplines for Domestic Regulation."

90 EU-Japan, "EU-Japan EPA," chap. 8(B) & 8(C); EU-Viet Nam, "EU-Viet Nam FTA," chap. 8(B) & 8(C).

91 Canada-Australia-Brunei-Chile-Japan-Malaysia-Mexico-New Zealand-Peru-Singapore-Viet Nam, "CPTPP," chap. 9; "USMCA," chap. 14.

dominant services exporters, the global commitments continue to rise while policy space shrinks.

Investment

Foreign investment poses one of the most difficult challenges to countries in the global trade regime—both those that seek further liberalization and those that fear it. "Economic theory, history and contemporary experiences all tell us that in order truly to benefit from foreign direct investment, the government needs to regulate it well."[92] Indeed, countries have historically had at their fingertips numerous creatively crafted investment measures aimed to protect domestic industry, preserve their current and capital account balances, create local backward and forward linkages, and otherwise strengthen their economy.[93] These measures address both foreign direct and portfolio investment—that is, both companies, and capital. At the same time, international investment agreements (IIAs) make up an enormous web of interwoven commitments that arguably protect foreign investors from the impacts of those measures. Table 2.5 lays out the current availability of those measures under various trade agreement models.

The WTO's TRIMs Agreement prohibits policies that violate national treatment or the general obligation to eliminate quantitative restrictions.[94] It then lays out an illustrative list of prohibited measures in an appended annex.[95] Under the TRIMs Agreement, countries may not require that foreign investors achieve a certain level of domestic content in their goods or prefer domestic producers or products in their production process. They may not limit foreign investors' imports in relation to their local production or export levels. They may not require investors to acquire foreign exchange only through export, and they may not demand that investors sell a certain amount of their product within the domestic market.[96]

In bilateral and regional agreements, these rules expand, in part because they often incorporate wholesale the much older disciplines found in bilateral investment treaties (BITs). Investment commitments demand the right of establishment on par with national firms, fair and equitable treatment, compensation for both indirect and direct expropriation, expanded rules

---

92 Chang, *Bad Samaritans*, 96.
93 Thrasher and Gallagher, "21st Century Trade Agreements."
94 "General Agreement on Tariffs and Trade (GATT)," III, XI.
95 "Agreement on Trade-Related Investment Measures."
96 These performance requirements also may not be conditioned on any economic benefit. This is consistent with the rules on subsidies discussed above. "Agreement on Subsidies and Countervailing Measures."

Table 2.5. Investment checklist

Policy instrument	TRIMS	US treaties	EU treaties	S–S treaties
Restrictions on foreign investor establishment	√	x	Mixed	√
Domestic content, trade balancing and foreign exchange requirements	x	x	x	x
Local management, labor and technology transfer requirements*	√	x	√	√
Research and development obligations	√	x	Mixed	√
International transfer/payment restrictions	x	x	x	√

* For local labor requirements, local management requirements, headquarters restrictions, technology transfer and research and development, a country may not require them as a condition of entry, but, in some cases, may condition receipt of a benefit on them.

on unrestricted capital flows, and prohibitions on a longer list of firm-based performance requirements. Even more importantly, these commitments are often enforceable by investor–state dispute settlement, allowing countries to be sued outside their home courts by a private investor.

Specific policy prohibitions

Country parties to IIAs—which include almost every country in the world—face a slew of specific rules and additional disciplines over and above the rules of the WTO's TRIMs Agreement. The most widely discussed of those proscribe indirect expropriation, capital flow management measures, and requirements that foreign firms contribute jobs, technology and capital to the host state.

Indirect expropriation, also referred to as "measures tantamount to expropriation,"[97] folds domestic regulation of foreign investments (which undermine the value of an investment) into historical ideas of land and property seizures by rogue governments. Although international law has always permitted expropriation by sovereign states, it has also demanded that those takings occur (1) for a public purpose, (2) in a nondiscriminatory way, and (3) on payment of prompt, adequate and effective compensation. Definitions of

---

97 United States-Mexico-Canada, "North American Free Trade Agreement (NAFTA)," 1110.

indirect expropriation began to expand under NAFTA arbitration, including measures that result in "covert or incidental interference" with property rights, or which deprive the investor of a "reasonably-to-be-expected" return on investment.[98] For a while, indirect expropriation was the darling of injured investors—claiming that logging regulations, failures to grant permits and licenses, and even environmental regulations were "tantamount to expropriation."[99] Although the investor did not always succeed, there began to be a concern that countries would fail to regulate in the public interest for fear of an investor–state dispute.

Another set of provisions constraining the public welfare policy demand free transfers of capital flows between treaty parties. Despite the fact that capital flow management measures have been proven to offer financial stability and mitigate financial crises, even the WTO prohibits restrictions on international transfers and payments, except where the country is already in the midst of a crisis.[100] This provision is given careful attention in Chapter 5 of this volume; however, it is important to note in this context that the WTO rules on capital account restrictions remain in the GATS and thus only apply to scheduled sectors, while extra-WTO disciplines apply across sectors to all covered investments.[101]

Finally, bilateral and regional mechanisms often include many more prohibited performance requirements than the illustrative list in the TRIMs annex. Under the expanded rules, countries may not require foreign firms to hire from the local population, locate their headquarters in the host state, transfer cutting edge technology or, in some cases, even accomplish a given level of research and development.[102] This is particularly important because each of these prohibited requirements represents key contributions foreign firms are poised to offer when they cross borders. Put another way, firms and investment-exporting countries have specifically induced developing countries to open their borders with promises of new technology, jobs, training and infrastructure. Yet they are unable to demand that those promises are kept.

---

98 Glinavos, "Haircut Undone?"

99 Edsall, "Indirect Expropriation under NAFTA and DR-CAFTA: Potential Inconsistencies in the Treatment of State Public Welfare Regulations."

100 World Trade Organization, "General Agreement on Trade in Services (GATS)," XI, XII.

101 "USMCA," 14.9; EU-Singapore, "EU-Singapore IPA," 2.7; EU-Viet Nam, "EU-Viet Nam IPA," 2.8; Japan-Mongolia, "Japan-Mongolia FTA," 2.11.

102 EU-Japan, "EU-Japan EPA"; "USMCA"; Japan-Mongolia, "Japan-Mongolia FTA."

Establishment, standards of treatment and legitimate expectations

Piling on additional rules to protect investors has a minor impact compared with the general standards of treatment demanded under bilateral and regional investment treaties. Since investment disciplines under the WTO are so limited in scope, it does not take much for extra-WTO investment treaties to wildly exceed those commitments. Among the most important differences are those provisions extending a right of establishment to foreign investors. The right of establishment requires that foreign investors are allowed entry into the country (that is, establishment in the country) as a firm, on par with domestic investors seeking to establish a firm in the same sector. In other words, before an investor even enters the country, the potential host state owes it a level of treatment comparable with domestic firms. Provisions of this sort are found most often in treaties with the United States, Japan and the European Union.[103] Under these rules, countries may not even act as gatekeeper to protect nascent domestic industries from foreign competition within their borders.

In addition to the right of establishment, a provision ubiquitous among investment agreements ensures "fair and equitable treatment" for foreign firms operating in a host country. On its face, the words "fair and equitable" do not seem to add substantially more than existing nondiscrimination rules already demand. However, this provision, in part because of its vague meaning, has become the basis of many recent claims brought under these treaties. The most basic understanding, and the historical one, requires only that host states recognize due process and offer full police protection and security to foreign firms.

Investor–state tribunals, however, have expanded the meaning to include state measures that undermine an investor's "legitimate expectations."[104] Due to the broad interpretations of this standard by investor–state tribunals, newer treaties do attempt to circumscribe this reach by specifying that legitimate investor expectations arise only where there are "specific representations" by the host state promising regulatory stability or specific returns on investment.[105] Others narrow the scope of the provision by stating that fair and equitable treatment does not grant "additional substantive rights," or even that thwarted investor expectations on their own do not give rise to a violation.[106]

Standards of treatment are not about specific policies but are much further reaching than that—they cover measures of all sorts—from taxation to environmental regulation, from land reform to capital controls. For that

---

103 "USMCA," 14.4, 14.5; EU-Japan, "EU-Japan EPA," 8.7–8.9.
104 Antaris Solar GmbH and Dr. Michael Gode v. Czech Republic, www.italaw.com.
105 EU-Singapore, "EU-Singapore IPA"; EU-Viet Nam, "EU-Viet Nam IPA."
106 "USMCA," 14.6.

reason, it is difficult to list all the possible domestic laws that would be prohibited under them, though many topics are discussed in later chapters of this volume. But first, to understand the breadth of the reach of the investment regime, we must understand its main enforcement mechanism—investor–state disputes.

Investor–state arbitration

Investor–state dispute settlement (ISDS) has been a staple of international investment disputes since the Netherlands-Indonesia Bilateral Investment Treaty in 1968.[107] In 1966, the World Bank created the International Centre for the Settlement of Investment Disputes (ICSID), an institution established for the purpose of resolving investor–state conflicts outside of the domestic court systems. In those early years, the system acted as a much-needed protection for foreign direct investors providing capital, employment and infrastructure to the developing world. Its value lay "in its role as a restraint against unjustified expropriation or unfair treatment when governments changed political direction".[108]

By the mid-1990s, the number of standalone investment treaties and free trade agreements with investment commitments began to boom. More than simply offering investor protection, investment treaties became a sort of welcome mat that developing countries could put out indicating that they were open for business. By including an investor–state dispute mechanism, countries added credibility to their commitments.[109] Parallel with the increased number of investment treaties, investor claims filed per year skyrocketed from under 5 (before 1994), to between 30 and 50 after the year 2000.[110]

Many people today argue that the presence of ISDS "tilts the scales too far" in favor of the investors.[111] Structurally speaking, investment treaties are simply contracts between states that impose obligations on those states. Covered investors and their investments, then, are only third-party beneficiaries of those treaties and have no obligations of their own.[112] Consequently, in ISDS, investors are always the claimants and states are always the respondents.

Even if this asymmetry is not, in itself, alarming, evidence from arbitration outcomes could prove otherwise. Several studies have examined

---

107 Netherlands-Indonesia, "Netherlands-Indonesia BIT," 11.
108 Schultz and Dupont, "Investment Arbitration."
109 Wellhausen, "Recent Trends in Investor–State Dispute Settlement."
110 Schultz and Dupont, "Investment Arbitration."
111 Wellhausen, "Recent Trends in Investor–State Dispute Settlement."
112 Schultz and Dupont, "Investment Arbitration."

the outcomes in investment arbitration and determined that states (and their taxpayers) have paid some amount to investors, either through an award or settlement, two-thirds of the time.[113] Additional research shows that for countries most vulnerable to the high costs of investment arbitration, the percentages are even higher. Eighty-eight percent of all claimant investors are from high income countries, and the bulk of claims are filed against middle-income countries. Moreover, high-income respondent states are more likely to prevail than low-income states—46 percent compared with 27 percent.[114] These trends reveal fundamental imbalances within ISDS—both structurally between investors and states, and, in practice, between developed and developing countries.

Cross-Cutting Issues and Conclusions

As hinted above, international trade is changing. An increasing percentage of transactions take place, not in physical goods, person-to-person services and foreign direct investment, but by electronic means. The way we consume goods and services would be unrecognizable to those who crafted the backbone of our global financial institutions, including the GATT. As our consumption patterns change, so do the international rules, albeit a good deal more slowly.

The WTO has had in place a Moratorium on Customs Duties on Electronic Transmissions since 1998.[115] As the economy has evolved, this moratorium has had a larger and larger effect on countries that rely on tariffs for a substantial proportion of government income. Developing countries, in particular, have received between 20 and 50 percent of their income through tariffs.[116] As a result, by some estimates, those same countries lose an average of US$5–10 billion per year in potential revenue due to the Moratorium

---

113 Sweet, Chung and Saltzman, "Arbitral Lawmaking and State Power." Unfortunately, we cannot measure the percentage of awards that the investors or states *should have* won, as it would require second-guessing the facts and legal arguments of hundreds of investment cases. Schultz and Dupont, "Investment Arbitration." On average, claimants who won their case were only awarded 30 to 40 percent of the amount initially claimed. One could argue that claimants either inflate awards requests, knowing that they will get a small percentage of that, or that tribunals do a good job of constraining damage claims against states. Wellhausen, "Recent Trends in Investor–State Dispute Settlement." Ultimately, however, we do not know.

114 Schultz and Dupont, "Investment Arbitration."

115 "Declaration on Global Electronic Commerce."

116 Dutt and Thrasher, "Growing Share of Online Trade Undercuts Government Ability to Pull in Revenue."

above.[117] Although many WTO members have demanded that the Moratorium be lifted, the outcome is very uncertain. And a large group of countries with an interest in protecting the interests of the giants of electronic commerce have formed a coalition to maintain the Moratorium, among other policy proposals.[118] The transition to electronic transmission of goods has also bled into disciplines on trade in services. Many of the sectors included in the concept of electronic transmissions are in fact services sectors and therefore not subject to customs duties. Despite more than 20 years in discussion, the Councils on Trade in Goods and Trade in Services have not yet come to a conclusion about how to comprehensively govern this new kind of global trade.

As the way we do business changes, so has the trading environment. The realities of climate change and the COVID-19 pandemic have illuminated real tensions between the individual needs of each country—to keep its constituents safe and kick-start a flagging economy—and those of the world— to contain the worldwide impacts of these crises. Each of these crises requires agility by governments to respond collectively and independently. Over the longer term, new experiments in industrial policy aimed at promoting economic development and diversification will require continuous monitoring and revision based on their outcomes.[119] While some treaties permit this, the majority are putting greater and greater constraints on industrial and trade policymaking.

It is worth noting that a posture in favor of industrial policy for development has to grapple with the realities of industrial policies as deployed by developed countries as well. If we propose a treaty regime with more policy flexibility, we may also be allowing developed countries to support their own national "champions" of industry—companies such as Facebook, Amazon, Apple, Netflix and Google. However, the primary tools in the toolkit for developed countries are often already permitted under trade rules. Advanced research and development, investment in higher education and subsidies in key services sectors without strings attached (such as export performance or local content requirements) are largely outside the scope of goods, services and investment rules. Meanwhile, those policies may be politically and financially unavailable to many developing countries, which do not have the fiscal backing and investment capital available for such projects.

---

117 Dutt and Thrasher; Banga, "Growing Trade in Electronic Transmissions: Implications for the South."

118 Ismail, "E-Commerce in the World Trade Organization."

119 Aiginger and Rodrik, "Rebirth of Industrial Policy and an Agenda for the Twenty-First Century," 192.

As the following chapters demonstrate, these implications for industrial policies are only the beginning. International trade and investment commitments reach into every area of domestic policymaking. And understanding the impacts of the treaty texts enables us to see how future trade integration needs to change—toward a more flexible, multilateral approach which acknowledges the structural change needed for development. The rest of this volume lays out the implications of the overreach of the current rules and proposes alternatives to the current trend that just might give countries the policy flexibility they need.

Chapter 3

TRADE-RELATED ASPECTS OF INTELLECTUAL PROPERTY, INVESTMENT RULES AND ACCESS TO MEDICINES

As major pharmaceutical companies worldwide scrambled to develop new vaccines to battle COVID-19, the wealthiest countries have likewise scrambled to secure early access to those vaccines. The result has been a wildly unequal distribution in which some countries will complete vaccinations by mid-2021 and others will still be waiting well into 2023.[1] Although there is a myriad of reasons for this inequality, some scholars have identified strict protection of intellectual property as one part of the problem. In particular, many are concerned that a failure to share knowledge surrounding developing and manufacturing the vaccines has resulted in fewer suppliers and, ultimately, global shortages.[2]

In general, the rules governing intellectual property (IP) aim to balance the encouragement of innovation with the needs and rights of those consuming it. However, this balance has become particularly contentious, when wealthier countries prioritize incentives for knowledge creation in a way that decreases access to necessary medicines, or in this case, vaccines.[3] During 2020 and early 2021, the urgency of finding the right balance of IP protection and access to innovative products and ideas reached its zenith. The COVID-19 pandemic has revealed how the current trade and investment regime can present a major roadblock to access to almost every product and service needed to address this public health crisis.

---

1 Twohey, Collins, and Thomas, "With First Dibs on Vaccines, Rich Countries Have 'Cleared the Shelves'"; Callaway, "The Unequal Scramble for Coronavirus Vaccines—by the Numbers."

2 Vawda and Baker, "COVID-19: The Time for Procrastination over Patents Is Over"; "What Will It Take To End The COVID-19 Pandemic?"

3 Vawda and Baker, "COVID-19: The Time for Procrastination over Patents Is Over"; Shadlen, "Policy Space for Development in the WTO and Beyond: The Case of Intellectual Property Rights."

Many have written about the urgency of making available, through facilitating and liberalizing global trade, the tests, masks, ventilators, medicines and vaccines that are necessary for all countries combating the pandemic.[4] Others have pointed out that we need to temporarily remove or fundamentally change patent protection for certain medicines so that more companies—both innovators and generic manufacturers—can be testing the impacts of potential anti-viral medicines and vaccines.[5] This chapter demonstrates that international cooperation to meet global challenges involves ample policy flexibility in IP, delinking nontrade areas from trade enforcement measures, and, especially, focusing on building long-term capacity building in countries in need of development.

Liberalizing Trade for Public Health

Trade in personal protective equipment, medical devices and treatments and vaccines has been in the spotlight since March 2020 when the United States and Europe began to take real notice of COVID-19. Given that the liberalization of trade in goods is widely touted as the most efficient way to development, trade theory argues that this will create more wealth and increase overall global welfare. As noted in previous chapters, the global liberalization of trade has certainly corresponded with a period of prolonged global growth.

Critics of the orthodoxy pushing liberalization for development point to two weaknesses in the argument, however. First, the rapid pace at which we are forcing this trade liberalization on developing countries gives them far less time to adjust to the natural economic restructuring than today's developed countries had when they were at a similar level of development. The industrial revolution in the United States and Europe took place under the watchful eye of the state, carefully protecting industries of importance and cushioning the fall of industries threatened by competitive imports. The United States undertook this change slowly, over roughly 150 years. Contrast that with the flexibilities given to developing countries in WTO agreements, which allow them 5 to 10 years to adjust their policies and get in line to fully implement the agreements. Many of those flexibilities are gone today.[6]

---

4 Gertz, "Reopening the World"; Baker, "The 'Lower Drug Costs Now Act of 2019'"; World Health Organization, World Intellectual Property Organization, and World Trade Organization, *Promoting Access to Medical Technologies and Innovation: Intersections between Public Health, Intellectual Property and Trade*; World Trade Organization, "WTO Contribution to the United Nations 2020 High Level Political Forum."

5 Vawda and Baker, "COVID-19: The Time for Procrastination over Patents Is Over."

6 Chang, *Kicking Away the Ladder: Development Strategy in Historical Perspective*; Chang, *Bad Samaritans*; Gallagher, *Putting Development First*.

Second, trade liberalization tends to reorder economies, undermining those industries unable to compete in the global economy and strengthening those industries that are already competitive. This should lead to not only an increase in the quantity of goods traded worldwide but also a concentration of those goods produced in certain countries.[7] Countries that don't have competitive manufacturing industries can find themselves de-industrializing and moving back toward an economy based on natural resources or primary agriculture.[8]

Nevertheless, in the context of a global pandemic, increased access to imports of medical goods seems like the right approach. Trade liberalization proponents argue that by increasing the quantity of these medical goods worldwide, producer competition will also increase, driving down prices and improving consumer welfare. Policies that divert or impede trade in essential medical products right now, even to address local shortages or pursue long-term gains for certain countries have met widespread disapproval.[9] The open question, however, is whether trade facilitation will actually lead to an increasing quantity of those goods, and whether other policy changes are required or merited.

At the time of this writing, the WTO predicts that, while global trade and (to a lesser degree) global GDP will decrease as a result of COVID-19, more optimistic outcomes will likely prevail—that trade volumes will only decrease by 12.9 percent and GDP by 2.5 percent.[10] In response to the pandemic, both the economic and public health impacts, governments have put in place a large number of trade policies and regulations—256 between October 2019 and May 2020. Of those, 57 percent were aimed at trade facilitation—increasing trade volumes in goods related to pandemic diagnosis, treatment and care—and 43 percent acted to restrict trade in those goods.[11] Most of the trade restrictions are aimed at driving up domestic access to essential medical goods and keeping them from being exported.[12]

---

7 Stiglitz, *Globalization and Its Discontents*.

8 Gallagher, *Putting Development First*; Stiglitz, *Globalization and Its Discontents*.

9 Trade Policy Review Body, "Report of the TPRB from the Director-General on Trade-Related Developments"; Broadman, "Protectionism Makes The Coronavirus Even More Lethal"; Wolff, Speech "COVID-19 and the Future of World Trade."

10 Trade Policy Review Body, "Report of the TPRB from the Director-General on Trade-Related Developments."

11 Trade Policy Review Body.

12 Although such restrictions have been highlighted in the media as particularly troubling, these are not really new. Trade restrictive measures have been increasingly the norm since the fallout from the 2008 financial crisis such that more than 8 percent of global trade is impacted by these restrictions. Thrasher and Gallagher, "Defending Development Sovereignty: The Case for Industrial Policy and Financial Regulation

Patent Protection and Public Health

Trade liberalization is not the only, or even the primary, way that we can increase access to the products needed to respond to this crisis. Indeed, the major intersection between trade and public health occurs in the trade-related area of IP protection. Unlike most other WTO agreements, the Agreement on Trade-Related Aspects of Intellectual Property Rights (TRIPS)[13] is more about regulatory harmonization (and ratcheting upward) than about de-regulation and lowering barriers to trade. It seems that while we want goods to be able to traverse borders with ease, we want ideas to stay put for as long as possible.

TRIPS entered the global trade regime in 1995, as a part of the single undertaking of the WTO along with the GATS. It was a product of several years of hard negotiations, wherein the United States and the European Union were seeking to extend patent protection for the newest technologies, produced by key innovative firms mostly located in North America and Europe. There was likewise a powerful lobby in the United States trying to cut down on piracy of their music and movies.[14] Although many low- and middle-income countries resisted, developed countries' interests prevailed and a new global agreement on IP rights was created.

From the very beginning, however, there was discontent about the outcome of the agreement.[15] Developing countries in particular felt that the demands of new global IP rules were not in their interest—not because IP protection was seen as unimportant, but because of the balance of interests involved. The importance of protecting IP for the purpose of encouraging its creation is relatively uncontroversial.[16] Discussions primarily center around *how much* compensation is necessary, and *how long* IP needs to be protected in order to encourage an optimal level of innovative ideas.[17] Pharmaceutical patents provide innovators with a monopoly rent for a time in order to compensate them for their innovation and encourage them to innovate more. Economic theory has shown that these incentives will increase the amount of innovation as long as there are few supply-side constraints like lack of human or financial capital. The flip side of that coin, however, is the monopoly rent compensation

in the Trading Regime"; Trade Policy Review Body, "Report of the TPRB from the Director-General on Trade-Related Developments."

13 World Trade Organization, "TRIPS."
14 Trebilcock, Howse and Eliason, *The Regulation of International Trade.*
15 Yu, "TRIPS and Its Discontents."
16 Sircar, "Public Health Emergencies: Reconciling TRIPS and IHR (2005)"; Williams, "Intellectual Property Rights and Innovation: Evidence from Health Care Markets."
17 Lietzan, Kesselheim and Olson, "Antitrust Concerns and the FDA Approval Process."

which, at least in the short term, does not lead to lower prices or increased consumer welfare.

If countries around the world push for stricter standards of IP protection in the name of innovation, we may see more new products but they will remain unaffordable for many. Moreover the problem of access to medicines was not invented with the pandemic; it was only made more visible. In the wake of COVID-19, access to medicines will continue to be an obstacle for many people around the world, in part due to the IP rules in the global trade regime.

Some experts argue vigorously that strong IP rights are essential to support innovative research and development in the pharmaceutical sector just as in other innovation-driven sectors.[18] In fact, there have been some studies that did find a correlation between IP rights and increased innovation.[19] Meanwhile, other scholars argue that IP protection as practiced in today's developed countries is not necessary to produce innovation, and that the current system creates monopolies that naturally drive up prices too much. Both stories may be true, though the evidence seems to lean toward the latter argument.

Whether Stricter Intellectual Property Rules Limit Access to Medicines, and How

Many experts have undertaken to find out whether, in fact, changes in policy toward increased IP protection actually cause prices to rise, and, correspondingly, reduce access to those medicines. The studies generally take one of two approaches: predictive studies using econometric analyses to determine price changes prior to a proposed policy change, or econometric studies after the policy change has gone into effect to see whether prices have indeed risen and by how much. By and large, predictive studies show that stricter IP rules lead to higher medicine prices, as well as increasing medicine expenditure by states and individuals, and, consequently, lower availability of those medicines.[20] Studies that take place after the fact draw similar conclusions but to a slightly less uniform extent.[21]

---

18 Kuhlik, "The Assault on Pharmaceutical Intellectual Property"; Finston, "India: A Cautionary Tale on the Critical Importance of Intellectual Property Protection"; Lybecker, "Intellectual Property Protection for Biologics."

19 Williams, "Intellectual Property Rights and Innovation: Evidence from Health Care Markets."

20 Trachtenberg et al.; Working Group on Trade, Investment Treaties and Access to Medicines, "Rethinking Trade Treaties and Access to Medicines: Toward a Policy Oriented Research Agenda."

21 Trachtenberg et al., "Trade Treaties & Access to Medicines: What Does the Evidence Tell Us? | Global Development Policy Center."

These econometric studies, while useful, come with major limitations. In order to glean meaningful findings, they are often extremely narrow in scope—for example, looking only at the market for one therapeutic drug in one country.[22] Studies of this sort must then extrapolate from the narrow context to draw general conclusions. This strategy may lack robustness due to the ways different therapeutic treatments respond in the market. Moreover, researchers face a lack of available data and can often fail to account for exogenous factors affecting prices that may confuse results.

One type of exogenous factor—one that may help explain the difference between predictive studies and studies that examine impacts after the fact—is the political economy at work in a given context. In particular, it helps to understand how countries mobilize domestic stakeholders to bring about policy change and promote access to medicines.[23] The story of the AIDS crisis in South Africa is often told to bring home this point. In the late 1990s, South Africa allowed parallel importation of various antiretroviral medicines to offer their citizens access to the cheapest medicines on the global market. In response, several developed countries, backed by key pharmaceutical MNCs brought a complaint under the TRIPS agreement, arguing that allowing imports from places like India, which had not patented those treatments, violated the agreement. Despite the strong voices behind it, the case was dropped within a month—in large part because of international publicity (and shaming) made possible by groups like Oxfam and Medecins Sans Frontieres. The whole affair led to the drafting and adoption of the Doha Declaration on TRIPS and Public Health,[24] which sets the gold standard for access to medicines and international IP protection.[25] South Africa continues to lead the world in promoting access to medicines within the international trade regime.[26]

Civil society and domestic political actors have been active in many other countries as well, using the power within their grasp to make medicines more affordable. Brazil, for example, established a new institution called

---

22 Islam et al., "The Social Costs of Graduating from Least Developed Country Status: Analyzing the Impact of Increased Protection on Insulin Prices in Bangladesh"; Chaudhuri, Goldberg and Jia, "Estimating the Effects of Global Patent Protection in Pharmaceuticals: A Case Study of Quinolones in India."
23 Working Group on Trade, Investment Treaties and Access to Medicines, "Rethinking Trade Treaties and Access to Medicines: Toward a Policy Oriented Research Agenda."
24 World Trade Organization, "Doha Declaration on Public Health."
25 't Hoen, *The Global Politics of Pharmaceutical Monopoly Power: Drug Patents, Access, Innovation and the Application of the WTO Doha Declaration on TRIPS and Public Health.*
26 South Africa, "Intellectual Property and Public Interest: Beyond Access to Medicines and Medical Technologies towards a More Holistic Approach to TRIPS Flexibilities."

the Secretariat of Health, Science, Technology and Strategic Inputs, which works together with the Ministry of Health to support health policy goals.[27] Since the government had extended certain guarantees of universal access to key medications, it had a keen interest in keeping prices of newly patented medicines down and actively negotiated with manufacturers as well as issued (or threatened to issue) compulsory licensing to drive prices down.[28]

Rules Governing Trade-Related Intellectual Property Rights: Flexibilities and Limitations

All of these policies, however, are limited to some degree by the multilateral trade and investment regime. The TRIPS agreement marked a new era of globalized minimum standards of IP protection for access to medicines. Before TRIPS, many developing countries did not grant patents for pharmaceutical products at all, often because they viewed the costs of granting patents on medicines as exceeding the benefits. Policy was informed by a sense that pharmaceutical patent protection in an individual low-income or lower-middle income country could only interfere with the rights of a patent holder in a limited way and was not likely to discourage innovation.[29] In the late 1970s and early 1980s, pharmaceutical patenting began to proliferate as innovators and their host states recognized the benefits of increased patent protection. Even then, there was no universally accepted standard of pharmaceutical patent protection, however, and countries had different patent term lengths, patent requirements for different types of pharmaceutical products (e.g., active ingredients, compositions and formulations, medical uses), and data protection duration, among others.[30] TRIPS changed this, reducing this space for cross-national diversity and requiring all WTO countries, except least developed countries (LDCs), to allow patents on pharmaceutical products.

As TRIPS entered into force, WTO members that had previously declined to patent medicines were required by 2005 to begin offering patents (lasting for 20 years from the date of application) for pharmaceuticals and to create a process by which they maintained priority for all patent applications filed after

27 Fonseca, Shadlen and Bastos, "Integrating Science, Technology and Health Policies in Brazil: Incremental Change and Public Health Professionals as Agents of Reform."

28 Shadlen, *Coalitions and Compliance: The Political Economy of Pharmaceutical Patents in Latin America.*

29 Shadlen, Sampat and Kapczynski, "Patents, Trade and Medicines: Past, Present and Future."

30 Shadlen, Sampat and Kapczynski, "Patents, Trade and Medicines: Past, Present and Future."

1995.[31] Although TRIPS set new minimum standards, it left member states some degree of policy space on how to achieve those standards.[32] The TRIPS provisions allowing for discretion in their implementation have come to be known as flexibilities, described in detail in Table 3.1. Countries could use those flexibilities to facilitate access to medicine under the new regime.

One of the most basic flexibilities is rooted in the way TRIPS laid out its patent requirements. Article 27 maintained relatively common standards of patentability: novelty, inventive step and industrial applicability. However, countries have implementation flexibility with respect to the stringency or leniency of such standards. For example, stricter patenting standards are particularly important in eliminating unwarranted patents and patent evergreening—the extension of patent exclusivities by minor tweaks to known products.

The most prominent examples of countries incorporating this flexibility are Argentina, Brazil and India.[33] Under India's Section 3(d), for instance, new forms of existing drugs are not eligible for a patent unless they demonstrate improvements in efficacy. Section 3(d) came under attack when the India's patent office refused to patent Novartis's key cancer treatment, Glivec. As a modification of an existing substance, it was not patentable under Indian law. Although Novartis sued in Indian courts, the Supreme Court upheld the decision and secured India's right to maintain high domestic patentability standards.[34]

WTO members are likewise explicitly permitted (but not required) to exclude "mere discoveries," diagnostic and therapeutic methods, as well as new uses and methods of use of known substances, among others.[35] This provision is important for purposes of access to essential medicine because it gives member states the discretion, for example, to decide whether to grant patents on certain biotechnological inventions or new uses for an existing medicine.[36] TRIPS also required a certain amount of disclosure in the application of a patent which identified all known practical methods of carrying out the invention, as well as the best-known mode and any additional patent applications in other jurisdictions.[37]

31 *India—Patent Protection for Pharmaceutical and Agricultural Chemical Products*, wto.org.

32 Shadlen, Sampat and Kapczynski, "Patents, Trade and Medicines: Past, Present and Future."

33 Shadlen, *Coalitions and Compliance: The Political Economy of Pharmaceutical Patents in Latin America.*

34 Gabble and Kohler, "To Patent or Not to Patent? The Case of Novartis' Cancer Drug Glivec in India."

35 World Trade Organization, "TRIPS," 27.3.

36 Correa, "Unfair Competitions under the TRIPS Agreement: Protection of Data Submitted for the Registration of Pharmaceuticals."

37 World Trade Organization, "TRIPS," 29.

Table 3.1. Recognizing TRIPS "flexibilities" in specific TRIPS provisions

Flexibility	Definition
Exclusions from patentability (Art. 27.3)	Could exclude from patentability "mere discoveries," surgical, diagnostic and therapeutic methods, genes or extractions from naturally occurring matter, new uses and methods of use of known substances, among others.
Standards of patentability (Art. 27)	Could impose high/strict standards of patentability, especially concerning combinations of prior art, novelty, inventive step and industrial applicability.
Disclosure (Art. 29)	Could require applicant to disclose all known practical methods of carrying out the invention, and the best-known mode, as well as corresponding applications in other jurisdictions.
Patent revocation and opposition (Arts. 32 and 62.4)	Could permit both pre- and post-grant opposition procedures with broad standing rights and easy-to-use administrative procedures. Could also establish broad grounds for revoking patents, including inequitable conduct, fraud, non-payment of patent maintenance fees, failure to make required disclosures, and failure to satisfy requirements/standards of patentability.
Bolar/Early working (limited exceptions (Art. 30))	Could create exceptions allowing generic manufacturers to use the patented invention for the purpose of seeking regulatory approval before the patent expires. Includes both commercial and noncommercial research rights, for domestic use and for export, and for pharmacy formulation and individual use.
Compulsory licensing and government use (Arts. 31 and 44.1)	Could establish broad grounds for issuing a government authorization for use of an invention without the consent of the patent holder, including excessive pricing, refusal to license, denial of access to an essential facility, and failure to supply sufficient quantities of a drug, among others. Licenses in the case of national security or public health crises allowed without prior negotiation. Public, noncommercial-use or government-use licenses without prior negotiation. Production for export licenses pursuant to Art. 31bis or, possibly, by an Art. 30 limited exception (although such an interpretation is not established in WTO jurisprudence). Judicial licenses also allowed with clear, efficient and easy-to-use administrative procedures and remuneration guidelines.

(continued)

Table 3.1. (*cont.*)

Flexibility	Definition
Parallel imports (Art. 6)	May choose whichever domestic rule of exhaustion they like. Under the adoption of an international exhaustion rule, for example, products marketed by the patent owner or with the patent owner's permission in one country may be imported into another country without the approval of the patent owner. Furthermore, practices related to parallel importation cannot be challenged under the WTO dispute settlement system.
Data protection (Art. 39)	Must protect undisclosed test data only from unfair commercial use and other disclosure unless "necessary to protect the public or unless steps are taken to" protect against unfair commercial use.
LDC waiver (Art. 66.1)	LDCs are not required to recognize patents on pharmaceuticals, as well as data rights, mailbox obligations and market exclusivity, currently extended by the TRIPS Council to the year 2033.
Competition policies (Arts. 8.2 and 40)	Must prevent abuse of IP rights by right holders, practices that unreasonably restrain trade or adversely affect international transfer of technology. Also, must prevent licensing practices or other IPR conditions that restrain competition, adversely affect trade and impede transfer of technology.
Enforcement flexibilities (various)	Not required to impose border measures for suspected patent infringement of goods in transit (Art. 51). No requirement of criminal penalties for patent violations (Art. 61). Although injunctions must be an available remedy, it is also permissible to limit remedies to adequate remuneration like that provided for compulsory and government-use licenses (Art. 44). Although provisional measures must be possible, their use is not mandatory (Art. 50). Although compensatory damages must be an available remedy for infringement, alternative measures damages based on market value, selling price, or deterrence are not required (Art. 45).

Source: Working Group on Trade, Investment Treaties and Access to Medicines, "Rethinking Trade Treaties and Access to Medicines: Toward a Policy Oriented Research Agenda"; Baker, "A Sliver of Hope: Analyzing Voluntary Licenses to Accelerate Affordable Access to Medicines."

Once a patent application has been filed, TRIPS permits pre- and post-grant opposition procedures whereby interested parties can help screen applications for the requisite patent criteria and disclosure inadequacies.[38] Limited exceptions to patent rights, recognized in Article 30, allow WTO members to adopt important exceptions in their domestic laws aimed at enabling access to essential medicines. The Bolar[39] or early-working research exception is especially important to enable generic medicine producers to begin working on developing a generic version of a medicine and submitting it for regulatory approval while the patent is still active.[40]

One of the most widely discussed flexibilities preserved by the TRIPS Agreement is the right of states to grant compulsory licenses in order to gain more affordable access for their constituents to an essential medicine. Clarified by the Doha Declaration, TRIPS affirms the rights of the parties to balance the interests of IP rights holders and the public's need for essential medicines. It does so by confirming countries' broad discretion to define the grounds for compulsory licenses, including identification of what constitutes an emergency that would permit expedited licensing. Countries may grant compulsory licenses in the case of a national emergency or public health crisis without prior negotiation with the patent holder, as well as for public, noncommercial or government use. Later revisions to Article 31 (Article 31*bis*) permit members to also produce licensed medicines for export and import if the importing countries lacks manufacturing capacity to make use of compulsory licensing.[41] What started as a temporary waiver in 2005 was approved as an amendment to the TRIPS Agreement and ratified by the required two-thirds of WTO membership in 2017.[42]

Selecting a patent exhaustion regime (national, regional or international) is likewise an important flexibility under TRIPS. Through the principle of

---

38 World Trade Organization, "TRIPS," 32.

39 The term Bolar comes from a United State Federal court case in which Bolar Pharmaceutical Company argued that their use of a patented drug fit into an experimental use exception. The Federal Court rejected this argument but the name has stuck in referring to other research exemptions outside of the United States. Roche Product, Inc. v. Bolar Pharmaceutical Co., 733 Federal Second; Hantman, "Experimental Use as an Exception to Patent Infringement."

40 Gleeson et al., "The Trans Pacific Partnership Agreement, Intellectual Property and Medicines: Differential Outcomes for Developed and Developing Countries."

41 Baker, "Ending Drug Registration Apartheid: Taming Data Exclusivity and Patent/Registration Linkage"; Abbott and Reichman, "The Doha Round's Public Health Legacy: Strategies for the Production and Diffusion of Patented Medicines under the Amended TRIPS Provisions"; World Trade Organization, "TRIPS," 31bis.

42 New, "WTO Members Celebrate Treaty Amendment on Medicines Access, Look Ahead."

exhaustion, once a patent owner has sold a patented product for the first time, they *exhaust* their right to control further exploitation and the buyer can use, sell (or export), license or destroy the product as they wish. Choosing international exhaustion allows pharmaceutical products, whose patent rights are exhausted in one country, to be imported into another without the patent owner's permission.[43] This is known as parallel importation. For some lower- and middle-income countries, parallel importation theoretically provides the opportunity for increased access.[44]

A few flexibilities are derived from the absence rather than the presence of treaty language. TRIPS lacks any specific mention of patent term extensions, for example, which would allow patent holders to receive longer patent periods for regulatory or patenting delays. Data protection in TRIPS Article 39 only requires countries to protect undisclosed test data from "unfair commercial use" unless "necessary to protect the public or unless steps are taken to" protect against unfair commercial use[45]—a much narrower standard of protection than the so-called data exclusivity provision, included in many preferential trade agreements (discussed below).

Some flexibilities go far beyond rights limited to patent holders. Competition rules in TRIPS prevent IP right holders from abusing their rights in ways that "unreasonably restrain trade and adversely affect the international transfer of technology" as well as impeding competition.[46] TRIPS also includes various rules on enforcement that allow member countries to protect IP in flexible ways. It does not require that states impose criminal penalties for patent violations, for example, and gives broad discretion in enforcing remedies for infringement.[47] Finally, although this is not directly related to a specific policy choice, LDCs benefit from the adoption and subsequent extension of a transition period for providing patent and data protections for pharmaceuticals until 2033, which gives them additional time to develop pharmaceutical patenting rules and capabilities.[48]

---

43 Krikorian and Szymkowiak, "Intellectual Property Rights in the Making."
44 It is worth noting that international exhaustion may also disincentive-ize patent holders from making those drugs available in the exporting market. Shadlen, Sampat and Kapczynski, "Patents, Trade and Medicines: Past, Present and Future."
45 World Trade Organization, "TRIPS," 39.
46 World Trade Organization, "TRIPS," 8.2, 40.
47 World Trade Organization, "TRIPS," 44, 45, 61.
48 Islam et al., "The Social Costs of Graduating from Least Developed Country Status: Analyzing the Impact of Increased Protection on Insulin Prices in Bangladesh."

In its recent submission to the WTO, South Africa notes that WTO members have "retained important public health flexibilities that can be used to adapt their IP law, policies and practices to meet human rights and public health objectives."[49] The report of the High-Level Panel on Access to Medicines observed the same only four years earlier. Flexibilities that they mentioned included many listed here—from compulsory licensing to patentability criteria, parallel importation and competition rules.[50] Despite this, there are still many countries that do not take advantage of these flexibilities.

One of the most remarkable of underused flexibilities is the compulsory license. In theory, the COVID-19 pandemic seems tailor-fit for such licenses. Given the added opportunities for LDCs under Article 31 *bis*, countries around the world could cooperate to make sure that testing, protective wear and ventilators are made available almost immediately (as soon as manufacturing can ramp up) for developing countries in need. Countries are able, under TRIPS, to engage in research and development to test and prepare for the manufacture of pharmaceuticals even prior to the end of a patent term. So while medicines are being tested, every country with capacity should be able to have access to the materials and data needed to develop treatment in parallel. The same should be true of vaccines. Once treatment and vaccines are available, countries can again issue compulsory licenses to get access to those products at affordable prices.

Nevertheless, compulsory licenses are only infrequently used, and an export-based license under Article 31 *bis* has only been attempted once— by Canada exporting an antiretroviral to Rwanda.[51] Since the onset of the pandemic, many more countries have sought compulsory licenses, as well as government-use licenses, for possible treatments, equipment and technology.[52] Still, the problem of access to medicines does not begin and will not end with

---

49 South Africa, "Intellectual Property and Public Interest: Beyond Access to Medicines and Medical Technologies towards a More Holistic Approach to TRIPS Flexibilities."

50 UN Secretary-General, "Report of the United Nations Secretary-General's High-Level Panel on Access to Medicines: Promoting Innovation and Access to Health Technologies."

51 Houston and Beall, "Could the Paragraph 6 Compulsory License System Be Revised to Increase Participation by the Generics Industry"; Sircar, "Public Health Emergencies: Reconciling TRIPS and IHR (2005)."

52 World Health Organization, World Intellectual Property Organization, and World Trade Organization, *Promoting Access to Medical Technologies and Innovation: Intersections between Public Health, Intellectual Property and Trade*.pp.205–206.

the pandemic. And the flexibilities inherent within the TRIPS rules are still exploited very little. One reason for this may lie in the web of extra-WTO agreements that contain language that ratchets up the IP commitments of their treaty parties.

Ratcheting Up Intellectual Property Protections with Regional and Bilateral Agreements

The language of TRIPS and its subsequent legal interpretation is fairly well-understood and discussed. The newer regime of free trade agreements and bilateral investment treaties, however, has further expanded IP rights to effectively undermine the flexibilities available in TRIPS. Researchers have found that approximately 90 percent of all trade agreements signed since 2009 include IP rules, and of those, at least one-third include provisions that increase IP protection for pharmaceuticals.[53] Furthermore, while the vast majority of these treaties originate with the United States, or countries in the European Free Trade Association, newer treaties among low- and middle-income countries have also begun to increase IP commitments.[54]

The provisions that restrict flexibilities in trade and investment agreements are thus called TRIPS-plus provisions, many of which are summarized in Table 3.2. Though, as noted above, not all extra-WTO treaties include each of these provisions, as a group they act to ratchet up overall IP commitments globally. Moreover, no treaty appears in a vacuum and many newly negotiated agreements borrow language from contemporaneous treaty drafts, creating a feedback loop of increasingly greater IP protection.

TRIPS-plus provisions impact access to medicines by introducing new standards in patentability, revocation and exceptions, inserting new rules to protect innovators, and adding new enforcement requirements for IP infringement.[55] Traditional standards of patentability, the TRIPS standard, still present in some extra-WTO treaties, require that inventions meet a threshold of novelty, involve an inventive step and are capable of industrial application.[56] Most treaties then exclude diagnostic, therapeutic and surgical methods for human treatment, as well as microorganisms and microbiological processes.[57] TRIPS has little to say

---

53 Wu, "Intellectual Property Rights."
54 Wu, "Intellectual Property Rights," 212.
55 Working Group on Trade, Investment Treaties and Access to Medicines, "Rethinking Trade Treaties and Access to Medicines: Toward a Policy Oriented Research Agenda."
56 China-Georgia, "China-Georgia FTA," 11.8.
57 "USMCA," 20.36.

Table 3.2. TRIPS-plus measures with implications for access to medicines

Measures	Mechanism of Impacting Access
Old provisions; New standards	
Eased standards of patentability	Requires patents on (1) new uses or methods of use of known medicines, and (2) new forms for known substances regardless of therapeutic efficacy. Lowers standards on novelty, inventive step (changed to "obviousness") and industrial applicability (changed to "usefulness"—both terms as used in the United States).
Limitations on patent revocation/ opposition	Limited grounds for patent opposition/ revocation by government.
Weakened limited exceptions for patent use	Restriction on the use by nonpatent holder of early working/Bolar provisions in obtaining third-market registration. No exception or weak exception for noncommercial and commercial research and educational use of patented technology. No exception permitted for prior use of patented technology.
New provisions	
Patent term extension	Extensions for delays in processing patent applications, medicines registration and marketing and other regulatory delays.
Elimination of patent exceptions	Requires patents on diagnostic, therapeutic and surgical methods for treatment of humans.
Patent registration linkage	Restricts the medicine regulatory authority's ability to register a generic medicine whenever an originator merely claims that a patent would be infringed.
Data exclusivity	Gives exclusive rights to regulatory data to the patent holder and prohibits medicine regulator's reliance on, or reference to, innovator's submission data in reviewing registration applications of generics. Includes the possibility of extending data exclusivity upon submission of additional clinical data not available at the time of the original submission.

(continued)

Table 3.2. (*cont.*)

Measures	Mechanism of Impacting Access
Enforcement measures	
Increased civil and border measures remedies	Deterrent civil remedies, such as damages based on average retail price. Requires seizure of goods in transit, mandatory destruction and allows third-party enforcement.
Broadened criminal remedies	Criminal sanctions for patent violations (beyond TRIPS requirement for criminal trademark counterfeiting and copyright piracy only).
Investor–state dispute settlement provisions	Inclusion of IPRs as covered investment, which permits ISDS claims based on patent decisions.*

* Although this table is quite comprehensive in terms of the IP and investment provisions that directly impact access to medicines, it lacks additional IP rules that might affect delivery of medicines, including trade secrets and in some cases trademark. It also does not include a much broader set of treaty provisions that have potential impacts on core pharmaceutical policy objectives, which include such provisions as procedural requirements for national pharmaceutical pricing and reimbursement, government procurement rules, rules on state-owned enterprises and designated monopolies, among others. For a detailed discussion of these aspects of trade agreements, see Gleeson et al., "Analyzing the Impact of Trade and Investment Agreements on Pharmaceutical Policy: Provisions, Pathways and Potential Impacts."

Source: Gleeson et al., "Analyzing the Impact of Trade and Investment Agreements on Pharmaceutical Policy: Provisions, Pathways and Potential Impacts"; Working Group on Trade, Investment Treaties and Access to Medicines, "Rethinking Trade Treaties and Access to Medicines: Toward a Policy Oriented Research Agenda."

on the subject of domestic patent revocation and allows limited exceptions to the exploitation of patent rights as long as they do not "unreasonably prejudice" the interests of the patent holder.[58]

A new wave of IP treaty commitments is changing the contours of those rules. Instead of demanding an inventive step and industrial application, these standards have eroded to "non-obviousness" and "usefulness."[59] Some treaties have even required patents for new *uses* of known medicines or new *forms* of

---

58 World Trade Organization, "TRIPS," 30.
59 "USMCA," 20.36.1, fn. 29.

known substances.[60] They also set strict limits for patent revocation—only where the patent failed to meet initial standards of patentability or in the case of outright fraud.[61] And the limited exceptions of TRIPS Article 30 are further constrained through specific regulatory review exceptions, narrowing the traditional scope of exceptions to exclusive rights.[62]

The new treaty wave has likewise adopted new provisions that further limit policy options available to member states. One of the most common new provisions requires parties to extend patent terms when there are delays in the patenting process to comply with regulatory requirements or gain marketing approval.[63] Another new rule links marketing approval for generic medicines to the registered patent status of the original product. This often triggers automatic infringement actions, delaying marketing approval for up to two and half years.[64] One proposed treaty text even demanded that parties recognize patents for diagnostic, therapeutic and surgical methods.[65]

The extent to which countries protect the data underlying patent applications is a major area of change in new trade agreements. The TRIPS standard does require that member countries protect that data against "unfair commercial use."[66] New treaty language expands that protection such that clinical trial data is not disclosed for any reason for five to twelve years.[67] Data exclusivity rules, as they have been called, can delay access to the market for generic drugs if they are required to generate their own test data or where the market exclusivity extends past the patent protection of a drug.[68] Data exclusivity provisions have become more prevalent as the United States and the European

---

60 US-Korea, "US-Korea FTA," 18.8.1.

61 "USMCA," 20.38.

62 "USMCA," 20.47.

63 "USMCA," 20.46.2; Canada-EU, "CETA," 20.27; EU-Japan, "EU-Japan EPA," 14.35.

64 Baker, "Ending Drug Registration Apartheid: Taming Data Exclusivity and Patent/ Registration Linkage"; Son et al., "Moderating the Impact of Patent Linkage on Access to Medicines."

65 Gleeson, Tienhaara and Faunce, "Challenges to Australia's National Health Policy from Trade and Investment Agreements."

66 World Trade Organization, "TRIPS," 39.3.

67 EU-Japan, "EU-Japan EPA," 14.37; Canada-EU, "CETA," 20.29; "USMCA," 20.48.1.

68 McCall and Quinn, "The FDA Process, Patents and Market Exclusivity"; Shadlen, Sampat and Kapczynski, "Patents, Trade and Medicines: Past, Present and Future."

Union have pushed for these heightened standards in their agreements. Even China has begun to introduce strict data exclusivity rules into its domestic law—six years for new chemical entities and twelve for biologics.[69]

To enforce its IP rules, the TRIPS agreement requires that member states provide effective enforcement measures to prevent and compensate for IP right infringement. At a minimum, countries must empower their judicial authorities to issue injunctions against infringing goods, damages to compensate for the injury and order the infringing goods to be disposed of or destroyed. Criminal procedures and penalties are required only in the case of "willful trademark counterfeiting and copyright piracy."[70]

New enforcement mechanisms add teeth to the increased IP protection already present in the FTAs. Some treaties provide for more deterrent civil remedies, specifying damages based on the average retail price of the original goods.[71] Others demand that counterfeit goods are not only seized but also destroyed in transit if they are found to infringe on patent rights.[72] They also expand the requirement for criminal sanctions far beyond the narrow context found in TRIPS.[73]

When IP is considered a type or form of investment covered by investment protection commitments, the enforcement toolkit expands further.[74] In that case, regulations that undermine the value of that investment by allowing infringement on patent or data exclusivity rights might run afoul of investor protections under the agreement and make countries subject to investor–state disputes for their public health policies. These challenges can prove very expensive, especially for low-income and lower-middle-income countries, even if the investor-claimant is unsuccessful.[75] Provisions outside of IP chapters, like these, are not often mentioned in the debate surrounding access to medicine but can have a direct effect on medicine pricing and availability.

At the time of this writing, three different countries have faced investor–state dispute challenges initiated by pharmaceutical companies. Gilead

---

69 Wang, "The China Drug Administration Proposes a Working Procedure for Pharmaceutical Study Data Protection."

70 World Trade Organization, "TRIPS," 41–61.

71 US-Korea, "US-Korea FTA," 18.10.5; Canada-EU, "CETA," 20.48.

72 EU-Japan, "EU-Japan EPA," 14.42, 14.51.

73 US-Korea, "US-Korea FTA," 18.10.27.

74 Canada-EU, "CETA," 8.1; Canada-Australia-Brunei-Chile-Japan-Malaysia-Mexico-New Zealand-Peru-Singapore-Vietnam, "CPTPP," 9.1.

75 Gleeson et al., "The Trans Pacific Partnership Agreement, Intellectual Property and Medicines: Differential Outcomes for Developed and Developing Countries."

Sciences (a company incorporated in the United States) brought a claim against Ukraine after failing in domestic courts to secure exclusivity in the country for Sovaldi (for hepatitis C). In Colombia, Novartis threatened a claim when Colombia prepared to issue a compulsory license on its prized cancer medication, Gleevec (Glivec). Eli Lilly sued Canada based on the Canadian domestic court's application of the "promise doctrine" whereby patents must live up to their (medicinal) promises in order to maintain patent protection.[76] Only the latter of those three resulted in a decision, but all three highlight the susceptibility of countries' IP laws when covered by trade and investment treaties.

Ukraine and Colombia both settled with the pharmaceutical companies, deciding to negotiate for lower prices rather than pursue the domestic policies they had originally implemented.[77] In Canada's case, the arbitration tribunal decided in favor of the state, that Canada's revocation of Eli Lilly's patents was not a violation of the investment treaty's fair and equitable treatment standard because it was rooted in established Canadian law. Countries without the promise doctrine on the books, however, might find themselves liable for voiding a pharmaceutical patent—even if that patent did not live up to its promised utility.[78]

Concluding Thoughts

Each treaty has a slightly different articulation of these protections for innovators. In most cases, we don't know the full import of these provisions because they have not been tested. Some experts have even argued that it is "too soon to tell" the impacts of these provisions since many countries did not have to introduce pharmaceutical patenting until 2005. Those earliest patents have not yet expired and thus the possible extensions of those patent terms, the impact of data exclusivity, and patent and registration linkage are yet to be seen.[79]

There have been some efforts to quantify the impact of key IP provisions on pharmaceutical policy space and, by extension, on access to medicines.[80] Independently, there have been other efforts to measure the overall depth of

76 Baker and Geddes, "The Incredible Shrinking Victory."
77 Baker and Geddes, "The Incredible Shrinking Victory."
78 Baker and Geddes, "The Incredible Shrinking Victory."
79 Shadlen, Sampat and Kapczynski, "Patents, Trade and Medicines: Past, Present and Future."
80 Gleeson et al., "Analyzing the Impact of Trade and Investment Agreements on Pharmaceutical Policy: Provisions, Pathways and Potential Impacts."

the trade treaty regime as it relates to IP protection,[81] as well as the reach of the international investment regime, including its potential impact on the same.[82]

The impact of the pandemic is still working its way through the global economy and health systems. Some argue that using this crisis to push for greater opening of the global economy will further undermine the financial and fiscal stability of developing countries attempting to rebuild in its wake.[83] Others argue forcefully that trade restrictive measures will decrease access to diagnostics, devices, treatments and vaccines and slow down the rate at which countries can recover.[84]

This crisis could present "an opportunity to learn from, and strengthen multilateral cooperation to address coming challenges."[85] A global pandemic offers a condensed picture of larger systemic issues that need multilateral solutions, like climate change. If we learn from our current context, collective public health interests may take precedence over strict IP protection. And hopefully investor–state disputes that challenge domestic health and medicine policies will come under increased scrutiny.[86]

Addressing a global pandemic, while it demands a collective action, does not demand increased trade rules commitments. To encourage cooperation, future treaties need to focus on building domestic and global capacities to meet these challenges.

---

81 Hofmann, Osnago and Ruta, "Horizontal Depth"; Wu, "Intellectual Property Rights."
82 UNCTAD, "The Changing IIA Landscape: New Treaties and Recent Policy Developments"; UNCTAD, "Investor-State Dispute Settlement Cases Pass the 1,000 Mark: Cases and Outcomes in 2019."
83 Gallagher and Kozul-Wright, "Breaking Out of the Double Squeeze: The Need for Fiscal and Policy Space during the COVID-19 Crises."
84 Baldwin and Tomiura, "Thinking Ahead about the Trade Impact of COVID-19."
85 Blanchard, "The Role of Deep Agreements in a Post-COVID-19 World: Round Table and Q&A."
86 Blanchard, "The Role of Deep Agreements in a Post-COVID-19 World: Round Table and Q&A."

Chapter 4

LAND GRABS, LAND GOVERNANCE AND INTERNATIONAL INVESTMENT COMMITMENTS*

Since 2000, the world has experienced a large, sudden increase in large-scale transnational land transactions. State-owned and private corporations, as well as private investors of agricultural land have purchased or (where land is not saleable) acquired long-term leases on large swathes of land for food, biofuel and (more recently) clean energy production.[1] At their most extreme, these transactions result in illegal dispossession of land and forcible transfer of the population living there.[2] The majority of these transactions are more nuanced in their design and impacts, however. Governments, seeking foreign investment for development and an infusion of capital, sell or lease government land to large corporations for food or energy plantations. Foreign direct investment (FDI) of this sort, as with all foreign investment, has long been considered a boon to countries seeking economic growth, diversification and development. Consequently, most (but not all) of these transactions take place between investors based in the United States, Europe and wealthy East Asian states, and regions with large amounts of rural land that is relatively less-developed, such as sub-Saharan Africa, Southeast Asia, Central and South America and Eastern Europe.[3]

---

* This chapter first appeared as a Background Paper for the Global Development and Environment Institute at Tufts University, co-authored with Dario Bevilacqua and Jeronim Capaldo.

1 Smaller and Mann, "A Thirst for Distant Lands: Foreign Investment in Agricultural Land and Water."

2 International Criminal Court, "ICC Tackling Global Challenges." The International Criminal Court has found this behavior to fall under the category "Crime Against Humanity," over which it asserts jurisdiction in member states. Rogers and FIDH, "Questions & Answers: Crimes against Humanity in Cambodia from July 2002 until Present."

3 Borras Jr. et al., "Towards a Better Understanding of Global Land Grabbing"; Smaller and Mann, "A Thirst for Distant Lands: Foreign Investment in Agricultural Land and Water." This experience is not exactly unique to developing countries. The experience of Native American groups, after experiencing centuries of violations of their land rights,

Despite its promises, however, large-scale land investment deals have resulted in increased inequality, widespread displacement of people and the destruction of natural resources. In many of these rural areas, indigenous communities and small agricultural villages have been living and subsisting on that land for centuries. Most of these traditional farmers do not have formal titles, even if they are available, and so the government can easily (and even inadvertently) sell the land, making them *de facto* trespassers on their own property. Even efforts at land reform through title and registration schemes have left local communities with increasingly tenuous and uncertain claims to their land.

The presence of these land "grabs," so named for their negative impacts on local populations, as a source of investment is hardly new, and arguably is simply part of the economic and social transformation in many developing countries.[4] In recent years, though, a sudden, large demand for rural land has been driven in part by the commodity boom of the mid-2000s, as well as by an ideological shift to promote foreign investment of all kinds, and global crises in finance and climate.[5] During and after the financial crisis in 2008, international investors gained an interest in buying large tracts of land for agriculture and (eventually) energy production when many other markets began to dry up.[6] A growing awareness of the impacts of climate change has also led to increasing large-scale land transactions for wind and solar farms and biofuel production.[7]

Today's small-scale land holders face extreme economic pressure, without which they likely could have continued farming for many more decades without secure land titles. Between the pressure from MNCs and their home states, and competition from other developing countries, their tenure is increasingly uncertain.[8] The most recent trends show that while the number

---

continue to fight against projects like the Dakota Access and TransCanada Pipelines. Nichols, *Theft Is Property: Dispossession and Critical Theory*; TransCanada Corporation and TransCanada Pipelines Limited v. United States of America, italaw.com.

4 "Oakland Institute | Reframing the Debate Inspiring Action"; Anseeuw et al., "Land Rights and the Rush for Land: Findings of the Global Commercial Pressures on Land Research Project."

5 Cotula, "Land Rights and Investment Treaties: Exploring the Interface"; Lavers, "Patterns of Agrarian Transformation in Ethiopia: State-Mediated Commercialisation and the 'Land Grab'"; Sikor, "Tree Plantations, Politics of Possession and the Absence of Land Grabs in Vietnam"; Cotula and Berger, "Trends in Global Land Use Investment: Implications for Legal Empowerment."

6 Cotula, "Land Rights and Investment Treaties: Exploring the Interface."

7 European Commission, "2009 Renewable Energy Directive."

8 Anseeuw et al., "Land Rights and the Rush for Land: Findings of the Global Commercial Pressures on Land Research Project."

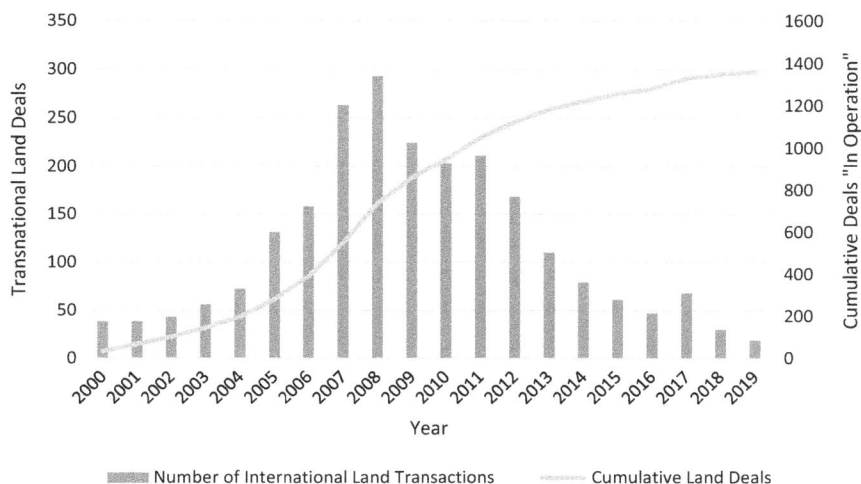

Figure 4.1. Transnational land deals and cumulative deals in operation

of new transnational land deals have begun to decline, the surge of deals between 2005 and 2013 are now at the implementation stage and have begun to have a larger impact on the ground.[9] What we see now is more than 2,300 large-scale transnational land deals under contract, amounting to 79.4 million hectares of land worldwide (Figure 4.1), only 14 percent of which is in productive use.[10]

To respond to this reality, national governments have often taken an active role by enacting laws that protect vulnerable agricultural landholders and traditional communities, putting limits on foreign investments in domestic law at the front end of those transactions, and by putting the brakes on foreign investment through nonrenewal, renegotiation or termination, when it is clear the impacts are a net negative for local populations. Unfortunately, the negative externalities of these large-scale land purchases are reinforced and facilitated through our current network of IIAs. To resolve the tension between national goals and IIA commitments, this chapter highlights both the importance of policy flexibility—in the presence of narrower and shallower agreements, and a deference to host state institutions in conflicts over its own land.

---

9 Cotula and Berger, "Trends in Global Land Use Investment: Implications for Legal Empowerment."

10 landmatrix.org, "Data: All Deals."

Investment Liberalization: Putting Limits on Policy Space

As Chapters 5 and 6 discuss in more detail, the governance of investment activities and movement of capital has reached a global dimension. Correspondingly, states have recognized the need to set rules, to pose limits and to protect the investors (for instance, from expropriation) and to coordinate those on a global scale. As proponents of investment liberalization argue, a company is entitled to make investments all over the world, and it is useful to have common principles and common rules governing such activity. At its best, the legal harmonization of this field helps the movement of capital all around the world and encourages private investors to use their money to create growth.

It comes up again and again, in each new context discussed here, but it is worth reiterating: investor protection has become a top priority for both investor home states and the host states that receive them. Host states are promised higher employment, economic growth and diversification into new sectors, new technology and, by extension, overall increases in human capital development through workforce training and experience all through the successful establishment and operation of foreign investment. Unfortunately, evidence of growth from FDI is mixed at best.[11] Research has found that such investment has a positive effect only where specific preconditions are present, including projects with shared domestic and foreign ownership,[12] investment in a country with a strong human capital base able to absorb the new technology,[13] and in countries that are relatively more developed.[14]

Nevertheless, investment exporters, most often countries at higher levels of per capita income and development, tend to put pressure on trading partners to increase investment liberalization in the interests of their MNCs. Investment liberalization generally means offering special protection to foreign investors—demanding equal treatment with domestic investors, and removing regulatory barriers that would interfere with the establishment, management and operation of their businesses. There is likewise pressure from fellow developing countries, who are competing for developed country FDI and all that it promises. This has led to a race among developing

---

11 Cotula and Berger, "Trends in Global Land Use Investment: Implications for Legal Empowerment"; Smaller and Mann, "A Thirst for Distant Lands: Foreign Investment in Agricultural Land and Water."

12 Smarzynska Javorcik, "Does Foreign Direct Investment Increase the Productivity of Domestic Firms?"

13 Borensztein, Gregorio and Lee, "How Does Foreign Direct Investment Affect Economic Growth?"

14 Alfaro et al., "Does Foreign Direct Investment Promote Growth?"

country regulators in particular, competing with each other to lower barriers and improve (read: remove) regulatory conditions in order to attract foreign capital.

To respond to pressures from investment exporters and competitive importers, states have offered extensive tax breaks for foreign corporations, sold or leased land at below-market prices and, in the most extreme cases, even cleared their own citizens from the land to make room for large-scale plantations.[15] Incentives have also included administrative and marketing support, guaranteed prices and government purchase of the goods produced, removal of rules restricting foreign ownership of companies and land, and even more direct forms of support in the form of subsidies. Moreover, some countries have been found to loosen other policies aimed at protecting general interests (such as the environment, health and labor rights), which may conflict with investment interests or delay the progress of an investor's production. Many of these policies make their way into private concession agreements between the individual investor and the host state. Concession agreements attempt to provide stability and promised returns on investment in exchange for a more long-term, committed presence by the investor.

Parallel to this trend and amplified by it, there is also a large and growing network of IIAs that has a two-fold effect on domestic policies. First, countries involved in treaty negotiations often proactively liberalize their investment law in order to seem an attractive investment destination and potential treaty partner to the other party—this is especially the case for low-income countries pursuing FDI. Second, once those treaties are in place, future changes to domestic law are much more difficult to achieve. In this way, they act to "compound shortcomings in national land governance," which expose traditional cultures and small holder villages to land and food insecurity.[16]

As noted in Chapter 2, investment treaties have been broadly criticized for restricting policy space by dictating which laws states can and cannot implement and prioritizing the protection of foreign investment over states' interests. Where investment agreements do not make specific demands on domestic policymaking, critics of the investment regime point out that ambiguous rules may cause a regulatory chill in states where they cannot run the risk of breaching the agreement. And of course, most of these commitments are backed up by giving investors the right to sue their host states in private arbitration for a breach of the agreement. For developing countries with less fiscal space, this presents a particularly onerous burden due

---

15 Mousseau and Mittal, "Country Report: Mozambique"; Mousseau and Mittal, "Country Report: Tanzania"; Mousseau and Sosnoff, "Country Report: Ethiopia."

16 Cotula, "Land Rights and Investment Treaties: Exploring the Interface."

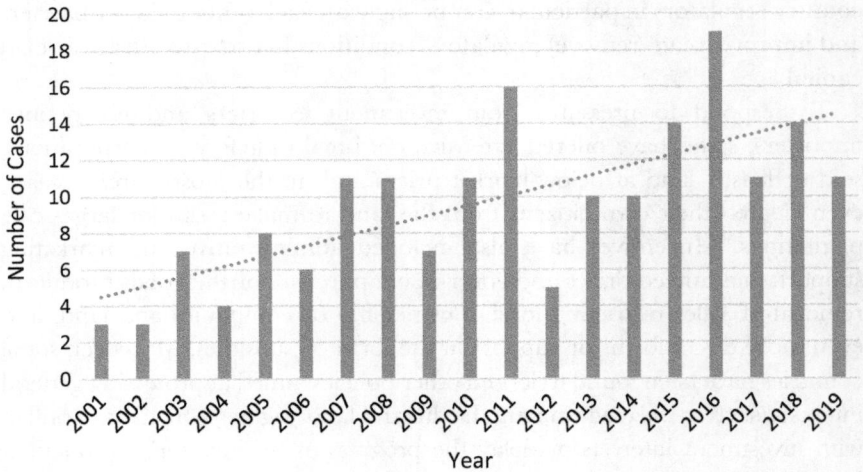

Figure 4.2. Number of investor–state disputes involving land-use investments, 2000–19

Source: UNCTAD Investment Policy Hub, "Investment Dispute Settlement Navigator."

to the costs of arbitration and (potentially) large awards for the investor if the state loses (see Chapters 2, 5 and 6).

Although there have not been any investor–state disputes contesting the treatment of large-scale land investors to date, there have been a growing number of cases involving land use investments, most of which deal with extractive industries.[17] Moreover, evidence has shown that at least 64 percent of documented transnational land investments are protected by investment treaties, and thereby subject to ISDS.[18]

In the global context, the international treaties that aim to increase free trade, competition and free movement of services and capital are more comprehensive and enforceable than the ones aimed at protecting noneconomic interests. In other words, we could say that while rules governing trade, competition and investment are becoming global norms, health and environmental protection, social and labor rights, and so on still are mainly issues of international negotiation and domestic regulation. As a result, countries have fewer tools and incentives for protecting social interests than economic ones, exacerbating the insecurities and vulnerabilities of their

---

17 Cotula and Berger, "Trends in Global Land Use Investment: Implications for Legal Empowerment."

18 Cotula and Berger, "Trends in Global Land Use Investment: Implications for Legal Empowerment."

constituents. In a globalized economy, as long as there is no cultural and political consensus on the way states should protect such underrepresented interests, the economic ones will always prevail.

As we have already seen, in the context of industrial policies and intellectual property protection, the actual language of the international trade and investment commitments matter. Some treaty provisions prohibit policies that countries have been using for hundreds of years, while others attempt to carve out exceptions and create space for policymaking. Just like in other investment contexts, large-scale land transactions involve competing interests and the treaty text itself must be balanced in a way that does not disregard the human rights, environmental and social impacts of those transactions.

International Investment Agreements

BITs have been commonplace since the 1950s. During the 1980s and 1990s, especially, the number of agreements soared, and today there are more than 3,000 in effect globally.[19] There has been a downward trend in recent years for several different reasons. Widespread criticism of investor–state dispute settlement as it impacts domestic policymaking is one driver of such a decline. Some countries have wholesale terminated all investment treaties to protect against such policy impacts.[20]

A much more powerful driver, however, is the trend toward broader and deeper integration. Standalone BITs have been set aside in favor of full-fledged mega-regional free trade agreements with commitments in goods and services trade, investment protection, intellectual property rules, competition policies and more. In 2019, the European Union agreed to terminate all intra-EU investment treaties in favor of a regional investment policy.[21] The region has begun to negotiate trade and investment agreements as a bloc— a process already completed with Singapore and Vietnam.[22] Britain's exit from the European Union is likely to result in an increase in new investment treaties with the European Union and other trading partners. Meanwhile, at the multilateral level, WTO reform has on its agenda a new investment facilitation agreement by which proponents hope to address transparency

---

19 UNCTAD Investment Policy Hub, "International Investment Agreements Navigator."
20 Ross, "India's Termination of BITs to Begin"; Olivet, "Why Did Ecuador Terminate All Its Bilateral Investment Treaties?"
21 Poland was the most active states to begin that process. UNCTAD, "The Changing IIA Landscape: New Treaties and Recent Policy Developments."
22 EU-Singapore, "EU-Singapore FTA"; EU-Singapore, "EU-Singapore IPA"; EU-Vietnam, "EU-Vietnam FTA"; EU-Vietnam, "EU-Vietnam IPA."

concerns, lowering barriers to administrative procedures and international cooperation.[23]

While the network of trade and investment treaties grows, countries experiencing the challenges of large land purchases have to make policy choices that may run afoul of these treaties. Many countries have existing laws to minimize the commercialization of land rights.[24] These include limitations on foreign land ownership by duration, land area, or to specific forms of land use. Countries might also require government authorization for foreign land acquisition, or even ban foreigners from owning land completely. The Voluntary Guidelines on the Responsible Governance of Tenure of Land, Fisheries and Forests,[25] established by the Food and Agriculture Organization, recommends that states establish key tenure rights for indigenous and traditional cultures, protect small holder agriculture, and recognize the interdependence of rights between their constituents. In order to implement these principles, countries may impose stricter standards for local community participation, free, prior, and informed consent, and impact assessments, or place land-area ceilings on these transactions. All of these may balance the rights and obligations of various stakeholders, but they also have the potential to increase costs and delay project implementation for foreign investors.[26]

Outside of land governance laws, investor–state concession agreements may also give rise to conflict. If the investment proves to have more negative social or environmental impacts than originally foreseen, states may refuse to issue or renew environmental permits, renegotiate or terminate contracts, or resist new negotiations initiated by the investor. Moreover, when communities and villages assert their own rights in legal and extra-legal ways, states can be held responsible for damaged property and even for the delay resulting from domestic court cases.

By comparing various existing and proposed treaty texts, we can see that those treaties act as barriers to states trying to improve land governance and care for the most vulnerable communities displaced due to these large-scale investments. As noted above, the mere presence of investment treaty negotiations can have an impact on investment law in the host country. Many countries liberalize (deregulating and removing old barriers to foreign-held

---

23 Notably, the Joint Ministerial Statement explicitly excludes investment protection and investor–state dispute settlement from the negotiating agenda. "Joint Ministerial Statement on Investment Facilitation for Development."

24 Cotula, "Land Rights and Investment Treaties: Exploring the Interface."

25 Committee on World Food Security and Food and Agriculture Organization, "Voluntary Guidelines on Land Tenure."

26 Cotula, "Land Rights and Investment Treaties: Exploring the Interface."

investment) in anticipation of a new treaty, signaling their preparedness for these commitments. If those unilateral measures result in an agreement, future changes may be more difficult to make.

Preestablishment protection

The impact of investment treaty commitments can be seen even before foreign investment enters the host state. Many of the standard treaty provisions require that states remove limitations on foreign ownership. This is made possible through preestablishment rights (mentioned in Chapter 2), often linked to national treatment and MFN treatment nondiscrimination provisions. While there is some variation in whether treaty texts include these rights, most of the newest mega-regional trade agreements, the CPTPP, the RCEP and the USMCA (NAFTA 2.0), do contain them.[27] Even European trade agreements have begun to incorporate the same language in the nondiscrimination provisions and adopt market access provisions, typically found in services agreements that prohibit limitations on foreign investors outright.[28]

The implications for large-scale land purchases are clear. Any existing or proposed land laws limiting the form, quantity, proportion or location of foreign land ownership would violate these preestablishment clauses.

Fair and equitable treatment: A "minimum" standard?

Once states admit foreign investors to own or lease land in their territory, additional standards of treatment come into play. Large-scale land purchases are tied to investor–state concession agreements, the contents of which are usually not open to the public. Nevertheless, the environmental externalities that those countries experience, unexpected social pushback from affected communities and the inherent instability of investments based on commodity markets suggest that the long-term nature of the concession agreements is not sustainable.

Countries attempting to respond to these realities by initiating renegotiation with the foreign investor, refusing to grant the needed environmental and other permits for the investor to operate or terminating the contract altogether face the uncertain terms of the so-called minimum standard of treatment or

---

27 Canada-Australia-Brunei-Chile-Japan-Malaysia-Mexico-New Zealand-Peru-Singapore-Vietnam, "CPTPP," 9.4-9.5; "USMCA," 14.4-14.5; "RCEP," 10.3-10.4. Note that Cambodia, Loas, Myanmar and Vietnam are excluded from coverage under this provision. "RCEP," 10.4, n. 18.

28 EU-Japan, "EU-Japan EPA," 8.7–8.9.

"fair and equitable treatment" (FET) standard, ubiquitous among modern investment treaties. At its most basic, the FET standard protects foreign land investors from egregious host state behavior—arbitrary regulation, outright taking of their property and lack of protection under the most basic laws of the state. As the concept of legitimate investor expectations creeps into our understanding of that standard, however, it is easy to see that concession agreements may be just the sort of document to create an expectation of long-term viability, which these host country policies undermine.

Perhaps the most troubling outcome of this standard is the vagueness of its text and the resultant diversity of interpretation. One arbitration tribunal identified thirteen different but overlapping articulations of that standard from recent jurisprudence.[29] While some interpretations keep FET narrow in its reach, others seem to protect against any legal change that undermines "reasonable expectations or guarantees of stability." Some tribunals emphasize a country's right to regulate in the public interest,[30] while others point out that even general legislation might give rise to legitimate expectations of legal stability.[31]

Indeed, even the United States and European Union have seen problems with the expansive interpretation. The United States has expressly excluded investor expectations from the purview of FET.[32] Meanwhile, the European Union has elected in some cases to simply include a short illustrative list of potential violations,[33] or even omit reference to this standard of treatment entirely.[34]

Still, even the narrowest understandings of FET may expose host country governments to arbitration risk under these investment agreements. The Comprehensive Economic Trade Agreement (CETA), between the European Union and Canada, for example, acknowledges that where a host state extends explicit assurances to the investors on which they rely, such as a concession contract, reneging on those commitments amounts to a violation. The concession agreements often contain regulatory stabilization clauses and put obligations on the host state to live up to their promises of special tax and regulatory treatment and other supports. Moreover, newer treaties are only the beginning of a trend in recasting the FET standard. The vast majority

29 Antaris GMBH and Dr. Michael Gode v. The Czech Republic, www.italaw.com paragraph 360ff.
30 EU-Vietnam, "EU-Vietnam IPA."
31 Antaris GMBH and Dr. Michael Gode v. The Czech Republic, www.italaw.com paragraph 360.
32 "USMCA," 14.6.
33 Canada-EU, "CETA," 8.10.
34 EU-Japan, "EU-Japan EPA."

of the world's investment treaties continue to contain vague references to the minimum standard of treatment that could be interpreted as broadly as the tribunal would like given the circumstances.[35]

Indirect and direct expropriation

The same state behavior that may give rise to an investor–state claim under the FET standard also may implicate the provision governing direct and indirect expropriation or nationalization. When it becomes painfully clear that the host state cannot keep the terms of a concession contract, they may attempt to slow down the process, change the terms of the agreement or cancel it. In instances of traditional nationalization, customary international law requires that such takings take place *only* (1) in a nondiscriminatory way, (2) for a public purpose, (3) in accordance with due process and (4) on payment of full compensation (see Chapter 2).[36]

While direct expropriation is a clearly understood concept, indirect expropriation is arguably as vague a standard as FET. Indirect expropriation encompasses government action which so diminishes the value of an investment that the results are "tantamount to" a direct taking of the property.[37] Investors have used this provision to challenge environmental measures that ban the use of their products,[38] refusal to issue environmental permits and licenses so that the investment can get underway,[39] reversals of previously promised government incentive programs due to market instability and more.[40] All of these undoubtedly had a large negative financial impact on the foreign investor, but was it equivalent to removing all value and control

---

35 The divergence of opinion is well documented in a recent case against the Czech Republic under the European Energy Charter Treaty. Antaris GMBH and Dr. Michael Gode v. The Czech Republic, www.italaw.com.

36 Nicholson, "The Protection of Foreign Property under Customary International Law"; Methanex Corporation v. the United States of America, 44 International Legal Materials. Taken as a whole, these criteria reflect a Western approach, focusing not on the reasons for the expropriation but on the way it is performed. Porterfield, "State Practice and the (Purported) Obligation under Customary International Law to Provide Compensation for Regulatory Expropriations."

37 United States-Mexico-Canada, "North American Free Trade Agreement (NAFTA)," 1110.

38 Methanex Corporation v. the United States of America, 44 International Legal Materials.

39 Metalclad Corporation v. The United Mexican States , italaw.com.

40 Antaris GMBH and Dr. Michael Gode v. The Czech Republic, www.italaw.com; Foresight Luxembourg Solar 1 S.A.R.L., et al. Claimants v. The Kingdom of Spain Respondent, italaw.com.

from the investment? If it does constitute a legal indirect expropriation, what constitutes "full compensation" for the loss of an investment and who gets to decide? That line of questioning rarely illuminates a consistent standard.

A new model of treaty text has begun to include clarifying language that "except in rare circumstances, non-discriminatory regulatory actions [...] designed and applied to protect public welfare objectives, such as public health, safety and the environment, do not constitute indirect expropriations."[41] Under the CPTPP, indirect expropriation is not carefully defined, but two parties have made specific reference to their domestic land laws as the standard for due process in the context of land expropriation.[42] The trade agreement between the European Union and Japan, however, stands out by removing all references to expropriation, although they have not yet concluded an investment protection agreement that would likely introduce these concepts more fully.

Full protection and security: state responsibility for nonstate actors

In the context of land investments of this sort, state behavior is not the only action which can give rise to violations of an investment treaty. When rural villages or indigenous people groups protest against the investment, peacefully or not, or when domestic and international civil society organizations challenge the legitimacy of that same investment, investors have, in other contexts, sued the state for failing to provide full protection and security. The full protection and security standard usually accompanies FET in provisions outlining the minimum standard of treatment afforded to foreign nationals. At a *minimum*, they should be protected from vandalism to their property, attempts to stop production at their plant, and frivolous lawsuits that delay their establishment and operation.[43] Yet large-scale land purchases very often result in resistance from local populations displaced by the new owner of the property.[44]

---

41 Canada-EU, "CETA," Annex 8-A; "USMCA," Annex 14-B.
42 The two countries are Brunei Darussalam and Malaysia. Canada-Australia-Brunei-Chile-Japan-Malaysia-Mexico-New Zealand-Peru-Singapore-Vietnam, "CPTPP," 9.8, n. 18.
43 Cotula, "Land Rights and Investment Treaties: Exploring the Interface," 19.
44 Mousseau and Mittal, "Country Report: Mozambique"; Mousseau and Mittal, "Country Report: Tanzania"; Mousseau and Sosnoff, "Country Report: Ethiopia"; Mittal, "Nicaragua's Failed Revolution: The Indigenous Struggle for Saneamiento."

Enforcement mechanisms: investor–state disputes

None of these provisions would have much impact on host state policy space without an enforcement mechanism. ISDS was created to protect investors from allegedly inequitable outcomes found in host state adjudication. It was set up to provide a neutral framework that would impartially judge between the investor's financial interests and the host government's political and regulatory interests. Many believe it to be the only reasonable way, currently available, to guarantee rights that have been granted to the investors and states.[45]

Just as in the case of industrial policy making and public health crises, investment treaties lay an onerous burden on states to protect foreign purchasers of large swaths of their land, but have no similar obligations for the investors themselves; the rights and responsibilities ensconced in IIAs are all one-sided. As noted above, local resistance to these purchases is widespread; land-based conflict is now the norm.[46] In light of that, the potential for disputes between investor and host country have increasing importance.

The probability of land disputes also grows as we remember that land purchases rose during a commodity boom in the mid-2000s and seem to have subsided in the wake of it. Moreover, with only 14 percent of the purchased land in production, any promised economic boon to the host state seems partial and unreliable. For low-income countries selling or leasing their land to the highest international bidder promising efficient food or biofuel production, jobs for local residents, and development to the region, only to have the land lay fallow when the commodity markets (notoriously unreliable) shift again, is a big financial burden. If policy responses then expose them to further risk of high-cost arbitration, then countries can be paralyzed to address the real needs of their populations.

There are other treaty provisions that may interfere with policies addressing the challenges of land governance. Rules prohibiting performance requirements may increase the likelihood of regulatory chill in sectors with high demand from foreign investors. Countries may not be able to put in place general rules for investors in rural land that create backward and forward linkages in the economy, increase the likelihood of local hiring and training, and encourage technology transfer.[47] Moreover, as Chapter 5 discusses in more detail, rules that demand free transfer of capital mean that states with

---

45 Schwebel, "In Defense of Bilateral Investment Treaties."

46 Mousseau and Mittal, "Country Report: Mozambique"; Mousseau and Mittal, "Country Report: Tanzania"; Mousseau and Sosnoff, "Country Report: Ethiopia."

47 Canada-Australia-Brunei-Chile-Japan-Malaysia-Mexico-New Zealand-Peru-Singapore-Vietnam, "CPTPP," 9.10; "USMCA," 14.10; EU-Japan, "EU-Japan EPA," 8.11; China, "RCEP—Draft Investment Text."

Table 4.1. New treaties and selected investment provisions

	Right of establishment	Full protection and security	Fair and equitable treatment	Indirect expropriation	Investor–state dispute settlement
CPTPP	√	√	*limited*	√	√
EU-Japan	√	x	x	x	x
EU-Singapore (IPA)	x	√	√	√	√
CETA	√	√	√	√	√
USMCA	√	√	*limited*	√	√

Note: EU-Japan stands out as a treaty with very few of these key investment provisions (the lack of provision indicated by an "x").

large-scale land purchases may not be able to control capital flows related to those investments in order to stabilize the flow of capital into their territory.[48]

Another approach is needed. As the following stories show, the countries that experience the downsides of these large-scale land purchases need an approach to IIAs that does not expose them to risk when they improve domestic land governance, attempt to alter concession agreements in the interests of their constituents, or when the displaced people groups resist their own displacement through the local courts or organized protest. Other models exist that would allow this kind of policy space, the details of which follow.

Land Investments and Land Conflicts

There are four illustrative responses that governments have had to large-scale land purchases which help us to see both the extent and the limits of investment treaties as instruments of investor protection: indifference, reliance on domestic law to keep investments in line, reversing course when investments seem to cause problems and minimizing investor reach.

---

48 Canada-Australia-Brunei-Chile-Japan-Malaysia-Mexico-New Zealand-Peru-Singapore-Vietnam, "CPTPP," 9.9; "USMCA," 14.9; EU-Japan, "EU-Japan EPA," 9.2.

State indifference to investment outcomes

In some cases, states are actively courting foreign investors pursuant to their own development policy and are seemingly indifferent to the plight of traditional communities within their borders. Ethiopia is one such case, where the government's goal of becoming a global sugar exporter has resulted in policies that prioritize large-scale sugar plantations and displace the pastoralist communities that have lived there for centuries.[49] They built dams to provide irrigation and energy to those plantations and the communities have been resettled into areas for subsistence farming.[50] The government has promised these groups jobs, education and access to technology but the execution was not well done. Although Ethiopian law, on paper, requires the use of environmental impact assessments and consultations with local tribes, they are poorly enforced and there is no evidence that they have actually taken place with these pastoralist people groups. In fact, the evidence points in the opposite direction—that government officials would prefer to dispense with these communities and have used the military to force tribal groups off their land.[51]

Nicaragua's experience is similar. In areas where indigenous and Afro-Nicaraguan communities are threatened by the presence of large-scale land purchases, as well as individual settlers from other parts of the country, the law enforcement does not seem to protect the land rights of those communities. Law 445, enacted in 2003, promised them land reform, reliable land tenure and titles and protection from those who would illegally inhabit those lands. Nevertheless, the laws are not adequately enforced and many people's lives and livelihoods are at stake.[52]

In these cases, the presence of investment treaties is not the root of the problem for displaced people groups. In the case of Ethiopia, at least, the government is a willing partner with any investors who would want to grab land, and in Nicaragua, the government is indifferent, at best.[53] Rather, the

---

49 Flores and Mittal, "Engineering Ethnic Conflict: The Toll of Ethiopia's Plantation Development on the Suri People"; Anon., "'How They Tricked Us': Living with the Gibe Dam and Sugar Plantations in Southwestern Ethiopia."

50 Anon., "'How They Tricked Us': Living with the Gibe Dam and Sugar Plantations in Southwestern Ethiopia."

51 Flores and Mittal, "Engineering Ethnic Conflict: The Toll of Ethiopia's Plantation Development on the Suri People"; Mousseau and Sosnoff, "Country Report: Ethiopia."

52 Mittal, "Nicaragua's Failed Revolution: The Indigenous Struggle for Saneamiento."

53 Mousseau and Sosnoff, "Country Report: Ethiopia"; Mittal, "Nicaragua's Failed Revolution: The Indigenous Struggle for Saneamiento."

role of investment treaties is to reinforce the status quo and resist future policy changes.

Governments make policy changes all the time. With an investment treaty in place, country leaders will have a more difficult time making changes that substantially diminish the value of the investments from the treaty partner. Ethiopia has BITs with South Africa (2008), China (1998) and Malaysia (1998), all major players in sugar plantation investments (see Table 4.2), and all three treaties have a broad FET standard, including full protection and security, and ISDS. On those standards alone, if Ethiopia should choose to shift gears and attempt to protect their agro-pastoralist communities in the future, it may face pushback from those investors.

Leveraging domestic law

Cameroon's story illustrates another possible government response—of leveraging domestic law to hold investors accountable in large-scale land purchases. In one instance, Herakles Capital (a US oil company) failed to acquire the right licenses and permits and even used bribes to facilitate its way once they began to set up shop in Cameroon.[54] As a result, they faced domestic court cases challenging their activity, a temporary injunction against their operation as well as local protests. The original concession agreement with Herakles was quite expansive, even allowing the right to a private security force and stating that the agreement takes precedence over national laws. Nevertheless, since the injunction was lifted, the whole operation has stalled and seems to have fallen apart.

Socfin (a Belgian palm oil company) faced a similar experience when it attempted to expand their palm oil plantation. Local affected communities resisted the expansion through the legal system and, as a result, the company chose to relinquish the area back to the government.[55] Cameroon has old BITs with the United States (1989) and Belgium (1980), and both of those treaties contain broad FET clauses, full protection and security, protection against indirect expropriation and, of course, investor–state disputes. Although in neither case did Cameroon face ISDS for the domestic legal processes limiting the reach of those investors, they were at risk. However the international investment regime should not act to discourage countries from responding through domestic legal processes.

---

54 Mousseau, "Herakles Exposed: The Truth behind Herakles Farms: False Promises in Cameroon."

55 Some villagers still do not feel safe and have claimed that they are still using 20K hectares of that land (now rent-free). Mousseau.

Table 4.2. Relevant treaties and their investment protection provisions

	Right of establishment	Full protection and security	Fair and equitable treatment	Indirect expropriation	Investor–state dispute settlement
ETHIOPIA		art. 3(1)	art. 3(1)	art. 5(1)	art. 7
– S. Africa BIT		art. 3(1)	art. 3(1)	art. 4	art. 9
– China BIT		art. 2.2	art. 3(1)	art. 5	art. 7
– Malaysia BIT					
CAMEROON	art. II.2	art. II.4	art. II:4	art. III.1	art. VII
– U.S. BIT		art. 3.2	art. 3.1	art. 4.1	art. 10
– Belgium BIT					
MOZAMBIQUE	art. VI	art. II.3	art. II.3	art. III.1	art. XI
– U.S. BIT	art. 1(e)	art. 2(2)	art. 2(2)	art. 5(1)	art. 2(2)
– U.K. BIT		art. 4	art. 4	art. 12	art. 17
– China BIT			art. 9	art. 9	art. 9
– Japan BIT			art. 3.2	art. 5	
– Brazil BIT					
– India BIT					
VIETNAM	art. 9.10	art. 9.6	art. 9.6	art. 9.8	art. 9.18ff
– CPTPP		art. 2.5	art. 2.5	art. 2.7	Ch. 3, Sec. B
– EU IPA					

Reversing course on foreign investment

Often, going through the domestic legal process is not enough to protect local communities. Some countries have seen the writing on the wall and realized that these large land investments are more trouble than they're worth. In Mozambique, as with many developing countries, domestic law requires that investors consult with nearby communities before acquiring a lease for land considered to be unused. In the mid-2000s, when investors were not fulfilling promises of increased employment and environmental protection, Mozambique faced widespread land conflicts. In the wake of literally hundreds of these disputes, the government quickly reduced new large-scale (more than 10,000 hectares) agricultural concessions between 2009 and 2011, and by 2013, they had stopped altogether.[56]

Mozambique has active BITs with the United States, the United Kingdom, China, Japan, Brazil and India, all of which are major investors in its agricultural sector (see Table 4.2). Almost universally, these treaties contain

---

56 landmatrix.org, "Data: All Deals."

an unqualified FET provision with full protection and security guaranteed for foreign investors, protection against indirect expropriation and investor–state disputes for conflict resolution. The treaties with the United States, Japan and Brazil also grant preestablishment rights to investors so that if Mozambique opened land investments to their domestic investors, they would have to do the same for foreign investors from those countries.[57] By disengaging from the process of large-scale land transactions, Mozambique was able to greatly reduce the risk posed by new investments; however, the current BITs remain a problem for communities affected by existing agricultural investments. Moreover, future policy decisions for Mozambique will be constrained by the terms of those treaties.

Ex ante disengagement: minimizing investor reach

Vietnam presents a somewhat unique response to the challenges related to large-scale land deals. As a country, it has only experienced a handful— mostly in the timber sector.[58] Surprisingly, its domestic small-scale farmers are fairly able to compete with larger foreign investors and roughly two-thirds of productive tree plantations in the country are held by rural households with just a few hectares of property—double the average in the region.[59] This is due to the longer term impacts of Vietnam's import substitution industrialization policies—industrial policies that built up key industries through state planning and protected them with tariffs in the mid-twentieth century. A large paper mill was built creating a need for a large timber industry to keep it operating at capacity. When communism fell, the government experienced an authority crisis and responded by allocating land to households in rural villages for long-term use—this, in a country where no individual ownership of land was permitted.[60] In addition to access to land, Vietnam created a Bank for Social Policies, which had outlets all throughout the rural areas. As a result,

---

57 In its BIT with the United States, Mozambique carved out its land law that requires, among other things, community consultations by foreign investors. In a letter exchanged between the parties, Mozambique agrees to "implement the provisions of its [Land Law], and any other provisions of law that relates to the same […] subject matter, in a manner that" does not discriminate against US investors.

58 Since 2009, Vietnam has experienced only 8 successful large-scale (>10,000 ha) land grabs. landmatrix.org.

59 Sikor, "Tree Plantations, Politics of Possession and the Absence of Land Grabs in Vietnam."

60 Sikor, "Tree Plantations, Politics of Possession and the Absence of Land Grabs in Vietnam."

tree farmers had access to capital at favorable rates and with no collateral necessary. Once the country did decide to liberalize investment, it did so in the wood processing sector, reinvigorating the downstream markets for these smallholder tree farmers.

Vietnam has not been a very active participant in the BIT regime. At the same time, it recently completed negotiations as part of the CPTPP, which extends all the most expansive protections to foreign investors (see Table 4.2). It is also party to an Economic Partnership Agreement and Investment Partnership Agreement with the EU—one of the first such treaties under the European Union's new region-wide investment policy approach. The EU-Vietnam treaty commitments have many similarities with other mega-regional agreements. It differs, however, in key areas—by explicitly recognizing the right to regulate, even if it negatively impacts the value of an investment (2.2), omitting preestablishment rights (2.3–2.4), maintaining an exemption to national treatment for its forestry sector (Annex 2) and containing a modified expropriation provision with respect to land in Vietnam.[61]

Another African Model

Yet again, these examples highlight the need for a new approach.

The newest mega-regional trade agreement to enter into force, the AfCFTA (2019), has opted to omit investment commitments altogether. As the world moves toward deeper integration, however, it is helpful to have a set of best practices for countries negotiating and signing new treaties. The Southern African Development Community (SADC) has developed just such a model, which aims to address the risks countries are exposed to under investment treaties.

In the first place, the SADC's model BIT eschews rights of preestablishment in favor of a more deferential approach. Instead the parties agree to admit investments in accordance with a good faith application of their laws. Vietnam's investment treaty with the European Union adopts that approach—requiring national treatment and MFN treatment only with respect to the operation of foreign investments.

As we've already seen, countries are attempting to contain overly expansive interpretations of FET by expressly limiting its reach.[62] The SADC text goes further by suggesting a standard of fair *administrative* treatment—a clearly procedural rather than substantive standard.[63] This concept further reserves

---

61 EU-Vietnam, "EU-Vietnam IPA."
62 "USMCA," 14.6; Canada-EU, "CETA," 8.10.
63 Southern African Development Community and Mann, "SADC Model BIT," 5.1.

the rights of states to regulate, as long as the processes do not deny justice or due process to foreign investors.

A procedural standard like fair administrative treatment could provide the additional policy space needed for governments with failed, underperforming or conflict-ridden agricultural investments in their territories, and that need to withdraw permits and licenses, or even the whole concession agreement. It might also make space for new regulations improving and enforcing standards for environmental assessment or community consultation.

The other main investment protection standard that poses problems for countries facing the negative externalities of land deals is the rule governing indirect expropriation. Absent a full set of investment commitments, countries may elect to omit the expropriation standard completely,[64] but the overwhelming trend is in the opposite direction.[65] The SADC model treaty offers a different solution to limit the scope of the expropriation provision—remove the requirement of nondiscrimination. Unfortunately, expropriatory acts are almost always specific acts of taking property for government purposes, and can rarely be considered nondiscriminatory. The same goes for countries responding to specific instances of large-scale land transactions gone wrong, making the government legally liable in the event of a land conflict. In the context of a modern land deal, were the host state to take back the land or withdraw the long-term lease from an agricultural investor due to a land conflict or some other public purpose, it would almost always be considered a discriminatory act because that investor is treated differently from other investors.

By removing the requirement that an expropriation (indirect or otherwise) be nondiscriminatory, a country may still be required to compensate the investor in some way, but otherwise would not be subject to investor–state arbitration. Indeed, each of the provisions of investment treaties only interfere with domestic policymaking inasmuch as they are enforceable, usually through investor–state disputes. As in other contexts, the strongest critics suggest that investor–state disputes should be discarded in favor of a state–state mechanism. Though some early drafts of the RCEP show that some parties would like

---

64 EU-Japan, "EU-Japan EPA."

65 Prior to 2019, the EU did not commonly include much in the way of investment provisions in their Economic Partnership Agreements. Investment commitments were negotiated separately in bilateral investment treaties with individual European states, giving the misleading impression that the European Union did not have extensive investment commitments. With the introduction of a regional policy on investment, however, it is clear that the EU prefers the same protections for investors as the United States and Japan. EU-Singapore, "EU-Singapore IPA"; EU-Vietnam, "EU-Vietnam IPA."

investor–state dispute settlement, there are others who believe that those proposals will not prevail, and the matter has been tabled for the moment.[66] In treaties where the parties insist on investor–state arbitration, however, the SADC model treaty proposes that host state counterclaims be more widely available, either on the basis on the concession agreement's investor obligations or some new obligations put on investors within the investment treaty itself.

Resolving a Specific "Trilemma"

Although the prevalence of large-scale land deals seems to be on the decline (see Figure 4.1), that does not mean that countries are in the clear for future land rushes. The commodity boom that precipitated these purchases in the mid-2000s is likely to appear again as commodity markets are subject to rapid price changes. Moreover, the economic impacts of the COVID-19 pandemic are predicted to result in a prolonged recession even more drastic than the 2008 financial crisis. In that case, investors may likely find themselves once more in search of alternative markets for investment. In addition, as countries actively seek out foreign investment to meet much needed capital demands, policymakers will be tempted to change policies toward a more open posture to foreign investment.

This reality makes clear the conflict between liberalizing investment policies and protecting the health and safety of people, as well as the environment. The trilemma articulated in Chapter 1 arises here in the specific case of land investment policy: governments cannot simultaneously pursue democracy, national sovereignty over their land and total investment liberalization. They must choose which of these they will prioritize over the others. Based on the concerns that have arisen out of the impacts of foreign land ownership and the expanding investment regime, giving investors ever greater influence over their host governments, governments must preserve the right to regulate (and in some cases, take back) their agricultural land, protecting the rights and well-being of their citizens. This could be accomplished in a number of ways.

First, legal harmonization should be confined to formal/procedural guarantees, ensuring that nation states still maintain their policy space in deciding the content of their public regulatory policies. Instead of broadening and deepening economic integration, countries should be pursuing trade agreements which allow shallower integration. In this context, land governance as well as large-scale investments for agricultural and energy productions

---

66 UNCTAD, "The Changing IIA Landscape: New Treaties and Recent Policy Developments." "RCEP," 10.18.

should be left to the political discretion of the government in accordance with democratic consensus rather than left to the market to regulate.

Second, disputes involving large-scale land purchases, like disputes involving public health and industrial policies, ought to be relegated to state–state dispute settlement with a strong preference for the exhaustion of local remedies prior to pursuing treaty disputes due to their sensitivity and the vulnerabilities of the communities at risk. As international tribunals are called to analyze national policies on land governance, their reach should be well-defined and limited to avoid undue interference with national policymaking. Countries are going to need to be even more active in the policy realm in the coming months and years to respond to the fallout surrounding the COVID-19 pandemic, and the newest treaty texts defining international investment commitments will make significant difference in whether they will face investor challenges for those policy changes.

Chapter 5

CAPITAL FLOW REGULATION AND TRADE AGREEMENTS: AN EMPIRICAL INVESTIGATION*

Beginning in the mid-2000s, a wave of new thinking overtook the economics profession on the question of the flow of capital across borders. According to what has been called the new welfare economics of capital controls, unstable capital flows to emerging markets can be viewed as a negative externality on recipient countries.[1] Therefore, regulations on cross-border capital flows are seen as a tool to correct for market failures that can make markets work better and enhance growth, rather than worsen it.[2] This is a marked departure from the accepted view during the 1990s, when the IMF (and others) put pressure on borrowing countries to liberalize their capital accounts with the same vigor that they liberalized trade.

According to the new research, externalities are generated by capital flows because individual investors and borrowers do not know what the impacts of their financial decisions will be on the financial stability of any particular nation. A common analogy for this effect is the case of an individual firm not taking into consideration its contribution to (and the costs of) urban air pollution when pricing its products. Just as, in the case of pollution, the polluting firm can accentuate the environmental harm done by its activity, in the case of capital flows, a foreign investor might tip a nation into financial difficulties and even a financial crisis. This is a prime example of a market failure, which calls for policy interventions to correct it and make markets work more efficiently.

---

* All econometric analysis and Figure 5.5 are courtesy of Sarah Sklar, the co-author of our paper Gallagher, Sklar and Thrasher, "Quantifying the Policy Space for Regulating Capital Flows in Trade and Investment Treaties: A G24 Working Paper."

1 Gallagher, *Ruling Capital*.

2 This work has been developed by economists Anton Korinek, Olivier Jeanne and others and is summarized by Korinek in the August 2011 issue of the *IMF Economic Review*. Korinek, "The New Economics of Prudential Capital Controls."

This idea is not entirely new, of course. Even during the formation of the World Bank and the IMF, Keynes and his colleagues acknowledged that capital flows must be regulated in order to prevent crises and "maintain an independent monetary policy."[3] Exercising control over capital flows allows for more policy space to increase employment and financial stability. The new research, however, brings those mid-twentieth-century calculations up to date and models global capital flows and controls in a broader context. As a result, it has gained credence with international financial institutions who view it as offering a more rigorous justification for policy action on capital flows.[4]

Under these circumstances, regulations on cross-border financial transactions can be effective to smooth the inflows and outflows of capital and protect developing economies. Most existing regulations target highly short-term capital inflows, usually conducted for speculative purposes. For example, Colombia's 2007 regulations required foreign investors to set aside a percentage of their investment in the central bank, which helped that nation escape some of the damage from the global financial crisis.[5] Magud, Reinhardt and Rogoff (2018) conducted an exhaustive review of the econometric literature on this matter for the National Bureau of Economic Research and, while ambivalent about the role of capital controls in general, conclude that regulations on capital inflows have been effective in preventing financial instability and that controls on outflows in the case of Malaysia during the Asian financial crisis of the 1990s were effective as well.[6]

The IMF study that set the stage for a broader acceptance of capital flow management found that capital controls helped buffer some of the worst effects of the 2008 financial crisis in some developing countries.[7] In light of these findings, the IMF now endorses the use of capital account regulations as a part of the macroeconomic policy toolkit. On December 3, 2012, the IMF made public an Executive Board–approved institutional view on capital account liberalization and the management of capital flows. In a nutshell, the IMF's new institutional view is that nations should *eventually* and sequentially open their capital accounts, and maintain capital flow management measures or capital controls in the toolkit to smooth the capital flow cycle.[8] Indeed, since

---

3 Gallagher, *Ruling Capital.*
4 For a full review of this literature, see Gallagher.
5 Coelho and Gallagher, "The Effectiveness of Capital Controls."
6 Magud, Reinhart and Rogoff, "Capital Controls: Myth and Reality."
7 Ostry et al., "Capital Inflows."
8 In general terms, cross-border financial flows and capital flows refer to the movement of finance and investment across borders. Consequently, capital flow management measures, capital account regulations and capital controls all synonymously pertain

the institutional view has been in place, the IMF has advised several countries to put in place regulations through their annual surveillance consultations and reports (Article IV reports) and has even required countries to put in place regulations as a condition for borrowing in an economic crisis.[9]

Trade and investment treaty rules, however, have not undergone a parallel shift. In fact, a growing number of trade and investment treaties generally prohibit restrictions on capital flows, also called transfers, and minimize the scope and number of exceptions to that rule. Many papers have pointed toward the problems that trade and investment treaties create for domestic policymaking in general and capital flow management measures in particular.[10]

Government policies like those proposed by the IMF are therefore on a collision course with the rules that govern international trade. The research laid out in this chapter seeks to examine the extent of that collision in order to make better recommendations to policymakers involved in negotiating and implementing trade agreements. The findings demonstrate how much FTAs, especially those with investment commitments, exacerbate the challenges that countries face in a financial crisis. While the treaty-making trend over time shows broader and deeper trade agreements, the evidence in this chapter once more highlights the importance of pushing back against that trajectory so that countries have the policy space to maintain financial stability.

There is a growing body of literature that attempts to quantify and analyze the text found in trade and investment treaties.[11] One particular effort by Thompson, Broude and Haftel[12] established a comprehensive textual coding framework for measuring policy space in BITs. Their framework was adapted to quantify the amount of policy space for capital controls and other financial stability measures in FTAs. With this framework in hand, the overall policy space in the global trade regime for deploying capital flow management measures before and during a financial crisis can be measured.

---

to the regulation of cross-border flows of capital. International Monetary Fund, "The Liberalization and Management of Capital Flows: An Institutional View."

9 See Grabel and Gallagher, "'Capital Controls and the Global Financial Crisis"; Gallagher and Tian, "Regulating Capital Flows in Emerging Markets."

10 Siegel, "Using Free Trade Agreements to Control Capital Account Restrictions: Summary of Remarks on the Relationship to the Mandate of the IMF"; Siegel, "Capital Account Restrictions, Trade Agreements and the IMF"; Thrasher and Gallagher, "21st Century Trade Agreements"; Coelho and Gallagher, "The Effectiveness of Capital Controls."

11 Viterbo, *International Economic Law and Monetary Measures*; Dür, Baccini and Elsig, "The Design of International Trade Agreements"; Broude, Haftel and Thompson, "The Trans-Pacific Partnership and Regulatory Space"; Thompson, Broude and Haftel, "Once Bitten, Twice Shy?"

12 Thompson, Broude and Haftel, "Once Bitten, Twice Shy?"

Setting the Stage for Capital Flow Liberalization: WTO and WTO+ Rules

Commitments at the WTO, as well as bilateral and regional FTAs limit countries' ability to respond to and prevent financial crises using capital controls.[13] They do so primarily through commitments in trade in services and liberalized investment regimes.

Under the WTO, especially the GATS, capital account regulations are principally bound by the fundamental standards of MFN treatment, national treatment and market access standards. If the capital control measure has a more detrimental impact on one trading partner than the rest, the MFN rule would apply. For bound sectors under a country's services liberalization schedule, capital controls that interfere with the supply of financial services (or other services) from abroad would violate national treatment and likely be considered a prohibited market access limitation as well.[14] Moreover, the mandate for negotiating rules on domestic regulation (under GATS article VI) could require that capital controls "do not constitute unnecessary barriers to trade in services" or are "not more burdensome than necessary," though those rules are not yet in place.[15] There are exceptions, of course, permitting capital flow measures for balance of payments crises and "prudential reasons," the exact scope of which has yet to be determined.[16] Many consider these exceptions to be weak and not a reasonable defense for long-term capital control measures that facilitate counter-cyclical stability. States may enforce these commitments through the (now beleaguered) WTO Dispute Settlement Mechanism.

Outside of the WTO, many countries are also members of broad-coverage FTAs with investment chapters, which ratchet up commitments to liberalize the countries' capital accounts.[17] A common investment provision laying out the rules for free capital transfers states that capital must be allowed to flow between trading partners "freely and without delay."[18] Bilateral and regional trade agreements are not homogeneous, however, and the rules vary among treaty partners. Trade agreements that have chapters on trade in financial services often prohibit limitations on financial transactions or assets. In treaties

---

13 Bilateral investment treaties (BITs), although outside the scope of this research, also play an important role in restricting policy space for CFMs.
14 Tucker, "The Looming GATS Conflict with Capital Controls."
15 Tucker, "The Looming GATS Conflict with Capital Controls."
16 World Trade Organization, "General Agreement on Trade in Services (GATS)," XII, Annex on Financial Services.
17 Siegel, "Capital Account Restrictions, Trade Agreements and the IMF."
18 "USMCA," 14.9.

where the United States is a party, regulations on cross-border financial transactions are considered actionable measures that can trigger enforcement in investor–state tribunals.[19] Other treaties contain commitments that mimic the rules under the WTO, containing limited constraints on policymaking and making allowances for crisis situations.[20]

A parallel regime of investment rules, governed by the more than 3,000 BITs in force, places limits similar to those in the strictest FTAs on countries' abilities to manage and regulate capital flows. By their sheer quantity, the role of BITs is likely much more constraining than the collective impact of the FTAs included in this study. The presence of these BITs points, then, to a much larger problem and the need for more research to understand the scope of policy constraints surrounding capital flows and financial stability.

Policy Space for Preventing and Managing Financial Crises: Gathering the Data

In order to empirically measure the policy space available in FTAs for countries attempting to implement capital account regulations for financial stability and to respond to crises, we create a composite index that measures the relative policy flexibility of one treaty over another. With the composite index in hand, we perform statistical and legal analyses to examine the global reach of those treaties with the least flexibility for nations to regulate cross-border finance.

To create the composite index, we categorize the language of just over 300 preferential trade agreements signed between 1960 and 2018, identified primarily by their notification to the WTO Regional Trade Agreements database. We rely on data gathered with the help of Deborah Siegel, former senior council of the IMF, as part of a World Bank project on deep integration in trade agreements. The Content of Deep Trade Agreements project seeks to quantify the degree of liberalization measures across the global spectrum of trade and investment treaties.[21] Our team compiled a list of questions designed to illuminate how treaties interact with domestic capital flow regulation.[22]

---

19 Viterbo, *International Economic Law and Monetary Measures*; Siegel, "Using Free Trade Agreements to Control Capital Account Restrictions: Summary of Remarks on the Relationship to the Mandate of the IMF"; Siegel, "Capital Account Restrictions, Trade Agreements and the IMF."
20 Hagan, *Transfer of Funds*; Viterbo, *International Economic Law and Monetary Measures*.
21 Siegel, Gallagher and Thrasher, "Movement of Capital"; Hofmann, Osnago and Ruta, "Horizontal Depth"; World Bank, "Content of Deep Trade Agreements."
22 We coded nearly 300 bilateral and regional trade agreements according to their treaty texts governing capital account activity. We chose the treaties based on their notification to the World Trade Organization under Article XXIV and the Enabling Clause.

From our research, we determined that five key questions captured the fundamental differences in policy space between treaties:

(1)   What is the scope of the commitment to liberalize capital account transfers, if any?

(2)   Is there some general or specific exception for monetary, fiscal or macroeconomic policies such as a safeguard against balance of payments and other crises?

(3)   What is the scope of the "prudential measures" exception in financial services, if any?

(4)   Is there investor–state dispute settlement available for capital flow regulation measures that violate free transfers commitments?

(5)   Are there any limitations, in the case of financial crises, to investor–state claims?

With these data, we measure the level of policy space (flexibility) of a particular treaty by creating a composite score, and then examine the collective level of policy space across the global treaty system.

Creating the composite score

In order to create the composite index and measure the overall flexibility of a treaty, a numerical value between 0 and 1 was assigned for each of the five indicators above, where 1 indicates the highest amount of policy flexibility.

The *scope* of the commitment to liberalize capital account transfers is measured by assigning 1 to treaties with no "free transfers" commitment (see Table 5.1). The *depth* is then calculated by counting the sections of the trade agreement that contain free transfers commitments. Such a commitment can generally be found in provisions governing the treatment of foreign investment, trade in services, and, more specifically, trade in *financial* services. Where free capital account transfers commitments only cover bound services transactions, the treaty receives 0.75. If it covers only investment transactions, it receives 0.50. This distinction is due to the limited reach of services commitments as compared with investment commitments in most treaties.[23] A trade agreement

---

The resulting database contained 93 fields of inquiry under six major headings: the scope of the rules on capital transfers, broad exclusions from those rules (for areas like bankruptcy and criminal law), safeguards for macroeconomic crises, flexibilities within financial services, general exceptions and enforcement measures. For a full discussion of the coding process, Siegel, Gallagher and Thrasher, "Movement of Capital."

23 Services commitments are usually limited to bound sectors using a positive list approach (a sector is only bound by the rules if the country specifically binds it). By contrast,

Table 5.1. Depth of free transfers commitment (ordinal)

No free transfers commitment	1
Free transfers for liberalized services sectors only (excluding financial services)	0.75
Free transfers for foreign investment only	0.50
Free transfers for investment & services, services & financial services, or financial services & investment	0.25
Free transfers for all three	0

with free transfers commitments in two of the three sections receives a 0.25, while an agreement requiring liberalized capital flows in all three sections receives the lowest score of 0.

The second indicator measures any general or specific exceptions for monetary, fiscal or macroeconomic policies (Table 5.2). This includes carve outs for "monetary and exchange rate policy," general balance of payments safeguards and special annexes with carve outs for country-specific capital account regulations. Here we once more assign 1 to treaties that have no commitment to liberalize capital account transfers and therefore have no need of any exceptions to the rule. The presence of such exceptions are treated cumulatively, worth 0.25 each, and a trade agreement can receive up to a score of 0.75 if all three are found in the treaty text.[24]

Table 5.2. Policy exceptions (cumulative)

No free transfers commitment	1
General macroeconomic policy exception (BoP, macroeconomic difficulties, etc.)	0.25
Exception for monetary and exchange rate policy	0.25
Specific annex with exception for domestic macroeconomic policies	0.25

The third question measures the scope of a specific exception often found in provisions governing financial services commitments (Table 5.3). This exception, informally referred to as the prudential exception, allows treaty parties to put in place measures for prudential reasons, "including for the protection of investors, depositors, policy holders, or persons to whom a

---

investment commitments usually take a negative list approach (all investment sectors are bound unless specifically excepted).

24 Of the treaties with no such exceptions, 7 are treaties in which the United States is a party. The other two are "Canada-Peru Free Trade Agreement" and "Canada-Panama Free Trade Agreement." This suggests that such an approach is limited to the Americas.

Table 5.3. Prudential reasons exceptions (cumulative)

No free transfers in services or financial services	1
Exception for "safety, soundness" of financial institutions and service suppliers	0.25
Exception for the "integrity and stability of the financial system"	0.25
Exception for other prudential reasons	0.25
Exception contains a limiting footnote ("concerns only *individual* financial institutions and service suppliers")	−0.25

fiduciary duty is owed by a financial institution or cross-border financial service supplier, or to ensure the integrity and stability of the financial system."[25] In order to capture the import of this exception, we counted the presence of certain language included in the definition of "prudential reasons." In that way, a treaty with no commitment to liberalize capital flows in services or the financial services sector (thus, no need for this exception) receives 1. Each exception mentioned thereafter receives 0.25, with the highest possible score at 0.75. A small minority of treaties also contain a specific footnote designed to further restrict the scope of "prudential reasons."[26] Although the exact legal import of such a footnote has not been tested, negotiating history would suggest that the United States, at least, intends to narrow the exception so that it does not cover general capital flow management.[27] The presence of that footnote, therefore, brings a treaty score down by −0.25.[28]

The last two questions measuring policy flexibility in trade agreements calculate the potential impact of ISDS and any relevant limitations to its reach. This mechanism has been widely studied and criticized in recent years because of national sovereignty concerns and the financial burden it places on state-respondents in international investment arbitration.[29] Since an

---

25 "US-Peru FTA," 12.11.

26 See, e.g., "United States-Peru FTA." at Article 12.10, n 4.

27 See Taylor, "Testimony before the Subcommittee on Domestic and International Monetary Policy, Trade and Technology." (stating that the United States seeks "greater protection for US investors than the IMF Articles of Agreement and the GATS afford").

28 Commonly put, it states "The term 'prudential reasons' includes the maintenance of the safety, soundness, integrity or financial responsibility of individual financial institutions or cross-border service suppliers." See, e.g., KORUS Article 13.10, fn.5; Nicaragua-Taiwan FTA Article 12.10.1, fn.3; Australia-Chile FTA Article 12.11.1, fn.25.

29 Janeba, "Regulatory Chill and the Effect of Investor State Dispute Settlements"; Ikenson, "A Compromise to Advance the Trade Agenda"; Tienhaara, "Regulatory Chill and the Threat of Arbitration: A View from Political Science." For empirical research into the outcomes of international investment arbitration and a discussion of the corresponding structural imbalances within the ISDS system, see Schultz and

Table 5.4. Investor–state dispute settlement and its limitations

Investor–State Dispute Settlement (ordinal)	
No ISDS	1
ISDS for free transfers disputes	0
Limitations to ISDS (ordinal)	
No ISDS	1
ISDS provision contains some limitation (side letter, special rules for disputes concerning prudential measures, cooling-off period, etc.)	0.50
No limitation on ISDS	0

investor–state dispute mechanism, when included, applies to commitments in investment liberalization, the rules proscribing or limiting policy space to impose capital controls are given new teeth. In light of that reality, treaties that allow investor–state claims receive a score of 0, while treaties with no such option score 1. Not all investor–state provisions are created equal, however. In some cases, investor–state dispute provisions include special rules for disputes concerning prudential measures, or require that the investor honor a cooling-off period before bringing a claim. These limitations are captured by assigning 0.50 for treaties that contain them.

The result is a variable measuring the flexibility of the treaty in terms of the breadth and depth of the commitment to liberalize capital account transfers, relevant exceptions to that commitment, and its enforceability, which varies from 0 to 5 (See Table 5.5). We also identify the numerical scores with a four-color scale to further simplify the results and improve visualization. Treaties that score between 4 and 5 (green treaties) are those with no commitments to liberalize capital account transfers, or a very narrowly circumscribed commitment (e.g., in bound services sectors only), with broad macroeconomic exceptions and no enforcement through ISDS. Treaties with scores between 2.75 and 3.75 (yellow treaties) either have a limited scope to their free transfers provision with some policy or prudential exception, or have a broad scope with equally broad access to relevant exceptions. In either case, they contain no investor–state dispute enforcement. Orange treaties, those that score between 1.5 and 2.5, usually have a broad commitment to liberalize capital account transfers, along with broad exceptions and limitations to investor–state claims. They may also be treaties with a limited scope, limited exceptions, and

---

Dupont, "Investment Arbitration"; Wellhausen, "Recent Trends in Investor–State Dispute Settlement"; Sweet, Chung and Saltzman, "Arbitral Lawmaking and State Power."

Table 5.5. Descriptions of treaty scoring and color scale (with treaty examples)

Color scale	Description	Score (0–5)	Examples
GREEN	Treaties with no commitments to liberalize capital account transfers, or a narrowly circumscribed commitment with broad exclusions/ exceptions and no ISDS enforcement.	4–5	Andean Community (CAN) (1988), Argentina-Brazil Partial Scope Agreement (2016), CARICOM Protocol II
YELLOW	*Either* treaties with a limited-scope free transfers commitment, some policy and/or prudential exceptions and no ISDS, *or* treaties with broad scope as well as exceptions and no ISDS.	2.75–3.75	US-Bahrain (2006), EFTA-Georgia (2017), OECD Codes (2018),* China-Hong Kong (2012)
ORANGE	*Either* treaties with a broad free transfers commitment, broad policy and/or prudential exceptions and ISDS with limits, *or* treaties with limited-scope, some exceptions and unconstrained ISDS.	1.5–2.5	Pakistan-China (2009), Mexico-Panama (2015), Australia-Chile (2009), Chile-Mexico (1999)
RED	Treaties with broad free transfers (2–3) commitments, a lack of general safeguards for macroeconomic crises and ISDS.	0–1.25	NAFTA (1994), Canada-Peru (2009), DR-CAFTA (2006), Pakistan-Malaysia (2008)

* The OECD Code of Liberalization of Capital Movements differs substantially from typical trade and investment treaty texts. Because of its multilateral character, countries have made extensive reservations to the commitments and there are several broad exceptions for financial stability. On the other hand, it covers a very broad scope of types of financial flows (OECD, 2018).

unconstrained investor–state enforcement power. Our least flexible treaties, scoring between 0 and 1.25 (red treaties), have the broadest free transfers commitments, along with a general lack of safeguards and exceptions, and unbridled ISDS.

Calculating policy space across the global treaty system

To understand the impact of these treaty scores on the actual policy space for regulating capital flows, we begin with a simple tally: Counting the number of treaties according to each level of flexibility on our four-color scale. The treaties are then broken down based on whether the parties were in the Global North or the Global South in order to better understand the data and see how it impacts countries at diverse levels of development. We adopt the World Bank's Development Level indicator to identify high-income countries as the Global North and all others as the Global South. As such, treaties where all members are high-income we label North–North treaties, and where no members are high income, we label them South–South treaties; treaties with mixed membership count as North–South.

We also sought to calculate the percentage of global GDP and inward foreign investment governed by each treaty in order to understand whether the minority of least-flexible treaties had a broader impact than a simple tally would show. In order to avoid double counting, we count each country only once under its least-flexible treaty. By categorizing each country in this way, we also capture the potential multilateralizing effect of MFN clauses in these treaties.[30] As described in Chapter 2 and unpacked in somewhat more detail below, MFN clauses demand that treaty partners extend their best treatment to each other. This means that a country signing a new treaty with less policy space may effectively ratchet up all their other treaty commitments with respect to capital flow liberalization. To the extent that this effect is real, it could have a large impact on countries with many treaties in effect, even if most of them are highly flexible. In order to determine whether this ratcheting effect is possible in reality, we look to the legal literature to find whether courts and international tribunals have allowed claimants to import more stringent provisions from respondent countries' other treaties by way of an MFN clause.

As a final step, the trends of treaty flexibility are examined over time. This provides a clue as to the trajectory of the treaty regime as a whole with respect to capital flow management.[31]

---

30 Schill, *The Multilateralization of International Investment Law*; Johnson, "Ripe for Refinement: The State's Role in Interpretation of FET, MFN, and Shareholder Rights."

31 To perform these calculations and analyses, we collected additional attribute data for all countries who were a party to one or more treaty. All attribute data are from the World Bank's World Development Indicators dataset, with the exception of GDP, which is from the UN database, as it is a more complete dataset. The World Bank, "WDI"; UNDESA Statistics Division: National Accounts, "United Nations National Accounts Analysis of Main Aggregates." Data on bilateral FDI flows are from the IMF's Coordinated Direct Investment Survey (CDIS). International Monetary Fund, "IMF CDIS." We use reported investment inflows because inflow data are generally seen as more accurate than outflow. When inflow data were unavailable but partner countries had outflow data reported, we pulled this in to reduce missing data. All FDI and attribute data are from 2018. Since CDIS reports all EU participants separately, these data were aggregated to find overall EU FDI flows.

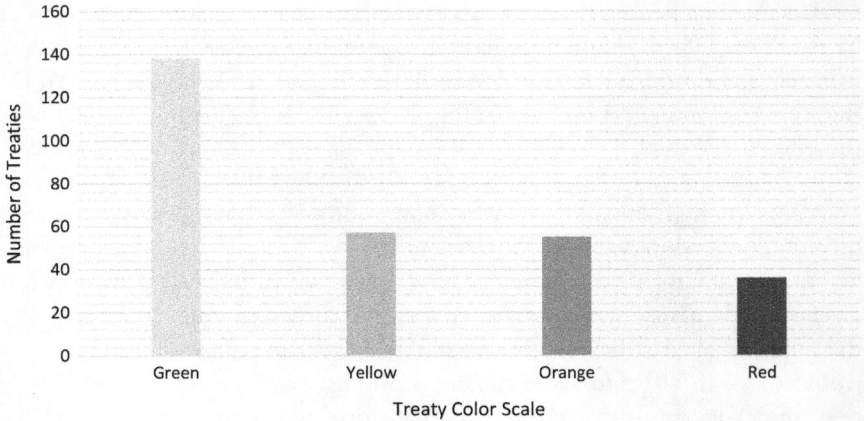

Figure 5.1. Treaties by color coding

The Impacts of Treaty Flexibility in the Global Economy

Overall, the findings were not surprising. A large majority of all treaties leave significant policy space for regulating cross-border finance in the world economy—only 12 percent of all treaties fall in to the highest category discussed above—and more than half do not govern capital flow management policy at all. However, when divided into three groups by development level, the distribution of less-flexible treaties suggests that there are significant negotiating power imbalances between developed and developing countries. Furthermore and most importantly, when weighted by the percentages of global GDP and foreign investment the treaty parties represent, those treaties in the least-flexible category represent 65 percent of global GDP and 55 percent of global foreign direct investment (FDI) flows. Moreover, international tribunals have allowed less-flexible treaty terms to be imported into flexible treaties through MFN clauses. Finally, the trend over time is concerning. New treaties in the world economy are more likely to be broader and deeper in scope and less flexible when it comes to managing capital flows.

Figure 5.1 exhibits the number of treaties by their relative level of flexibility. Here we see that more than half of the treaties have no capital transfer commitments at all, and the least-flexible treaties are quite rare. The average flexibility score over all treaties was 3.5—equivalent to a more flexible yellow treaty.

Treaty trends, income and development levels

When treaties are divided based on parties' development level, however, a new trend emerges. Figure 5.2 shows a much higher percentage of flexible treaties

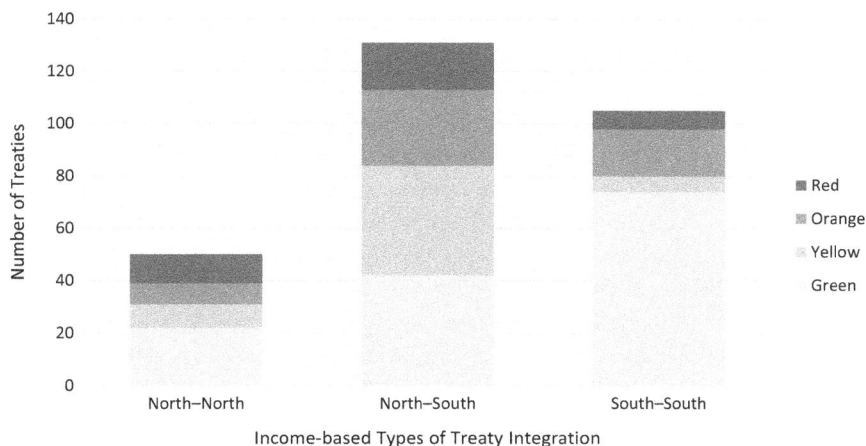

Figure 5.2. Policy space by trading partner

in South–South integration compared with North–South and North–North. North–South treaties, in particular, stand out because of the high percentage of treaties that contain the most demanding language with respect to capital flow liberalization. Figure 5.2 reveals that while developing countries tend to reserve flexibilities with their fellow developing country parties, they sign onto much more restrictive treaties with the Global North.[32]

Of course, trends among developing countries are very diverse. China's engagement in FTAs has drastically changed over the past 20 years, from being a reluctant treaty partner to being a regional leader, seeking broader and deeper trade agreements.[33] As noted in Chapter 2, certain regions, South America in particular, may have quite deep economic integration within the region while keeping policy flexibility vis-à-vis nonparty countries. Perhaps more importantly, however, the proportions of strict treaties in North–North treaties and North–South treaties are similar, suggesting that more developed countries are setting the agenda for final treaty texts. Together with the other evidence, this reality hints at a darker truth: while developing countries prefer more policy-flexible commitments, it is the preferences of the developed world

---

32 Gallagher, Sklar and Thrasher, "Quantifying the Policy Space for Regulating Capital Flows in Trade and Investment Treaties: A G24 Working Paper."

33 Hoadley and Yang, "China's Cross-Regional FTA Initiatives"; Rajan and Sen, "The New Wave of FTAs in Asia: With Particular Reference to ASEAN, China, and India."

that more often take precedence in income-diverse agreements, highlighting the likelihood of negotiating power imbalances.[34]

Previous research has shown that, of the countries that are parties to only one treaty, none have signed a treaty with one another but always with a country more integrated into the network of trade treaties.[35] Moreover, treaties with many co-signers are generally more flexible than those with fewer. Finally, the research demonstrates that bilateral treaties with one large country with significant capital outflows were much less flexible (R squared = .02, p < .008).[36] When more countries are involved in the negotiations, treaties tend to be more flexible with respect to capital controls. When combining FDI (discussed below), participant count, and year (discussed below) into a regression, the resultant model explains 30 percent of the fluctuation in treaty score.[37] In other words, later in time treaties that involve strong capital exporters and fewer participants tend to embody the strictest rules. These characteristics also lend more support to the theory that significant power imbalances pervade treaty negotiations.

On the surface, this is not surprising. Multilateral treaty negotiations will almost always have weaker commitments because there are more parties to assert their interests and fewer points of commonality. On the other hand, when combined with the highly correlated negative relationship between income diversity and treaty flexibility, it seems that bilateral North–South trade negotiations are weighted heavily in favor of developed country interests.

Treaty flexibility, GDP and foreign investment

When treaties are weighted by their relative amount of coverage of global GDP and financial flows (see Figure 5.3 and Figure 5.4), the picture in Figure 5.1 reverses—such that almost two-thirds of the world economy is covered by restrictive trade and investment treaties. While only 12 percent of treaties score below a 1.5, those treaty parties represent 65 percent of global GDP and 55 percent of global FDI inflows. In other words, foreign investment tends to flow to those countries with the least-flexible treaty commitments.

---

34 Siegel, Gallagher and Thrasher, "Movement of Capital."
35 Gallagher, Sklar and Thrasher, "Quantifying the Policy Space for Regulating Capital Flows in Trade and Investment Treaties: A G24 Working Paper."
36 Gallagher, Sklar and Thrasher, "Quantifying the Policy Space for Regulating Capital Flows in Trade and Investment Treaties: A G24 Working Paper."
37 Gallagher, Sklar and Thrasher. Outward FDI and year are both significant at p < .000 and participant count at p < .05.

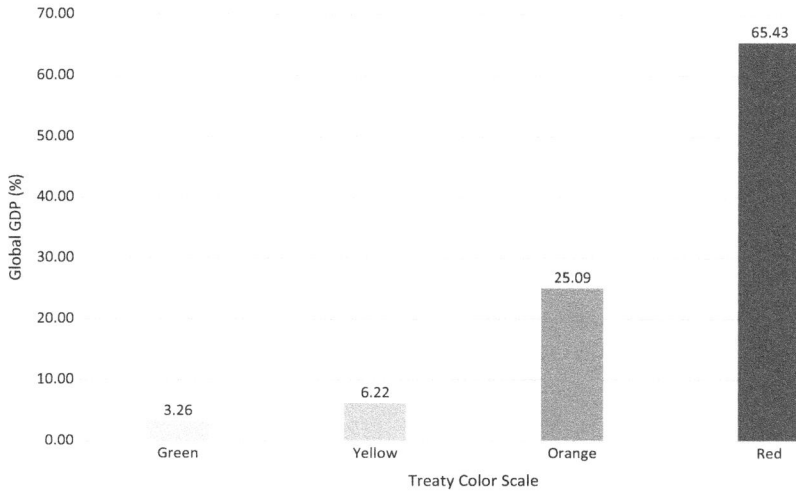

Figure 5.3. Treaty flexibility as a percentage of global GDP

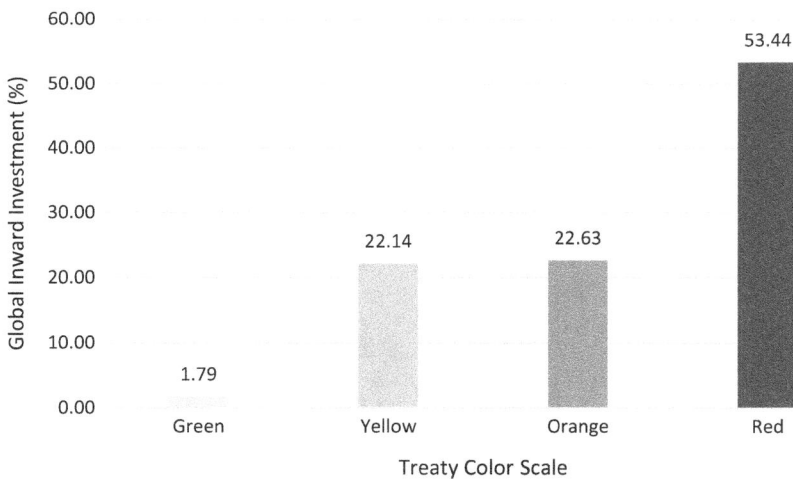

Figure 5.4. Treaty flexibility as a percentage of global FDI

The MFN effect

These impacts may be felt even more through the multilateralizing effect of the MFN treatment standard. In theory, the role of MFN clauses suggests that, for countries who sign red treaties, those which are least flexible, *all* of their capital inflows from *all* treaty partners may be subject to the same strict standard. MFN clauses, found in almost all modern treaties, demand that the treaty parties extend their best treatment to each other, including standards of treatment set in future treaties with third states.[38] Case law demonstrates that, in practice, states *have* used MFN provisions to attempt to import more-favorable conditions from third-party treaties, in particular in the BIT context.[39] There, the general rule holds that MFN clauses may incorporate more-favorable substantive conditions from third-party investment treaties.[40] In a few cases, the tribunal has allowed parties to use MFN clauses to import more-favorable procedural provisions for dispute settlement as well.[41]

On the other hand, tribunals have been reluctant to import access to investor–state disputes where the treaty limits such jurisdiction,[42] and an MFN clause may not be used to expand the scope of the treaty itself, either in time,

---

38 Schill, *The Multilateralization of International Investment Law*. This issue reveals an active debate as to the appropriate role of MFN provisions for "drafting in by reference" the more-favorable provisions of later treaties. Johnson, "Ripe for Refinement: The State's Role in Interpretation of FET, MFN, and Shareholder Rights."

39 In fact, the primary economic rationale articulated for these provisions was the multilateralizing aim to level the playing field and undermine attempts to extend different kinds of concessions to different trading partners. Schill, *The Multilateralization of International Investment Law*.

40 See, e.g., Pope & Talbot, Inc. v. Canada; CME Czech Republic B.V. v. The Czech Republic; EDF International S.A., SAUR International S.A. and Leon Participaciones Argentinas S.A. v. Argentine Republic. Schill, *The Multilateralization of International Investment Law*; Johnson, "Ripe for Refinement: The State's Role in Interpretation of FET, MFN, and Shareholder Rights." In both *Pope & Talbot v. Canada* and *MTD v. Chile*, the tribunal relied on more expansive provisions on "fair and equitable treatment" from other Canadian and Chilean treaties to find a violation of the treaty terms. MTD Equity Sdn. Bhd. and MTD Chile S.A. v. Republic of Chile; Pope & Talbot, Inc. v. Canada. See also, EDF International S.A., SAUR International S.A. and Leon Participaciones Argentinas S.A. v. Argentine Republic (incorporating an umbrella clause from a third-party BIT to expand the subject-matter jurisdiction of the BIT); White Industries Australia Ltd. v. The Republic of India (adopting a more-favorable "effective means" clause from another treaty); and CME Czech Republic v. The Czech Republic (importing the standard of compensation from another treaty). Johnson, "Ripe for Refinement: The State's Role in Interpretation of FET, MFN, and Shareholder Rights."

41 Emilio Agustín Maffezini v. The Kingdom of Spain; Gas Natural SDG, S.A. v. Argentine Republic. In *Maffezini v. Spain*, for example, the tribunal allowed the claimant "to rely on a shorter waiting period [from 18 months to 6 months] from a third-party BIT" in bringing a claim. Schill, *The Multilateralization of International Investment Law*.

42 In one case, the investor sought to expand the jurisdiction of the ISDS provision to cover contract claims by importing the broader consent to arbitration of the United States-Jordan and United Kingdom-Jordan BITs. Salini Costruttori S.P.A. and Italstrade S.P.A. v. The Hashemite Kingdom of Jordan; Schill, *The Multilateralization of International Investment Law*. In another case, however, the tribunal expanded the

or personal or subject-matter jurisdiction.[43] This final limitation on the reach of MFN clauses has particular importance for our case. The most flexible treaties, which simply do not cover capital account flows, would not be subject to the same ratcheting effect. Treaties that fall into the yellow, orange or red category, however, would not be able to claim such a limitation to subject-matter jurisdiction.

To better understand this effect, Figure 5.5 provides an up-close view of the MFN effect on investment flows among three partner countries. Bilateral ties between the countries are all yellow, meaning the least-flexible treaty both parties are a member to is yellow. However, the European Union and Morocco (MAR) have both signed less-flexible treaties with other partners. The European Union's least-flexible treaty is orange and Morocco's is red. Once a country signs such a treaty, they agree to refrain from discriminating against foreign capital flows relative to domestic capital flows. This prevents them from implementing restrictions on either the inflow or outflow of foreign capital. In this illustration, once Morocco signs a red treaty with any country, other nations that have treaties with Morocco may be able to use the MFN clause to extend those benefits to their own financial flows. Egypt and Morocco have only signed a yellow treaty together, however, if Morocco tries to place limitations on the flows of Egyptian capital, Egypt can sue for red-level protections based on the MFN clause. Moroccan flows to Egypt, however, are still yellow, giving Egypt more flexibility to implement restrictions.

---

subject-matter jurisdiction of the arbitration provisions by reference to another BIT with broader consent to jurisdiction. RosInvestCo. UK, Ltd. v. The Russian Federation; Johnson, "Ripe for Refinement: The State's Role in Interpretation of FET, MFN, and Shareholder Rights."

43 ADF Group Inc. v. United States of America; Emilio Agustín Maffezini v. The Kingdom of Spain; Técnicas Medioambientales Tecmed, S.A. v. The United Mexican States. Under NAFTA, the United States specifically excluded government procurement from MFN coverage, and for that reason, one private investor was unable to import better procurement provisions from another US treaty. *ADF v. US*. See also, *Maffezini v. Spain* ("the third-party treaty has to relate to the same subject matter as the basic treaty") and *Tecmed v. Mexico* (the tribunal did not extend the temporal applicability of a treaty based on the MFN provision). MFN also may not be used to avoid access to general exceptions—such as those that permit treaty derogation for the protection of human, animal or plant life, or in the case of national emergencies. See, *CMS v. Argentina* (in which the investor sought to avoid application of an emergency provision (permitting derogation from the treaty provisions) because other Argentine treaties did not have such a clause protecting the host state in the case of emergencies. Schill, *The Multilateralization of International Investment Law*.

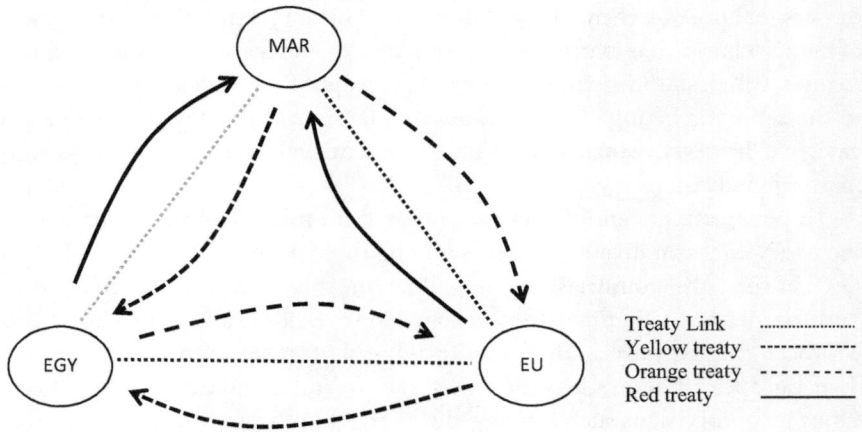

Figure 5.5. MFN effect

Moreover, earlier iterations of this research showed[44] that while bilateral financial flows between trade agreement co-signers account for 40 percent of global direct investment flows, 99 percent of these are governed by treaties with some free transfers commitments. By breaking down these flows further according to development level, we found that global FDI flows are almost entirely among developed nations. North–North flows account for 93 percent of global FDI. Next are North–South flows with 6 percent and South–North flows with 1 percent. South-South capital flows are negligible overall.[45] FTA-regulated FDI flows follow a similar pattern. More than 90 percent of treaty-regulated FDI flows pass between developed countries, and of those, a vast majority are governed by the least-flexible treaties. Financial flows going from the Global North to the Global South are also almost completely governed by the least-flexible treaty commitments.

Time trends

Finally, we find that treaties in the world economy are increasingly providing fewer flexibilities, as is the case in many other areas of treaty governance. When we examine treaties over time, we see a clear trend toward less flexible treaties,

---

44 Our earlier research relied on a different scoring system but the same attribute data for country parties. See Gallagher, Sklar and Thrasher, "Quantifying the Policy Space for Regulating Capital Flows in Trade and Investment Treaties: A G24 Working Paper."

45 Gallagher, Sklar and Thrasher, "Quantifying the Policy Space for Regulating Capital Flows in Trade and Investment Treaties: A G24 Working Paper."

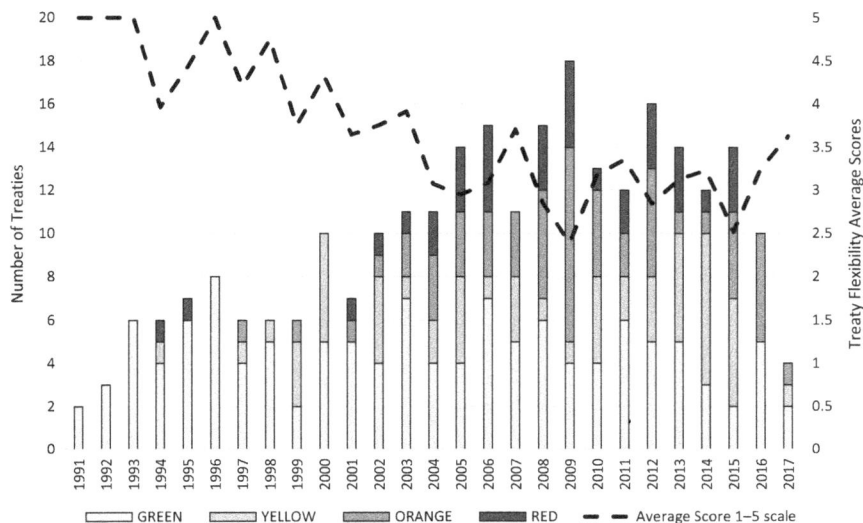

Figure 5.6. Shrinking policy space over time

mandating free capital flows along with other liberalizing commitments. Figure 5.6 shows the number of treaties by color code since 1991, as well as changes in the average treaty score—which has hovered between 2.5 and 3.5 since the 2008 financial crisis. If these trends continue into the future, the current low percentage of inflexible treaties provides only time-limited policy flexibility for countries seeking to regulate their capital account.

A regression of treaty score by year found a strong statistical correlation, with treaty year explaining approximately 14 percent of score variation.[46] This suggests that once more restrictive treaties were introduced, the terms and commitments began to spread across the treaty network. Recent years have seen a slight slowdown in this trend, with Britain's exit from the European Union and the United States' withdrawal from the Trans-Pacific Partnership. Despite this temporary slowdown, there is no evidence to suggest a substantial shift in trade treaty paradigm away from more stringent treaty standards. The European Union's expansive policy of economic partnership agreements, the ongoing ratification of the CPTPP and other mega-regional initiatives like the RCEP and the AfCFTA point toward a continuing trend toward broader and deeper economic integration in the rest of the world.

---

46 Gallagher, Sklar and Thrasher, "Quantifying the Policy Space for Regulating Capital Flows in Trade and Investment Treaties: A G24 Working Paper."

Conclusion

The international trade and investment treaty regime is increasingly restricting the policy space for regulating cross-border financial flows that is granted under the IMF Articles of Agreement and other international institutions. Although the vast majority of free trade agreements leave ample space to regulate capital flows, the older treaty models are falling out of use in favor of treaty texts demanding complete liberalization of capital flows and investment more generally. As we note above, the least-flexible treaties now effectively govern more than 65 percent of the world economy and 55 percent of FDI flows. MFN provisions allow countries with weaker protections for their exported capital to import higher standards under other treaties, further undermining much needed policy space for financial stability.

Many other efforts are being made to calculate policy flexibility across the broader trade and investment regime. The UN Conference on Trade and Development's Investment Policy Hub has, since our research began, mapped the content of almost 3,000 investment treaties, ripe for extensive research and analysis. The WTO's Regional Trade Agreements database allows researchers to search and categorize trade treaties by treaty terms from goods tariff schedules to services commitments and investment liberalization provisions. The World Bank, as well, has continued their work at the Content of Deep Trade Integration Project, which seeks to measure the depth of the global network of regional and bilateral agreements.

These efforts combined could prove useful for further empirical study as well as for policymaking. From a policy perspective, however, there seems to be a major inconsistency across the global economic governance system. Whereas the IMF board, the G20, and many other international institutions and governments all recognize the importance of capital account regulations to prevent and manage financial crises, the global trade governance regime increasingly seeks to remove that policy flexibility.

Research like this, however, is opening up the possibility for change. As the world faces various crises of food, energy, climate, public health and finance, country leaders will be looking for new approaches to old problems. Understanding the implications of signing onto strong capital-liberalizing treaty commitments is the first step to making domestic policy that can be good for all. Future integration, then, can be shaped with policy space for capital flow management and financial stability in mind. What is more, as we'll see in the next chapter, limitations to policy space addressing financial instability has enormous implications for countries facing unmanageable levels of sovereign debt.

Chapter 6

THE EMERGING ROLE OF INTERNATIONAL INVESTMENT AGREEMENTS IN SOVEREIGN DEBT RESTRUCTURING

Argentina has once more restructured its debt.[1] In May 2020, Argentina became unable to pay bondholders the interest on their bonds—this due in part to unsustainable growth of its debt-to-GDP ratio over the past few years, along with the acute economic downturn during the COVID-19 pandemic. The restructured bonds are now worth only 55 cents on the dollar, compared to their original value, which is still higher than they are trading on the open market.[2]

Argentina's economic woes are only Act Two of a much longer saga that began almost 20 years ago. And though Argentina has been through the ringer when it comes to sovereign debt, the country is not alone in its sovereign debt difficulties. Many experts believe this is just the tip of the iceberg—that, in the wake of the COVID-19 pandemic, we will experience a large-scale sovereign debt crisis on par with the Latin American debt crisis of the 1980s.[3]

This looming sovereign debt crisis is happening at a time when trade and investment liberalization is at its zenith. As repeatedly emphasized, despite the United States' apparent skepticism toward trade agreements and Britain's withdrawal from the European Union, the overall trend of the global economy is toward greater, broader and deeper integration.[4] The push toward lower barriers for trade in goods has been accompanied by a parallel trend toward fewer barriers to cross-border trade in services and foreign investment.

---

1 Smith, Mander and Wigglesworth, "Argentina Strikes Debt Agreement after Restructuring Breakthrough."
2 "Argentine Bonds Trade below Restructuring Level on Economic Woes."
3 Buchheit and de la Torre, "Sovereign Debt Restructuring: From the Brady Plan to Ecuador 2020"; Serrichio, "Kevin Gallagher, el profesor de la Universidad de Boston que defiende al país y ataca a los bonistas: 'El mundo está mirando a la Argentina.'"
4 Hofmann, Osnago and Ruta, "Horizontal Depth"; Siegel, Gallagher and Thrasher, "Movement of Capital."

Moreover, to facilitate all this trade, treaties increasing demand capital flow liberalization as well.

Trade and investment liberalization has the potential to provide greater access to capital at a time when countries are in need of external financing for development projects and policies. However, recent research on trade liberalization and government revenue shows that increased trade liberalization is correlated with decreases in government revenue.[5] This applies both to the lost revenue from lower tariffs, as well as a failure to replace that income with other taxation income.[6] At the same time, other policy constraints imposed by the WTO, FTAs and BITs all restrict the ability of country parties to recoup those losses of tariff revenue through other forms of taxation.[7] That same research also finds a correlation between increased trade liberalization and government debt service obligations.[8]

As trade liberalization contributes to an already overwhelming debt overhang, many countries face the additional challenge of a lack of any comprehensive and uniform regime for handling debt default and resultant restructuring. There are many proposals for reforming the regime. Some suggest improving the existing contractual approach with better collective action clauses and new provisions placed into sovereign bonds.[9] Others urge a reliance on a soft law approach—nonmandatory standards for restructuring set forth by the International Law Commission or a model law drafted for countries engaged in restructuring.[10] Still others recommend continuing to push for a multilateral treaty to govern sovereign debt, even if it is not feasible in the near-term future, relying on the contractual approach in the meantime.[11] Experts are each attempting to balance concerns for human

---

5 Dutt and Gallagher, "The Fiscal Impacts of Trade and Investment Treaties."

6 Rolland, "The Impact of Trade and Investment Treaties on Mobilization of Taxation in Developing Countries."

7 Rolland, "The WTO and Tax Mobilization for Developing Countries"; Rolland, "The Impact of Trade and Investment Treaties on Mobilization of Taxation in Developing Countries"; Montes, "Policy Space for Fiscal Revenue Mobilization under FTAs and BITs."

8 Dutt and Gallagher, "The Fiscal Impacts of Trade and Investment Treaties."

9 Eichengreen, "Restructuring Sovereign Debt"; Zettelmeyer, Trebesch and Gulati, "The Greek Debt Restructuring."

10 Howse, "Towards a Framework for Sovereign Debt Restructuring: What Can Public International Law Contribute"; Guzman and Stiglitz, "A Soft Law Mechanism for Sovereign Debt Restructuring Based on the UN Principles"; Guzman and Stiglitz, "Creating a Framework for Sovereign Debt Restructuring That Works."

11 Ocampo, "A Brief History of Sovereign Debt Resolution and a Proposal for a Multilateral Instrument"; Guzman and Stiglitz, "Creating a Framework for Sovereign Debt Restructuring That Works."

rights, equal treatment among creditors, and state sovereign immunity, as well as political and socioeconomic realities and moral hazard problems.[12]

One institution that has stepped into that role for the time being is the network of IIAs, which includes the universe of BITs and investment chapters in FTAs. By defining the term investment broadly, countries bring sovereign debt under the governance of investment treaty rules, including the right of establishment, national treatment, FET, rules governing expropriation and many other protections. ISDS makes it potentially easier for investors to acquire an enforceable judgment against sovereign debtors. Although this seems to be serving a need in the international community, these treaties are not set up to deal with the political and socioeconomic complexities of sovereign debt default.

This chapter does not argue in favor of one particular solution to the challenge of sovereign debt crises and restructuring, as that has been amply discussed.[13] Instead it argues that existing international legal norms must leave room for the experimentation and evolution, however slow, of a new sovereign debt restructuring (SDR) regime. Regardless of what form that might take, investment agreements should not replace a holistic approach to sovereign debt governance. New IIAs should step back from the arena of sovereign debt in order to ensure policy space for these discussions and negotiations so that a new regime can emerge. Even more critically, ISDS should not be the forum where we decide whether and how a country can restructure its debt. If investment treaty standards of treatment and dispute settlement must play a role temporarily, then it must do so taking into consideration the special role of sovereign debt in development and giving deference to the state attempting to manage its financial and fiscal stability.

Debt and Development

Governments taking on debt is not necessarily a bad thing. In some cases, governments are able to rely on domestic savings, both individual and corporate, to finance policies for structural change to the economy and economic growth. Most developing countries, however, lack the domestic

---

12 Gelpern, "Sovereign Debt: Now What?"; Buchheit and de la Torre, "Sovereign Debt Restructuring: From the Brady Plan to Ecuador 2020"; Guzman and Stiglitz, "Creating a Framework for Sovereign Debt Restructuring That Works."

13 Eichengreen, "Restructuring Sovereign Debt"; Gelpern, "Sovereign Debt: Now What?"; Guzman and Stiglitz, "Creating a Framework for Sovereign Debt Restructuring That Works"; Guzman and Stiglitz, "A Soft Law Mechanism for Sovereign Debt Restructuring Based on the UN Principles"; Paliouras, "The Right to Restructure Sovereign Debt."

savings to finance planned investment and must fill in the gap with foreign resources.

At the same time, borrowing money is inherently risky, and countries with a savings gap often do not have a choice about who to turn to for improved liquidity.[14] If the government is unable to turn that foreign currency into profitable investment and economic growth, and the savings gap grows over time, then nations may be unable to make interest payments on that debt, or to pay back the principle when a bond matures. Both internal factors (like low absorptive capacity to turn loans into successful income) and external factors (like contagion from other crises) may contribute to unsustainable debt overhang.

Developing country debt is most often denominated in foreign currency. As a result, high interest rates or inflation can cause the cost of debt service to skyrocket. Moreover, when left unchecked, debt markets tend to be pro-cyclical—during a boom both debtors and creditors are eager to do business, but when markets swing low, debtors are unable to roll over or increase their debt to meet their basic expenditure needs.[15] As Chapter 5 explains, these tensions are exacerbated in developing countries with strict capital flow liberalization commitments, as they would not be able to control rapid inflow and outflow of capital.[16]

Sovereign Debt Restructuring Past and Present

In the not-so-distant past, most sovereign debt was held by official bilateral creditors—country-to-country lending—and a handful of large banks. These creditors dealt with default through negotiations with debtor nations and among themselves. The group of creditors was small and the process was informal but relatively consistent.[17] By 1989, due in part to the experience of the Latin American debt crisis and the US Brady Plan, most banks traded in unpayable loans for discounted bonds.[18] This meant that private creditors now owned an increasing share of sovereign debt and that ownership was much more broadly dispersed.

---

14 Wiedenbrüg, "What Is Really Owed: Structural Injustice, Responsibility, and Sovereign Debt."

15 Thrasher and Gallagher, "Mission Creep: The Emerging Role of International Investment Agreements in Sovereign Debt Restructuring."

16 Gallagher, Sklar and Thrasher, "Quantifying the Policy Space for Regulating Capital Flows in Trade and Investment Treaties: A G24 Working Paper," 24.

17 Gelpern, "Sovereign Debt: Now What?"

18 Gelpern; Buchheit and de la Torre, "Sovereign Debt Restructuring: From the Brady Plan to Ecuador 2020."

In under ten years, the world was facing another financial crisis, forcing countries to attempt to restructure their debt now with large disaggregated groups of bondholders, most of which were disconnected from government finance officials and "uninterested in the public good."[19] In light of this new situation, and as the world began to prepare for a new millennium, civil society pushed for more debt relief and even debt forgiveness for the most distressed countries. The G-7 responded with various debt relief programs, most of which linked debt relief with promises of policy and governance reform, and the IMF became the primary institution through which countries sought debt relief.[20] Debt relief often took the form of a coordinated global bailout in which nations are given the cash to pay creditors in the short term in exchange for new loans or grants from the IMF, conditioned on new austere fiscal policy.

By 2010, the landscape of sovereign debt had changed still further. Emerging market nations, especially China, had begun to play a much more active role in lending to other countries. Rules that demanded free cross-border capital flows were becoming the norm, and bond trading on the market meant that the owners of sovereign debt could change at any time and no one knew for sure who held it. To top it all, the sheer magnitude of global sovereign debt exceeded what any international institution or group of countries would be able to satisfy. The most costly bailout until recently was the US$50 billion rescue package for Mexico's crisis in 1994. Once seen as an unthinkable bailout, it has become eclipsed by the staggering US$1 trillion rescue for Europe's more recent crisis. Bailouts also fell out of favor due to the concern for moral hazard created by guaranteeing payout for creditors even when they knew the loans to be exceedingly risky.

At this time, both creditors and debtors recognized the need for a different mechanism. The IMF suggested a treaty-based SDR mechanism, which would bind countries to a formal process in the case of default. Representatives from the United States, Mexico and Brazil pushed back and argued instead for the inclusion of collective action clauses in bond terms—a market-based mechanism that provided a way for creditor coordination in the case of restructuring negotiations and decreased the chances that holdout creditors would undermine the process.

SDR, modeled loosely after the private bankruptcy process, requires private creditors to bear some of the burden of the default and provides a way to distribute the financial burden between debtor and creditors. Alternatively called private sector involvement or a bail-*in*, SDR involves a formal change to debt contracts that is negotiated between creditors and debtors. This may include

---

19 Gelpern, "Sovereign Debt: Now What?"
20 Gelpern, "Sovereign Debt: Now What?"

Table 6.1. Sovereign debt restructurings, 1998–2015

	Duration (m)	Value (billion US$)	Haircut (%)	Participation (%)
Russia (1998–2000)	23	31.9	50.8	98
Ukraine (1999–2000)	4	1.6	18	95
Pakistan (1999)	4	.6	15	95
Ecuador (2000)	25	6.7	38.3	97
Uruguay (2004)	2	3.1	9.8	93
Argentina				
2005	42	43.7	76.8	76
2010	60	18	75	66
Argentina Total	*100*	*99.8*		*93*
Greece (2012)	4	206	53.3	94

Source: Thrasher and Gallagher, "Mission Creep: The Emerging Role of International Investment Agreements in Sovereign Debt Restructuring"; Gallagher, "The New Vulture Culture: Sovereign Debt Restructuring and Trade and Investment Treaties"; Poštová banka, a.s. and ISTROKAPITAL SE v. Hellenic Republic, www.italaw.com.

reducing the face value of the debt (called a discount), swaps (where new bonds with lower interest rates and longer maturities are exchanged for the defaulted bonds), and so forth. Losses or discounts are collectively referred to as haircuts.

Table 6.1 lists some of the major restructurings since the late 1990s, including the duration of the negotiations, the total face value of the bonds under restructuring, the haircut and the participation rate.

There are two primary threats to the SDR process: recalcitrant states and holdout creditors. On the one hand, payment on sovereign debt is ultimately unenforceable absent the will of the debtor state.[21] Both Argentina and Ecuador, in recent years have made that truth painfully obvious by refusing to engage with international creditors on the basis of their sovereign rights. As a result, both were, to some degree, cut off from international markets (at least until Argentina experienced a regime change), which is the main enforcement mechanism creditors have at their disposal.[22]

Refusal to pay, however, is a relatively rare occurrence. In fact, most countries are eager to negotiate some kind of deal that allows them to re-enter international financial markets as quickly as possible. Holdout creditors, on the other hand, seem to be a regular fixture in the SDR experience. Some view holdouts, or the threat thereof, in a positive light—ensuring that states

---

21 Gelpern, "Sovereign Debt: Now What?"
22 Feibelman, "Ecuador's 2008–2009 Debt Restructuring"; Buchheit and de la Torre, "Sovereign Debt Restructuring: From the Brady Plan to Ecuador 2020."

make the best possible offer to their creditors. They refuse to accept a bond discount or swap and thus put pressure on states to make a better offer.[23]

On the other hand, holdouts pose a real threat to the finality of any attempted restructuring. Although traditionally, restructuring has been considered successful when at least 90 percent of bondholders have tendered and received at least 50 percent of the value of their debt, holdouts refuse to accept that offer, leaving states to try to pay them in full and creating a perverse incentive for future creditors. There is also some evidence that certain investors, called vulture funds, purchase bonds when restructuring is imminent or has just occurred, using holdout litigation to drive up the value of their investment.[24]

Moreover, the recent experience with Argentina shed a different light on the potential difficulty posed by holdouts. When Argentina was unable or unwilling (or both) to pay holdout creditors the full value of its debt owed, they sued in the Southern District Court of New York on the basis of a *pari passu* bond clause. This clause states that the bonds "shall at all times rank at least equally with all its other present and future unsecured and unsubordinated External Indebtedness." On that basis, they argued that the bondholders who agreed to the restructured terms should not be paid on the new bonds unless the holdouts were also paid.[25] For the first time, holdout creditors were pitted not only against the debtor state but also against their fellow creditors.[26] Since then, the court has permitted a discrete number of payments made on the bonds governed by Argentine law, but payments continue to come due.[27]

The costs associated with SDR, including the high number of individual creditors and their geographical dispersion, the uncertain identification of those creditors in light of rapid bond trading, and asymmetric bargaining power between debtor and creditors, can be exacerbated by holdout litigation. In fact, since the 1990s, 50 percent of all restructurings resulted in lawsuits, with poorer countries more often on the defending side of those cases.[28] Most of those cases appear as contract cases in domestic courts.[29] These costs could be significantly

---

23 Buchheit and de la Torre, "Sovereign Debt Restructuring: From the Brady Plan to Ecuador 2020."
24 Gallagher, "The New Vulture Culture: Sovereign Debt Restructuring and Trade and Investment Treaties."
25 NML Capital, LTD., and others v. Republic of Argentina, 699 F.3d 246.
26 Buchheit and de la Torre, "Sovereign Debt Restructuring: From the Brady Plan to Ecuador 2020."
27 Judge Griesa, NML Capital LTD., and others v. Republic of Argentina.
28 Gelpern, "Sovereign Debt: Now What?"
29 Although outside of the scope of this chapter, some experts have pointed out that national courts deciding contracts are "ill-suited to the coordination task [of a sovereign default]" in part because as a sovereign debtor, that state has any number of legitimate

reduced with a swift and orderly restructuring process—a goal that would benefit all parties. It is in the interest of private creditors to support a regime that would prevent all creditors from rushing to exit given that such a run would jeopardize the collective value of the asset and keep a debtor solvent enough to pay debts. Of course it is in the debtors' interest to restructure debt in a manner that allows the nation to service its debt burden and begin to recover.

Bondholders as Protected Investors

In an interesting development, in addition to filing contract suits in domestic courts, some holdouts have filed investor–state disputes at the ICSID. Argentina first, then Greece, found themselves defending their restructuring in an investor-state dispute, each with a different outcome.

After Argentina announced a one-time bond exchange (in which it resolved to never hold a future swap with a better offer), 180,000 bondholders filed a claim under the Italy–Argentine BIT arguing that the restructuring effort amounted to uncompensated expropriation and a violation of FET.[30] The claim: US$4.3 billion. The first exchange took place in 2005, and 5 years later, Argentina announced one more exchange—this time offering only 25 cents on the dollar for willing bondholders—take it or leave it. Some of the investors accepted the offer, but US$1.2 billion remained with the claim.[31] As a result, the ICSID tribunal found jurisdiction over the dispute, in particular finding that the Italy–Argentina bilateral investment treaty included sovereign bonds as a covered investment. The tribunal never ruled, however, on the substance of the case, as the two parties agreed to a settlement in 2016, after Argentina elected a new president who campaigned on a platform of returning the country to international financial markets.[32]

As in all areas of trade and investment treaty governance, not all treaties are created equally. In the wake of the 2008 financial crisis, Greece restructured a catastrophic US$262.3 billion of sovereign debt in an attempt to maintain the stability needed to stay in the Eurozone.[33] Prior to the restructuring, Greece

expenditures that are hindered by one-off contract cases. These courts, however, are not set up to make political determinations about what states can and cannot afford to offer their creditors. Gelpern, "Sovereign Debt: Now What?"

30 Waibel, "Opening Pandora's Box."

31 Thrasher and Gallagher, "Mission Creep: The Emerging Role of International Investment Agreements in Sovereign Debt Restructuring"; Hornbeck, "Argentina's Defaulted Sovereign Debt: Dealing with the 'Holdouts.' "

32 Abaclat and others v. The Argentine Republic—Consent Award, www.italaw.com.

33 Zettelmeyer, Trebesch and Gulati, "The Greek Debt Restructuring."

took extensive steps to negotiate with its private creditors and even did so with the blessing of the European Union and the IMF. Greece also initially received a bailout package from Euro-area members and the IMF, with the promise to follow strict austerity measures and cut down on government expenditures.[34] Despite all the good will, however, it became clear that additional private sector involvement would be necessary to manage this unsustainable debt burden.

Greece, the European Commission and the IMF evaluated several different restructuring proposals, but in the end, it was the Greek Bondholder Act that did the heavy lifting. This Act retrofit collective action clauses—in which a supermajority of the bondholders could bind the rest to a negotiated bond exchange—into all sovereign bond contracts governed by domestic law. Along with several incentives built into the new bonds, these policies garnered the support of 96.9 percent of all bondholders.

Still, a small minority of holdouts, represented by Slovak bank Poštová banka, remained and sued under the Greece–Slovakia BIT.[35] Like the Argentine case, the tribunal never reached a decision on the merits of the case. This time, however, they also rejected the bank's standing as a covered investor under the treaty. The tribunal concluded that, although investment was defined generally as "every kind of asset," only "debentures of a *company* and any other form of participation in a company" (private bonds) were mentioned specifically in the text of the agreement.[36] Notably, the tribunal in the Greek case distinguished the text of the two treaties (the Italy-Argentina BIT and the Greece-Slovakia BIT) when coming to the decision to dismiss the case on jurisdictional grounds.

IIA Mission "Creep": Extending its Reach into Sovereign Debt

If bondholders are protected investors under some IIAs, how might those outcomes impact the burden- and risk-sharing of sovereign debt contracts? The initial gateway by which these agreements extend their jurisdiction over SDR is by adopting broad definitions of investment so as to include sovereign bonds within that definition. The archetype of this kind of definition can be found in the newly negotiated USMCA, which defines investment as "every asset an investor owns or controls," which "has the characteristics of an investment," including "bonds, debentures, other debt instruments and loans."[37] The contrasting stories of Argentina and Greece clearly demonstrate

---

34 Poštová banka, a.s. and ISTROKAPITAL SE v. Hellenic Republic, www.italaw.com.
35 Poštová banka, a.s. and ISTROKAPITAL SE v. Hellenic Republic, www.italaw.com.
36 Poštová banka, a.s. and ISTROKAPITAL SE v. Hellenic Republic, www.italaw.com.
37 "USMCA," 14.1.

that a narrower definition can keep these cases out of investor–state arbitration altogether.

Moreover, the outcome in Argentina highlights how important it is to understand how the rules of an investment treaty might map onto a restructuring process; in particular, to understand which rules would allow a creditor to walk away with a large award for damages against a country already in the middle of a debt crisis. What follows is just such a map.

The definitions of covered investment are not the only source of jurisdiction found in international investment arbitration. The convention governing the ICSID contains its own jurisdictional requirements, which many believe to put a limitation on expansive definitions within the treaties. Under *Salini v. Morocco*, the most widely cited case on the subject, to count as a protected investment, the transaction must involve "a significant commitment of resources, an economic risk [...], sufficient duration of the operation, a regularity of profit and return and a contribution to the development of the host state."[38] The tribunal in the Greek case above invoked *Salini* in dicta to say that even if the investment treaty had been ambiguous about including sovereign debt (which it was not), then the claim would have failed based on criteria similar to the *Salini* test. The bondholders' interests did not qualify for failure to share in the risks and contribute to the development of the Greek economy.[39] Certainly not all arbitral tribunals would apply *Salini* in such a strict way. An alternative view suggests that the criteria provide "useful guidance [but] do not create any jurisdictional requirements," an approach which would act to keep IIA jurisdiction expansive.[40]

Another provision that exposes the host state to ISDS jurisdiction is known as the umbrella clause. Present in some 43 percent of all investment treaties,[41] these clauses bring additional international obligations under the umbrella of the investment agreement's enforcement mechanisms. In this case, the treaty might extend its reach to the terms of the bond contract as a separate international obligation of the sovereign debtor.[42] As a result, the debtor

---

38 Salini Costruttori S.P.A. and Italstrade S.P.A. v. Kingdom of Morocco, 42 International Legal Materials paragraph 52; Waibel, *Sovereign Defaults before International Courts and Tribunals*.

39 Poštová banka, a.s. and ISTROKAPITAL SE v. Hellenic Republic, www.italaw.com.

40 Waibel, *Sovereign Defaults before International Courts and Tribunals*.

41 "Mapping of IIA Content | International Investment Agreements Navigator | UNCTAD Investment Policy Hub."

42 Although not determinative in the jurisdictional outcome, the Italian claimants in the Argentine case attempted to bring in an umbrella clause from the Chile–Argentina BIT by way of an MFN provision. The tribunal side-stepped these issues, holding that the claims were not purely contract claims and the umbrella clause was not necessary to reach them. Thrasher and Gallagher, "Mission Creep: The Emerging Role of

Table 6.2. International investment agreement governance of sovereign debt restructuring

Sovereign debt restructuring	IIA jurisdiction overlap
Issuing sovereign bonds	Broad definition of "investment"—bond holders become protected investors; right of establishment
Failure to pay interest payments	Free transfers rules, indirect expropriation
Negotiations with creditors	National treatment, fair and equitable treatment, free transfers rules
Restructuring proposing reduced face value, lower interest rates, longer maturities	National treatment, fair and equitable treatment, indirect expropriation, free transfers rules

state might be subject to lawsuits in the state court as well as investor–state arbitration.

Once sovereign debt is considered a covered investment under the treaty, the value of that investment is protected through a number of key provisions (Table 6.2). At each juncture of the SDR, different rules and standards of protection might apply. When a country issues sovereign bonds, it often inadvertently invites bondholders to be protected investors under all of their investment agreements, as described above. Indeed, only around 5 percent of all investment treaties explicitly exclude sovereign debt from their list of covered investments.[43] In a small minority of treaties, investors are also extended a right of establishment, which demands that countries extend to prospective foreign bondholders the same rights given to domestic bondholders to become established as investors and thus protected under the treaty before they even purchase the bonds.[44]

Once a country is facing a debt crisis and is unable to make interest payments on its bonds, the government may run afoul of the rules requiring free transfers, discussed in detail in the previous chapter. These provisions commonly state that current and capital account flows must pass into and out of the country "freely and without delay."[45] Approximately half of all FTAs

International Investment Agreements in Sovereign Debt Restructuring"; Abaclat and others v. The Argentine Republic—Decision on Jurisdiction and Admissibility, www.italaw.com.

43 "Mapping of IIA Content | International Investment Agreements Navigator | UNCTAD Investment Policy Hub."

44 "Mapping of IIA Content | International Investment Agreements Navigator | UNCTAD Investment Policy Hub."

45 "USMCA," 14.9.

notified to the WTO have provisions of this sort, and almost 100 percent of all investment treaties.[46] Delays on bond payments as well as temporary standstills on capital flows during restructuring negotiations could easily rise to the level of a free transfers violation, unless a relevant exception applies.[47]

Failure to make interest payments could also be considered an indirect expropriation if the value of a bondholder's investment is decreased considerably as a result, and the government is not able to offer compensation. As discussed in previous chapters, the standard for expropriation has expanded considerably since its days as a gatekeeper against widespread direct nationalization of foreign property. Today it includes also the indirect "or incidental interference with the use of property which [deprives] the owner [...] of the use of reasonably to be expected economic benefit of property."[48] While expropriations are not outright prohibited, a country carrying out debt restructuring would need to demonstrate the public purpose and nondiscriminatory application of the measures, and prompt, adequate and effective compensation after the fact—all part of the standard under customary international law.

The last requirement is where it gets complicated in the context of sovereign debt. Ideally, of course, the restructuring will result in some compensation for the loss of value to the creditor—better interest rates or terms for the exchanged bonds, for example. But the reality is that these are countries with no additional resources to spare for compensation. When mapped onto sovereign debt default, the expropriation standard would be regularly violated out of sheer necessity.

Once a government begins negotiations with creditors in order to restructure their debt and make changes to the bond contracts, a host of other provisions come into play. National treatment provisions (ubiquitous in trade and investment treaties), for example, require any negotiations for restructuring to offer foreign investors the same terms and conditions as domestic investors. This may, in fact, put additional burdens on domestic investors at a time when they need to revive the domestic financial system. In particular, domestic

---

46 Gallagher, Sklar and Thrasher, "Quantifying the Policy Space for Regulating Capital Flows in Trade and Investment Treaties: A G24 Working Paper," 24; "Mapping of IIA Content | International Investment Agreements Navigator | UNCTAD Investment Policy Hub."

47 In another case against Argentina, an ICSID tribunal ruled that its tax on outflows could be a violation of the free transfers clause, and was definitely an instance of "creeping" (slow-moving, eventual) expropriation. Gallagher, "The New Vulture Culture: Sovereign Debt Restructuring and Trade and Investment Treaties"; El Paso Energy International Company v. the Argentine Republic, www.italaw.com.

48 Glinavos, "Haircut Undone?," 483.

investors can experience a double adjustment during both debt default and restructuring. In addition to the haircut that all other investors receive, they also deal with the domestic realities that follow the restructuring—including slow growth, high unemployment and interest rates, and currency devaluation.[49] In addition to mitigating against these domestic realities, it may also purchase political buy-in for subsequent recovery and reform efforts to provide slightly better terms to domestic creditors.[50]

Another broad-reaching provision found in investment treaties is the FET clause. The FET standard has been the subject of some controversy in recent years—and is more extensively discussed in Chapter 4 of this volume. Nevertheless, for our purposes here, the most basic understanding of FET, and the historical one, is that it requires only the recognition of basic due process and explicitly does not grant additional substantive rights to the investors. The vagueness of the language, however, has lent itself to a wide variety of interpretations, some of which expressly include protection of the "legitimate expectations" of investors.[51] When restructuring negotiations have involved large decreases in the face value of the debt (as in Argentina), investors sued, in part on the basis of their "legitimate expectations" being unmet.[52] Even if the tribunal takes a narrower view of the standard, some more extreme take-it-or-leave-it approaches to the exchange may seem to undermine good faith and due process. In the Greek case, for example, the due process of retroactively inserting collective action clauses into bond contracts through an act of law could look suspiciously like changing the rules of the game and letting "legitimate expectations" fall to the wayside.

IIAs Mission "Creep": Policy Space within the Framework

Still, within this alarming framework of sovereign creditors as protected investors, there is some policy space built in for countries facing a debt crisis. In the first place, a small minority of IIAs have general exceptions for balance of payments crises or other serious macroeconomic difficulties.[53] This allows

---

49 Gallagher, "The New Vulture Culture: Sovereign Debt Restructuring and Trade and Investment Treaties."

50 Gallagher, "The New Vulture Culture: Sovereign Debt Restructuring and Trade and Investment Treaties"; Thrasher and Gallagher, "Mission Creep: The Emerging Role of International Investment Agreements in Sovereign Debt Restructuring."

51 Antaris GMBH and Dr. Michael Gode v. The Czech Republic, www.italaw.com.

52 Abaclat and others v. The Argentine Republic—Decision on Jurisdiction and Admissibility, www.italaw.com.

53 According to UNCTAD, only about 14 percent of IIAs have a balance of payments exception. By contrast, almost half (46 percent) of all FTAs notified to the WTO include exceptions for balance of payments. Gallagher, Sklar and Thrasher, "Quantifying the

Table 6.3. Existing safeguards in international investment agreements

Sovereign debt restructuring	IIA jurisdiction overlap
Failure to pay interest payments	Balance of payments exceptions for macroeconomic difficulties, prudential measures exceptions, 9-month cooling-off period
Negotiations with creditors	"Negotiated restructuring" carve out from investor–state disputes
Restructuring proposing reduced face value, lower interest rates, longer maturities	Balance of payments and prudential measures exceptions, "negotiated restructuring" carve out, 9-month cooling-off period

countries to restrict capital flows, especially the repatriation of funds back into the investor's home country, on a temporary basis—just long enough to address the immediate needs of the crisis. In this case, the IMF often oversees implementation of the article. Another similar provision, with a narrower scope, can be found among financial services commitments in broader treaties. As noted in the previous chapter, financial services provisions often include a prudential carve-out allowing state parties to "adopt or maintain [restrictive] measures [affecting financial services] for prudential reasons such as [...] ensuring the integrity and stability of the financial system."[54]

These two exceptions are essentially hypothetical—they have not yet been used to successfully fend off investor claimants. Indeed, it is generally understood that neither exception is crafted for the context of sovereign debt, but rather for the context of general financial regulation and capital controls (see Chapter 5).[55] However, given the close logical and practical nexus between the current debt crises sweeping the globe and the stability of the financial system (both individually and collectively), defendant states should keep these safeguards in mind as they face disputes for their crisis-era policies (see Table 6.3).

Of course many experts believe these exceptions, to the extent that they work at all, to be "too little, too late" for a country in the throes of a debt crisis.[56]

Policy Space for Regulating Capital Flows in Trade and Investment Treaties: A G24 Working Paper"; "Mapping of IIA Content | International Investment Agreements Navigator | UNCTAD Investment Policy Hub."

54 EU-Singapore, "EU-Singapore FTA," 8.50.

55 Waibel, *Sovereign Defaults before International Courts and Tribunals*; Viterbo, *International Economic Law and Monetary Measures*.

56 Guzman, Ocampo and Stiglitz, *Too Little, Too Late*.

Some more recently drafted treaties have attempted to address sovereign debt default head-on, by including an annex governing these specific circumstances. These Annexes lay out specific rules and act to formalize the previously *de facto* governance by these treaties of SDR. The main role of the annex is to limit the use of ISDS for investor claims about restructuring. For example, under the CPTPP, investor–state disputes are not allowed for negotiated restructuring, defined as a restructuring plan that involves at least 75 percent bondholder participation (except for national treatment and MFN treatment claims). It also requires that investors wait nine months before bringing claims as a sort of cooling-off period, which allows for *de facto* flexibility for countries involved in short-term crises.

New Trade and Investment Treaties and SDR: Avoiding a Collision Course

These flexibilities are a step in the right direction but more change is needed.

Global trade and investment are being remapped as we speak. The European Union is aggressively pursuing new trade agreements with partners all over the world, with a particular focus on Asia.[57] Brexit has forced Britain to re-establish linkages with various parts of the world in the form of new trade policy and new treaties.[58] China is expanding is regional reach through the RCEP, and the United States has renegotiated both its accord with Canada and Mexico (USMCA) and with Korea (KORUS). Moreover, it has begun negotiations with Kenya to transform a more aspirational agreement, a Trade and Investment Partnership Agreement, into a full-fledged FTA.[59]

Each of these approaches offers a slightly different approach to governing SDR. Many new treaties implicitly include sovereign bonds as a covered investment under the treaty (see Table 6.4). A few have language noting that investments must also satisfy at least some of the *Salini* criteria for investment characteristics.[60] Others note that official bilateral creditors do not qualify as protected investors.[61] At the same time, those same treaties almost universally

---

57 EU-Japan, "EU-Japan EPA"; EU-Singapore, "EU-Singapore FTA"; Canada-EU, "CETA."

58 Poulsen, "British Foreign Investment Policy Post-Brexit"; Larik, "Brexit, the EU-UK Withdrawal Agreement, and Global Treaty (Re-)Negotiations."

59 "Joint Statement between the United States and Kenya on the Launch of Negotiations towards a Free Trade Agreement | United States Trade Representative."

60 "USMCA," 14.1; US-Korea, "US-Korea FTA," 11.28.

61 Canada-Australia-Brunei-Chile-Japan-Malaysia-Mexico-New Zealand-Peru-Singapore-Viet Nam, "CPTPP," 9.1, n. 3.

Table 6.4. New trade and investment treaties and SDR: An illustrative list

	Sovereign debt as covered investment	ISDS	Balance-of-payments & Prudential except	Sovereign/public debt annex
EU-Singapore*	1.2 (I)	3.1 (I)	BOP: 4.4 (I), 8.50 (T) Prudential: 16.9 (T)	None
EU-Japan	*Inconclusive*	None	BOP: 9.4 Prudential: 8.65	None
CETA	*None*	8.18	BOP 28.4–.5 Prudential: 13.16	Annex 8-B
USMCA	14.1	14.D.3	BOP: 32.4 Prudential: 17.11	Appendix 2 (chapter 14)
KORUS	11.28	11.16	Prudential: 13.10	None
CPTPP	9.1	19.19	BOP: 29.3 Prudential 11.11	Annex 9-G
RCEP	10.1	Proposed for future Work Program, 10.18	BOP: 17.15 Prudential: Annex 8A, Article 4.	None.

* The EU-Singapore treaty comprises two parts—a general Economic Partnership Agreement (EPA) and an investment treaty. "(I)" denotes a provision from the investment treaty and "(T)" denotes a provision from the general EPA.

include exceptions for balance of payments and "prudential reasons," which could make such defenses more widely available if this trend continues.

Moreover, given the widespread criticism of investor–state disputes, most treaties have placed limits on investor suits in the context of sovereign default. The USMCA, for instance, only allows investor claims for national treatment and MFN violations, and for *direct* expropriations. Even then, discrimination claims based on the foreign investor's right of establishment are prohibited. Furthermore, the claimant must show damages arising out of the treaty breach.[62]

Negotiated restructuring annexes are also becoming more prevalent,[63] each limiting the scope of possible complaints by sovereign creditors and

---

62 "USMCA," 14.D.3.
63 Canada-EU, "CETA," Annex 8-B; Canada-Australia-Brunei-Chile-Japan-Malaysia-Mexico-New Zealand-Peru-Singapore-Viet Nam, "CPTPP," Annex 9-G; EU-Singapore, "EU-Singapore IPA," Annex 4.

mandating a cooling-off period for all claims unrelated to non-discrimination rules. The USMCA deploys an even more hands-off model that attempts to distance the treaty still further from sovereign debt governance.[64] Rather than a negotiated restructuring annex, the agreement explicitly does not allow claimants to bring bond contract terms under the umbrella of the treaty. It also states that investors may not bring restructuring-related claims under the agreement if the restructuring took place in compliance with the terms of the debt instrument.

Early negotiations of the RCEP showed some promise as countries that have historically lagged in development were setting the negotiating agenda. India, for example, submitted some interesting negotiating drafts, in particular, excluding sovereign debt explicitly in its definition of investment. Since India stood alone in refusing to sign the final agreement, however, the agreement did not take a form with Indian preferences. The final text includes provisions much like European and US models, including sovereign bonds within the list of covered investments, while placing ISDS on the Work Program for future negotiations (see Table 6.4).[65]

Conclusions and Policy Proposals

It is clear that treaty negotiators are aware of the regime overlap between sovereign debt and investment protection—and by and large they are wary of it. Nevertheless, as sovereign default threatens to become a global problem, we should be ever more conscious of the overreach of investment agreements into this realm, especially when the current regime of restructuring oversight is still very fragile.

The ability of holdout bondholders to use investment treaties to reclaim the full value of their bonds could further undermine the development of a new effective regime. SDR, by definition, changes the investment environment, reduces the value of an investment, allows a host government to effectively expropriate some of the loan, and often results in bonds held by domestic financial institutions and citizens being restructured differently than foreign bondholders. For that reason, when sovereign debt is counted as investment by an investment agreement, numerous conflicts could arise. Neither the Greek or Argentine cases made it past a finding on jurisdiction. As a result, we can only speculate how the substantive provisions of the investment treaties might have applied under each circumstance.

---

64 "USMCA," Appendix 2 (chapter 14).
65 "RCEP," Article 10.1, 10.18.

Although investor–state disputes have come under increasing criticism and newer treaties are placing boundaries around the scope of such claims, the vast majority of investment treaties in force today have an investor–state dispute mechanism.[66] As such imminent sovereign default is likely to give rise to more claims like *Abaclat* and *Poštová banka*. Limitations placed in public debt annexes are also not likely to have an immediate impact given that they are new features of the landscape and not yet available to most sovereign debtors.

Even if they were to become a new permanent fixture in international investment law, our legal norms must leave room for the development of a restructuring framework through experimentation and evolution. Regardless of the form of such a regime, investment agreements should not replace a more holistic approach, which addresses the stability of the system as a whole, alongside the sovereignty of the debtor nation, the needs of its constituents and the long-term sustainability of the foreign investment. Instead, investment agreements should take a back seat and allow other sovereign debtor–creditor transactions to take place in a separate space. The overarching goal of new treaties should be to cede policy space to governments and multilateral institutions so that negotiations and discussions can take place out from under the shadow of investor–state arbitration threats. To the extent that these treaties play a small role, they must give deference to the debtor countries, mindful of the special role of sovereign debt in development and managing financial crises.

In light of these realities, three concrete policy proposals stand out.

First, definitions matter. As demonstrated by the differing outcomes between the Greek and Argentine cases, the wording of the definition of "covered investment" matters greatly in the preliminary determination of jurisdiction. If there is no jurisdiction, then there is no case. In new trade and investment agreements and in renegotiating old ones, countries should consider excluding sovereign debt explicitly from coverage under the treaty and leaving SDR to other international fora.[67]

Second, where sovereign debt remains a covered investment, we need to improve sovereign debt exceptions and safeguards. This could be accomplished through modifications to existing exceptions—explicitly allowing sovereign default to be a circumstance in which restrictions on capital flows would be allowed, or making reference to sovereign default in a footnote within the prudential reasons exception such that the carve out would apply directly to the context of sovereign default. Box 1 provides example treaty text to accomplish this purpose.

---

66 "Mapping of IIA Content | International Investment Agreements Navigator | UNCTAD Investment Policy Hub."

67 The CETA is one of only a few new treaties to do this. Canada-EU, "CETA," 8.1.

Box 1. Proposed Balance of Payments and Prudential Reasons Exceptions for Sovereign Debt Restructurings

Article X.1 Restrictions in the case of serious balance of payments or external financial difficulties

1. Where a Party experiences serious balance-of-payments or external financial difficulties, or threat thereof, it may adopt or maintain restrictive measures with regard to capital movements or payments, including transfers.*

   * For clarity, when a party is unable to service its sovereign debt and is entering default, or the threat thereof, this constitutes "external financial difficulties" for purposes of this article.

Article XX.1 Prudential Carve Out

1. This Agreement does not prevent a Party from adopting or maintaining reasonable measures for prudential reasons, including:

   (a) the protection of investors, depositors, policy-holders, or persons to whom a financial institution, cross-border financial service supplier, or financial service supplier owes a fiduciary duty;
   (b) the maintenance of the safety, soundness, integrity, or financial responsibility of a financial institution, cross-border financial service supplier, or financial service supplier; or
   (c) ensuring the integrity and stability of a Party's financial system.†

   † For clarity, when a party is unable to service its sovereign debt and is entering default, or the threat thereof, this represents a threat to the integrity and stability of that party's financial system and should be considered an appropriate circumstance for adopting prudential measures.

A more controversial modification might be to eliminate the national treatment requirement for these restructurings. Since national treatment is one of the pillars undergirding these agreements, the allowance for discrimination in the case of restructuring would have to be carefully limited. However, if legitimate domestic financial interests are taken into account, these annexes would go a long way (together with other measures) to protect countries in default.

Finally, SDR should be subject only to state-to-state dispute resolution with a strong preference for exhausting local dispute remedies first. Investor–state disputes are a well-established practice for modern investment treaties. However, given the sensitive nature and complicated political realities of sovereign default, this context calls for a more collaborative process. Many current EU trade and investment treaties contain both a state–state process and an investor–state process. A proposed annex could simply preserve restructuring for state–state dispute resolution. This alternative approach could be modeled on a financial services safeguard present in the CPTPP, which states that in the case of an investor–state conflict over financial services, the authorities of the respondent state and the party of the claimant investor must meet together to make a determination of whether an exception applies in that context.[68] The determination of the authorities "shall be binding on the tribunal" adjudicating the dispute. That same provision could be read into a Public Debt annex (see, e.g., Box 2), such that the authorities of each party would have the chance to collaborate and determine whether a prudential reason exists for the restructuring.

As the world turns to bigger, broader and deeper trade and investment agreements, this is the perfect time to ensure that these treaties reflect the realities of sovereign debt in an environment with liberalized capital markets. In the meantime, policymakers must take stock of their existing treaty commitments and become aware of the ways that sovereign default and restructuring might expose them to arbitration risk.

IIAs have a broad scope. Just as they cover cross-sectoral contexts like capital flows and sovereign debt, these treaties reach into sector-specific policy in agricultural land reform, pharmaceutical development and access to medicines and energy policy. In each case, investors are protected not only from arbitrary or inconsistent state behavior but also from the instability that comes from necessary regulatory change. Countries are developing new

---

68 Canada-Australia-Brunei-Chile-Japan-Malaysia-Mexico-New Zealand-Peru-Singapore-Viet Nam, "CPTPP," 11.22.

Box 2. Model State–State Dispute Settlement Carve out for Sovereign Debt Restructuring

Article X.1. Investment Disputes over Sovereign Debt

...

2. If an investor of a Party submits a claim to arbitration under [the investment chapter] regarding the restructuring of sovereign debt, the following provisions of this Article shall apply.
   - (a) The respondent shall [...] submit in writing to the authorities responsible for sovereign debt restructuring of the Party of the claimant [...] a request for a joint determination by the authorities of the respondent and the Party of the claimant on the issue of whether the sovereign debt restructuring constituted an uncompensated direct expropriation or a most-favored nation violation [...]
   - (b) The authorities of the respondent and the Party of the claimant shall attempt in good faith to make a determination as described in subparagraph (a). Any such determination shall be transmitted promptly to the disputing parties and, if constituted, to the tribunal. The determination shall be ***binding on the tribunal and any decision or award issued by the tribunal must be consistent with that determination.***
   - (c) If the authorities referred to in subparagraphs (a) and (b) have not made a determination within 120 days of the date of receipt of the respondent's written request for a determination under subparagraph (a), the respondent or the Party of the claimant may request the establishment of a panel under [the state-state dispute settlement chapter] to consider whether and to what extent the sovereign debt restructuring violated the provisions listed in subparagraph (a). The panel [...] shall transmit its final report to the disputing Parties and to the tribunal.
3. The final report of a panel referred to in paragraph 2(c) ***shall be binding on the tribunal***, and any decision or award issued by the tribunal must be consistent with the final report.

approaches—due in part to the rising awareness of the impact of these treaties and efforts to make the content of, and comparison between, treaty texts more available. In the context of sovereign debt, we may be able to see change happen even more quickly, as countries are forced to respond to the looming crisis with ingenuity.

Chapter 7

TRADE AND INVESTMENT POLICY FOR CLIMATE CHANGE AND THE ENERGY TRANSITION

The evidence for climate change is strong. We are concerned for animal and plant extinction, as well as, in some of the worst case scenario modeling, the disappearance of entire landmasses and sources of arable land for our children and grandchildren. Worse, it is the people in vulnerable geographical areas, already suffering from natural disasters, lack of infrastructure, and weak governance who will be most at risk.[1] There remains some uncertainty about the short- and long-term impacts of climate change, as well as how much of the natural and human disasters we are facing is attributable to climate change as opposed to other factors.[2] Nevertheless, countries facing those challenges need a toolkit to address them, a toolkit that has been disappearing, along with the broader toolkit for industrial policy and development, since the middle of the 1990s.

Facing climate change, whether through increased regulation or coalition building with the private sector requires public buy-in for democratic countries. In the United States, for example, proponents of the Green New Deal rely heavily on their understanding of the priorities of the "average" American to attempt to garner public support. Research has shown that people of all ages and income groups identify themselves more strongly with their nation (at a federal level) than they do with humanity more broadly, their region of the world, their language group or even their local community or subnational unit.[3] Moreover, survey after survey shows that, while climate change is of concern for some, it is far outweighed by economic issues like jobs and gas prices, not to mention global challenge of the COVID-19 pandemic.[4] This

---

1 Janetos, "Why Trade Matters to a Climate Agreement"; Gore, "Extreme Carbon Inequality."
2 Shellenberger, "Why Apocalyptic Claims about Climate Change Are Wrong."
3 Rodrik, *Straight Talk on Trade*.
4 Bialik, "State of the Union 2019"; Gallup, Inc., "Most Important Problem." Although, among the youngest voters, climate change ranks #1. Loudenback and Jackson, "The 10 Most Critical Problems in the World, According to Millennials."

much is obvious. Constituents of countries around the world expect their governments to prioritize *them* over the needs of people elsewhere.

In response to this, many countries have adopted new laws and policies to kick-start the renewable energy sector to mitigate climate change and encourage energy transitions, while at the same time contributing to economic growth and the protection of their citizens.[5] These new laws, often called green industrial policy, are also relevant for foreign investors, prompting them to put their money in green energy while also contributing to the diversification of the local economy. The World Bank, the IMF and other international institutions have begun, albeit inconsistently, to support these laws through institutional policies prioritizing climate-friendly development projects.

Trade and investment treaties, however, by their very nature, slow down the process of legislative and policy change. In general, political and legislative stability and reliability is essential for a growing economy. That is part of why the world saw such positive global growth on the heels of successive GATT negotiations— companies could rely on lower barriers to trade over time without being concerned they would suddenly shift with a new government or administration. Unfortunately, the trend toward regulatory convergence offers not only stability and reliability but also problematic regulatory harmonization.[6] This means that country governments with very different population needs, factors of production, baskets of tradeable goods and, not to mention, geographical characteristics, must approach new regulation in largely the same way.

A different approach is needed. New trends in treaty negotiations as well as WTO and investor–state cases demonstrate that, despite the awareness of the need for government intervention, many countries' hands are tied. A handful of countries have begun to adjust their new investment agreements in response to the problems with regulatory convergence. Investment treaties, whose primary goal is to facilitate investment and protect the interests of foreign investors, arguably have the potential to promote climate-friendly investments through providing a stable investment climate.[7] At the same time, they may also have a chilling effect on government regulation aimed at meeting global climate goals by exposing them to ISDS.

We need treaties that allow countries to experiment with policies that correct for the environmental spillover effects of traditional industry while also responding to the needs of their constituencies. Rather than ratcheting up the

---

5 Cui and Lu, "Optimizing Local Content Requirements under Technology Gaps."

6 Rolland, "The Impact of Trade and Investment Treaties on Mobilization of Taxation in Developing Countries."

7 Sachs and Sauvant, "BITs, DTTs and FDI Flows: An Overview"; Tienhaara and Downie, "Risky Business?"

commitments in trade treaties to create enforceable standards in renewable energy and emissions targets, countries can cooperate with each other to build capacity through technical assistance and financing.

The Case for Green Industrial Policy

As Chapter 2 explains in some detail, industrial policy has always played a key role in development for both economic and political reasons.[8] Many of these measures were put in place to build backward and forward linkages within the local economy, encouraging an integrated industrial development.[9] Countries also relied on them to diversify their economies, introducing new businesses and sectors into certain states or regions.

The renewable energy market seems particularly well-suited to these policies, in part because it is a relatively new industry in most countries. Given that new industries are not immediately competitive internationally, they may, with some support, catch up within a reasonable amount of time.[10] Countries that cannot afford to directly subsidize their domestic green energy sector might want to use investment and industrial policies to a similar effect. Local content requirements, for example, may garner much needed public support for the higher costs of renewable energy projects by extending promises of new businesses and jobs up and down the supply chain.[11] As Joseph Stiglitz has pointed out, if a country needs to provide subsidies and other support to "try to undermine a massive distortion in an un-level playing field, you're going to want to appropriate as much of the gains […] as you can […] to ensure that as much of the benefit [as possible] can go to your producing economy, *especially if you're a developing country*."[12] The challenge of climate change in particular requires a long-term view that most governments do not have. In order to prioritize this, then, the benefits must be linked to more immediate concerns— like local jobs and economic growth.[13] In the long term, industrial policies that support new renewable energy sectors in a larger number of countries worldwide could result in an increased global supply of renewable energy and a greater ability to compete with fossil fuel prices. Indeed, in countries like

---

8 Nikièma, "Performance Requirements in Investment Treaties."
9 Stephenson, "Addressing Local Content Requirements in a Sustainable Energy Trade Agreement."
10 Stephenson, "Addressing Local Content Requirements in a Sustainable Energy Trade Agreement."
11 Nikièma, "Performance Requirements in Investment Treaties."
12 Stiglitz, Shoyer and Howse, "Climate Change, China and the WTO."
13 Meyer, "How Local Discrimination Can Promote Global Public Goods."

China and India, it would seem irresponsible to not have an internationally competitive solar and wind power sector.[14]

Market failures and distortions

Even if we argue that industrial policy is excessive state intervention in the market, as some have, the presence of structural market failures as well as sector-specific distortions give good reasons for challenging the dominant free-trade paradigm in this context. In the first place, as noted in various parts of this volume, highly integrated world markets in all sectors have "accentuated many of the pervasive market distortions" in the global economy.[15] These distortions work against the development goals of economic diversification, technological growth and increasing domestic production capacity, to name a few. Market failures like these extend beyond negative economic outcomes, often resulting in social, cultural and environmental externalities that are not immediately quantifiable.[16]

Nowhere are these distortions more evident than in the global energy markets. Negative environmental externalities occur when the prices in the economy do not adequately take into account the environmental costs of the production or consumption of a good.[17] Fossil fuels, both in their production and consumption cause irreversible damage. Current projections by the international environmental community indicate that we need to hold global warming to *below* 2 degrees Celsius by the year 2100.[18] In order to meet that goal, however, scientists estimate that approximately 75 percent of the fossil fuels still in the ground must remain there—and not be extracted and burned.[19] Continuing to rely on fossil fuel for energy has some very real (negative) consequences for our earth. Still, these external impacts are not calculated as a part of the cost of these goods.[20] As a result, the demand for fossil fuels has been kept artificially high. In order to compete with, and ultimately overtake, fossil fuels as our dominant energy source, governments must intervene to support the development and production of renewable energy.

---

14 Stiglitz, Shoyer and Howse, "Climate Change, China and the WTO."
15 Kumar and Gallagher, "Relevance of 'Policy Space' for Development: Implications for Multilateral Trade Negotiations."
16 Kumar and Gallagher, "Relevance of 'Policy Space' for Development: Implications for Multilateral Trade Negotiations."
17 Kumar and Gallagher, "Relevance of 'Policy Space' for Development: Implications for Multilateral Trade Negotiations."
18 Janetos, "Why Trade Matters to a Climate Agreement."
19 Vaughan, "Earth Day."
20 Janetos, "Why Trade Matters to a Climate Agreement."

In addition to the natural failures in the energy market, government support exacerbates this problem. Governments actively promote fossil fuel production and consumption, in the name of equitable access to energy and energy security, through subsidies, investment policies, the tax code and other domestic laws.[21] Research surrounding government support for the fossil fuel sector reveals that it is both ubiquitous and difficult to measure. There are essentially two broad types of subsidies: those offered to producers to overcome supply-side constraints and those aimed at consumers to increase demand.[22] As mentioned in Chapter 2, the definition of a subsidy is intentionally broad, including any "financial contribution by a government which confers a benefit."[23] In addition to grants and government loans, this includes tax breaks, royalty breaks, the provision of infrastructure, and goods and services offered at below market value. It also includes measures that transfer risk through providing cheaper financing, equity and guarantees. Despite the expansive scope of this definition, it may still leave out certain consumer subsidies, like price controls imposed by a government energy agency.[24]

This difficulty in defining fossil fuel subsidies makes it also difficult to measure. There have been various efforts to quantify the amount of government support for fossil fuels and for energy more generally. However, the lack of a full accounting of such subsidies make it likely that current estimates are well below the actual numbers.[25] One study compiled available data and calculated approximately US$588 billion for global fossil fuel subsidies in 2014.[26] The IMF proposed another approach that tallies not only traditional government subsidies but also the costs of climate change, local air pollution, congestion, accidents and road damage. This estimate suggested that these indirect (or "post tax") subsidies, when added to existing numbers amount to nearly US$5.3 *trillion*.[27] With that level of distortion in the energy market, it is not surprising that governments would need to employ subsidies and incentive programs to build up competing renewable energy industries.

Another factor that highlights the inequality in treatment between renewable and traditional energy sources is the absence of any fossil fuel

---

21 Timperley, "Explainer."
22 Timperley, "Explainer."
23 "Agreement on Subsidies and Countervailing Measures," 2.1.
24 Timperley, "Explainer." Even countries offering tax breaks for fossil fuel producers have resisted the categorization of "subsidy," as in the case of the United Kingdom.
25 Timperley, "Explainer." Offering a full discussion of the various attempts at defining and quantifying fossil fuel subsidies lies beyond the scope of this chapter.
26 Whitley and van der Burg, "Fossil Fuel Subsidy Reform: From Rhetoric to Reality."
27 Whitley and van der Burg, "Fossil Fuel Subsidy Reform: From Rhetoric to Reality."

subsidy challenges before the WTO dispute settlement body.[28] At the same time, there have been 10 disputes challenging local content requirements in renewable energy subsidy programs since 2010. Three of those resulted in the removal of the challenged measure or some retaliatory trade practice by the complainant state, and the rest have yet to be determined.

Experts debate the reason for this. It could be that countries judge the likelihood of success to be low in fossil fuel cases due to the "challenge of establishing that a fossil fuel subsidy will have 'adverse effects' and result in injury to other WTO members."[29] It could also be that states are just more likely to challenge measures in countries with diversified economies, which is where the majority of the renewable energy technologies are. A third hypothesis suggests that the novelty and visibility of these measures make them an easier target compared with comparable supports for the fossil fuel industry.[30]

Case Typologies: Challenging Policy Changes in the Renewable Energy Sector

As countries have made various attempts to promote the energy transition or mitigate climate change, there are three different types of cases or conflicts that have arisen. These cases show that international treaty commitments largely prohibit countries from using investment incentives to establish backward and forward linkages to the domestic renewable energy industry. Furthermore, when countries put in place investment incentive programs for renewable energy, they put themselves at risk for suit if the incentives are too successful, too quickly, and the government is unable to meet the demands of the investors while also keeping energy costs down for their domestic consumers. Finally, policies that attempt to phase out traditional energy sources (such as coal) may be targeted by those companies as also violating investment treaty obligations.

---

28 Van de Graaf and van Asselt, "Introduction to the Special Issue." Russia did bring a claim against the European Union on the basis of new policies governing the natural gas sector. Russia argued, *inter alia*, that the policy discriminated against Russian natural gas suppliers (though it was not a subsidy program). Russia prevailed on the basis of that claim and the European Union has appealed. European Union and its Member States—Certain Measures Relating to the Energy Sector—Report of the Panel, wto. org.

29 Van de Graaf and van Asselt, "Introduction to the Special Issue."

30 Van de Graaf and van Asselt, "Introduction to the Special Issue"; Tienhaara and Downie, "Risky Business?"

Nondiscrimination cases at the WTO

The first sort of cases to arise were nondiscrimination cases in which countries were sued for provisions in their energy incentive programs that aimed at creating backward and forward linkages in the economy around the renewable energy sector. These cases have made it clear that, under the rules of the WTO, countries may not employ local content, local hiring or local manufacturing requirements as a part of the incentive programs aimed at facilitating an energy transition. Local content requirements, as the name would suggest, are measures that require "firms to meet a minimum threshold of goods or services that must be purchased locally."[31] These requirements demand relatively little public expenditure and instead rely on the investor rules to establish links to the rest of the economy, thereby diversifying and developing across sectors.[32] Furthermore, by being tied to local industry and jobs, they are often more politically palatable than general renewable energy incentives.[33]

For that reason, they are a great fit in the renewable energy industry. A transition away from an old industry that represents a century or more of jobs for certain communities is scary, and rightly so. Offering those communities a lifeline and a hope that this transition will offer them new opportunities can be the difference between the takeoff of a renewable energy industry and further lags in development. For countries that seek a diverse economy that would like to benefit from new industrial opportunities, local content, manufacturing and hiring requirements make even more sense.

Employing local content requirements for renewable energy transitions is quite common—they have been documented in Brazil, China, India and South Africa, as well as the United States, Canada, Italy, Spain and France.[34] In Canada, India and the United States, however, those policies have been challenged and struck down by the WTO Appellate Body.

The first time that local content requirements came before a WTO panel was in 2011.[35] At that time, the European Union brought consultations against Canada for a program Ontario had introduced to encourage investments in renewable energy. The feed-in-tariff (or FIT) program simply paid a guaranteed rate to eligible generators of electricity produced from renewable

---

31 Cui and Lu, "Optimizing Local Content Requirements under Technology Gaps."

32 Nikièma, "Performance Requirements in Investment Treaties"; Stephenson, "Addressing Local Content Requirements in a Sustainable Energy Trade Agreement."

33 Meyer, "How Local Discrimination Can Promote Global Public Goods."

34 Cui and Lu, "Optimizing Local Content Requirements under Technology Gaps."

35 Canada—Certain Measures Affecting the Renewable Energy Generation Sector, wto.org.

sources.[36] One eligibility requirement, among many, was the purchase of local equipment to produce renewable energy. The European Union and Japan claimed that Canada had violated the TRIMs and the SCM Agreements—both of which prohibit local content requirements explicitly.[37]

In its defense, Canada argued that the FIT program was, at its heart, a government procurement program for energy production.[38] As in many countries, Canada's provinces regulate energy production and administer distribution.[39] The provinces are also responsible for granting permits and licenses and overseeing the retail price of energy to consumers. The FIT program guaranteed a price for renewable energy producers who were awarded contracts—essentially government procurement contracts.[40] The Appellate Body, however, disagreed. Based on the wording of the national treatment standard in the GATT, the Appellate Body noted that the products discriminated against (equipment used to produce renewable energy) were not the same as the product procured by the government (the renewable energy itself).[41]

Read narrowly, the government procurement exception in the GATT does limit the carve-out to the "products purchased for governmental purposes," which, in this case, would be the energy and not the energy-producing equipment.[42] And although this conclusion is intuitively reasonable, the outcome paved the way for numerous similar claims brought on these bases. On the heels of the *Canada-FIT* decision, both the United States and the European Union initiated domestic trade investigations into the Chinese solar industry, which resulted in countervailing duties from the United States and an agreement by China to voluntarily limit exports to the European Union.[43] China likewise brought a claim in 2012 against the European Union for measures substantially similar to Ontario's FIT program, which did not progress past the consultation stage.[44] A year after the conclusion of

---

36 Canada—Certain Measures Affecting the Renewable Energy Generation Sector, wto.org.
37 Canada—Certain Measures Affecting the Renewable Energy Generation Sector, wto.org.
38 *Canada—Certain Measures Affecting the Renewable Energy Generation Sector*, wto.org, para. 2.156.
39 Christian and Shipley, "Electricity Regulation in Canada."
40 *Canada—Certain Measures Affecting the Renewable Energy Generation Sector*, wto.org.
41 *Canada—Certain Measures Affecting the Renewable Energy Generation Sector*, wto.org, para. 5.79.
42 "General Agreement on Tariffs and Trade (GATT)," III:8.
43 Palmer and Walet, "China Agrees to Halt Subsidies to Wind Power Firms"; Emmott and Blanchard, "EU, China Resolve Solar Dispute—Their Biggest Trade Row by Far."
44 *European Union and Certain Member States—Certain Measures Affecting the Renewable Energy Generation Sector—Request for Consultations by China*, wto.org.

Canada-FIT, the United States brought a claim against India for the same policies, which was concluded on identical terms.[45] India then returned the favor in September 2016, bringing a complaint against the United States for a number of state-based renewable energy programs with local content requirements.[46]

Although the specifics of these policies are diverse, these have a key similarity: each challenged policy required that investors receiving incentives to produce and sell renewable energy, and to use locally sourced inputs for their production. Moreover, each defendant state attempted to claim that these policies fell into the category of government procurement—since the government was purchasing the energy to sell to its constituents. And in each case, the dispute settlement body articulated the narrow reach of the government procurement exception in the national treatment standard under the WTO. Since the local products receiving special treatment were not the same ones as those being purchased by the government, the exception did not apply.[47]

In the aftermath of the Canada-FIT case, an investor brought a subsequent arbitration case against Canada under the NAFTA for the same policies, which they subsequently lost. Mesa Power, a renewable energy company based in the United States, complained that the program discriminated on the basis of nationality and Canada argued that the reach of the government procurement exception under the NAFTA was broader than that of the GATT. The arbitral tribunal agreed.[48] While it is reassuring that an investor was unable to recover damages for this kind of policy, the WTO rules apply much more broadly, and measures that are struck down by the dispute settlement body must still be brought into compliance to avoid further challenges.

Fair and equitable treatment in rolling back renewable energy incentives

A second group of cases seem, at first glance, to be harnessing the power of the investor to promote and protect renewable energy policies once they are in place. In these conflicts, renewable energy investors in Europe responded to new policies and programs put in place to comply with the European Union's renewable energy directive.[49] In several cases, however, a confluence

---

45 *India—Certain Measure Relating to Solar Cells and Solar*, wto.org.

46 *United States—Certain Measures Relating to the Renewable Energy Sector* , wto.org.

47 Thrasher, "Policy Space for Jobs and Clean Energy: Trade, Investment Rules and Local Content Requirements in Renewable Energy Policies."

48 Mesa Power Group, LLC v. Government of Canada, italaw.com.

49 European Commission, "EU Renewable Energy Directive."

of factors made these new programs suddenly economically unsustainable and initially generous investment incentives were diminished or removed. Governments could not make good on their promises due to a combination of the global financial crisis, a rapid decrease of the cost of solar market inputs and investors crowding the market too quickly.[50] They had to respond to the resultant economic instability, and quickly.

While piling-on effects threatened to destabilize the economy and require the government to take on unsustainable debt, renewable energy producers and investors sued them for rolling back incentives offered initially. Spain, Italy, Poland, Bulgaria and the Czech Republic have all faced similar suits, all implicating commitments under Europe's Energy Charter Treaty (ECT). *Foresight Luxembourg Solar v. Kingdom of Spain* is the most recent decision in a long line of cases contesting Spain's regulatory rollback of its investment incentive programs targeting the solar industry.[51] Spain had to meet certain EU targets for moving toward renewable energy—29.4 percent renewable energy consumption by 2010—and put in place laws to implement those EU policy targets. The main law at issue was Royal Decree (RD) 661/2007, which, like Canada above, established a fixed FIT (guaranteed price) for solar facilities for their lifetime and priority access to the electrical grid.[52] The implementation of the law was wildly successful. Within four months, the installed photovoltaic capacity was already 85 percent of the target set in RD 661/2007, exacerbating an already unsustainable gap between the amount paid by retail customers and the costs of the support schemes.[53] Spain had to respond quickly, and immediately repealed and replaced RD 661/2007 with other incentives which promised a more reasonable and sustainable rate of return for investors, including a subsidy and priority access to the grid.[54]

Interpreting the FET standard of the ECT, the tribunal emphasized the importance of legal stability and protecting investors' legitimate expectations as part of that standard under the treaty.[55] Although the tribunal acknowledged that no investor has a reasonable expectation of a completely

---

50 Tienhaara and Downie, "Risky Business?"

51 Foresight Luxembourg Solar 1 S.A.R.L., et al. Claimants and The Kingdom of Spain Respondent, italaw.com.

52 Foresight Luxembourg Solar 1 S.A.R.L., et al. Claimants and The Kingdom of Spain Respondent, italaw.com, para. 69.

53 Foresight Luxembourg Solar 1 S.A.R.L., et al. Claimants and The Kingdom of Spain Respondent, italaw.com, para. 56.

54 Foresight Luxembourg Solar 1 S.A.R.L., et al. Claimants and The Kingdom of Spain Respondent, italaw.com, para. 57.

55 Foresight Luxembourg Solar 1 S.A.R.L., et al. Claimants and The Kingdom of Spain Respondent, italaw.com, para. 343–52.

frozen regulatory framework, the structure of Spain's incentive programs were such as to give assurances to investors that the programs would remain in place.[56] Furthermore, despite acknowledging the right to regulate in the public interest, the tribunal cautioned that it must not be limitless or investor protections will be rendered useless.[57] They found, ultimately, that the claimants had legitimate expectations which Spain had abrogated; in the end, Spain lost and was ordered to pay €39 million in damages.

These same measures were recently disputed in *Charanne, Isolux, Eiser, Novenergia, Antin, Masdar,* and *Greentech,* the latter five also decided in favor of the investor on FET grounds.[58] On the other hand the Czech Republic has had a different experience with respect to the ECT. After imposing an aggressive pro-solar policy, like Spain, which included tax exemptions, preferential connection to the grid, an FIT program and price stability guarantees, the Czech Republic experienced an energy crisis. Essentially, the excessive production of solar energy drove the market price down too far, making it too expensive for the government and the Czech citizens to back its price guarantees.[59] The Czech government responded by a severe rollback of the promised tax incentives.[60] Antaris GMBH and Dr. Michael Gode then sued under the ECT and the Germany–Czech bilateral investment treaty concurrently.[61]

In that case, the tribunal spent an extensive amount of time laying out the practice of previous investor–state tribunals in determining a breach of the FET standard, and specifying in particular what would give rise to

---

56 Foresight Luxembourg Solar 1 S.A.R.L., et al. Claimants and The Kingdom of Spain Respondent, italaw.com, para. 353–56.

57 Foresight Luxembourg Solar 1 S.A.R.L., et al. Claimants and The Kingdom of Spain Respondent, italaw.com, para. 363–364.

58 Charanne and Construction Investments v. Kingdom of Spain, italaw.com; Isolux Infrastructure Netherlands v. Kingdom of Spain, italaw.com; Eiser Infrastructure Ltd. and Energia Solar Luxembourg S.A.R.L. v. Kingdom of Spain; Novenergia II–Energy & Environment, SICAR v. Kingdom of Spain, italaw.com; Antin Infrastructure Services Luxembourg S.A.R.L. and Antin Energia Termosolar B.V. v. Kingdom of Spain, italaw.com; Masdar Solar & Wind Cooperatief U.A. v. Kingdom of Spain, italaw.com; Greentech Energy Systems A/S, Novenergia II Energy & Environment SICAR and Novenergia II Italian Portfolio S.A. v. The Italian Republic, italaw.com. It is important to note that these cases are all interpreting the Energy Charter Treaty (as opposed to a bilateral investment treaty) and therefore are more instructive for future cases involving the same treaty. Foresight Luxembourg Solar 1 S.A.R.L., et al. Claimants and The Kingdom of Spain Respondent, italaw.com, para. 385.

59 Antaris GMBH and Dr. Michael Gode v. The Czech Republic, italaw.com, para. 127.

60 Antaris GMBH and Dr. Michael Gode v. The Czech Republic, italaw.com, para. 94.

61 Antaris GMBH and Dr. Michael Gode v. The Czech Republic, italaw.com, para. 10.

legitimate investor expectations. The tribunal was incredibly precise, requiring clear and (usually) explicit representations made by the government in order to encourage the investment.[62] Moreover, it specified that general legislation on its own cannot give rise to an expectation of legal stability, emphasizing that "the State's rights to exercise its sovereign authority to legislate and to adapt its legal system to changing circumstances" are not affected by the FET standard.[63]

The tribunal's analysis says essentially this: the solar energy market looked good at first. Initially the government attempted to make minor changes to its incentive programs in order to maintain stability and not interfere with investor expectations. However, later statements by the government and other experts made it clear that the Czech solar market was in an unsustainable boom and would have to be adjusted drastically.[64] The claimants had some reason to be optimistic for a time, but in the end, they should have known that large regulatory change was coming. As a result, the claim failed and the Czech Republic was shielded from a potentially large award in favor of the investor.[65]

In 2018, the European Court of Justice ruled that the Treaty on the Functioning of the European Union precludes the use of investor–state dispute settlement between EU members, making these cases the last of a dying breed.[66] In response, 22 member states of the European Union made a declaration in January 2019 announcing their intention to terminate intra-EU BITs by December 6, 2019, and declaring that all investor–state dispute clauses in intra-EU BITs, including the ECT as it applies to EU member states, are "contrary to Union law and thus inapplicable."[67]

This has two correlative consequences. First, the European Commission has declared that if Spain paid compensation to the prevailing investors (in *Foresight* and others) in accordance with the arbitration awards, it would constitute state aid (also known as a subsidy) under EU law, and require approval by the European Commission.[68] Second, investors will have to bring future cases directly to the domestic courts of their host states. The

---

62 Antaris GMBH and Dr. Michael Gode v. The Czech Republic, italaw.com, para. 360.
63 Antaris GMBH and Dr. Michael Gode v. The Czech Republic, italaw.com, para. 360.
64 There is some suggestion that after the legal changes were proposed, there was a rush on the market by solar producers trying to take advantage of the benefits before they were withdrawn, which exacerbated the problem. Antaris GMBH and Dr. Michael Gode v. The Czech Republic, italaw.com, para. 389.
65 Antaris GMBH and Dr. Michael Gode v. The Czech Republic, italaw.com, para. 446.
66 Slovak Republic v. Achmea B.V., italaw.com.
67 European Commission, "EU Declaration on Achmea."
68 Power, "Novenergia v. Kingdom of Spain, the ECT and the ECJ."

Declaration is quick to assure readers that member states of the European Union are bound by EU law to protect investors and their investments to the same standards as those found in BITs.[69] Although this development is not limited to renewable energy cases, the prevalence of these cases in the past several years will limit the ability of European investors in solar and wind power to challenge government measures through ISDS.

While proponents of investor–state dispute settlement have pointed to these cases as evidence that it is a useful tool in combatting climate change, they also highlight the delicate tension states face between climate goals and economic stability.[70] Country governments when faced with the decision between raising energy prices to their constituents or removing investment incentives from foreign companies, chose the latter. Likewise, during a time of financial instability, they were hit with another financial burden—defending their policies before an international investment tribunal.

Incumbent investor–state cases

A third set of international disputes reveals a darker side of ISDS, demonstrating how the traditional energy sector is poised to strike back against aggressive energy transition efforts. Unlike the others, these have yet to be fully litigated in an international court, but in one case, it did result in a reversal of the attempted policies. In the United States, for example, TransCanada brought an investor–state dispute under the NAFTA when President Obama suggested that the Keystone XL pipeline extension (a TC Energy (formerly TransCanada) project) would not align with the United States' new energy priorities.[71] The investor demanded US$15 billion in compensation for future lost profits. The suit was dropped when President Trump announced a reissue of permits for the project.

Westmoreland, a US coal mining company in Canada, brought another NAFTA investor–state dispute targeting Alberta's new Climate Leadership Plan involving the closure and phase out of a number of coal fire generating plants. The investor argued, principally, that Alberta gave special payments to domestic generators, but neglected to offer those payments to Westmoreland, which constituted a violation of national treatment as well as the FET standard. Canada has pushed back, pointing out that any support offered by the government was for coal energy *generators* and not for domestic mining companies in competition with Westmoreland. The host state also noted that

---

69 European Commission, "EU Declaration on Achmea," 2.
70 Tienhaara and Downie, "Risky Business?"
71 Sachs, Merrill and Johnson, "Environmental Injustice."

the special payments should be protected under a carve-out for subsidies or grants,[72] and that in any case, Alberta had made no commitment to regulatory stability. On the contrary, the pendulum of climate regulations was swinging the other way.[73]

Meanwhile, Uniper, a German energy company in the Netherlands, has threatened to sue under the ECT for banning coal-fired power in the country by 2030. Documentation of the claim are not yet public, but analysts have suggested that Uniper may argue that the Dutch law violates the FET commitments along with rules about indirect expropriation.[74] This case, like those in Spain and the Czech Republic above, would be impacted by the ruling in *Achmea*, but the full impact is as yet unknown.[75] Either way, the cases brought by incumbent players in the fossil fuel industry demonstrate that countries seeking to make policy changes to undertake energy transitions are likely to meet with resistance through investor–state disputes.

Treaties and Domestic Policy at an Impasse

The three different sets of international cases drive home two important points: (1) countries need to, and do, constantly put in place policies that both address the specter of climate change and meet the short-term needs of their citizens, and (2) treaty texts do not seem forgiving of these government efforts. At the WTO, three-fourths of government, nongovernmental and private stakeholders currently rank "clarifying the role of trade policy in tackling climate change" as a high priority for the next ministerial conference negotiations.[76] Unfortunately, it ranks just behind "negotiating stronger rules on the use of subsidies and industrial policies" and even farther behind the priority for ramping up new rules in electronic commerce, investment facilitation and domestic regulation of services.[77] Clearly the priorities of WTO members and interested parties seem out of alignment with the interdependence of these short- and long-term goals.

Part of the effort to make sense of the trade-climate change nexus came in the form of another proposed plurilateral agreement (one negotiated among a subset of WTO members rather than at the multilateral level)—the

---

72 United States-Mexico-Canada, "North American Free Trade Agreement (NAFTA)," 1108.

73 Westmoreland Mining Holdings LLC v. Government of Canada—Canada's Statement of Defense, italaw.com.

74 Niemelä et al., "Risky Business."

75 Niemelä et al., "Risky Business."

76 Fiorini et al., "WTO Negotiation and Institutional Reform Priorities."

77 Fiorini et al., "WTO Negotiation and Institutional Reform Priorities."

Environmental Goods Agreement (EGA). The EGA aimed to lower tariffs among a narrow list of "environmental" goods like products that clean up pollution, help to produce renewable energy or are otherwise more environmentally friendly than traditional products (e.g., bamboo as a substitute for wood).[78] Critics of the agreement point out that the current average tariffs for the goods on this list are already so low, at 1.5 percent, that removing them will not "meaningfully address climate change."[79] Moving past the removal of tariffs, however, would mean liberalizing trade in environmental services and dismantling nontariff barriers—in other words, a broader and deeper trade integration.

Outside of the WTO, the number of new regional and bilateral trade agreements continues to grow and most of that activity includes IIAs. Ninety-six new investment treaties were signed since 2018 and only a small minority of them make any reference to climate change or renewable energy.[80] The majority employ the same boilerplate language of investor protection, which implicitly prioritizes liberalized investment regimes over climate change mitigation.

The baseline for investor protection and standards of treatment in modern IIAs is found in four key treaty provisions: MFN treatment, national treatment, FET and standards for expropriation, all of which have been discussed at length in prior chapters. The former two lay out the well-known standard for nondiscrimination in treatment of foreign investors, and the latter two are associated with customary international law standards of treatment, which often apply regardless of treaty commitments. In the context of the energy market, MFN treatment demands that energy inputs, services, investors and investments from a treaty partner receive the best treatment on offer (through tariffs, other taxes or regulation) as any other trading partner. National treatment states further that a country may not afford preference to their own energy inputs, services, investments, and so on, over those of its treaty partners, usually by taxation or regulation.

The FET standard ultimately protects against egregious or bad faith conduct by the importing or host state, but it may also protect firms from having their legitimate expectations thwarted by sudden policy changes. Rules governing expropriation prohibit new measures that indirectly strip away the value of an energy investment and that are not accompanied by the requisite compensation. Of the cases discussed above, the national treatment standard

---

78 APEC, "ANNEX C—APEC List of Environmental Goods."
79 Melo and Solleder, "The EGA Negotiations."
80 The number of signed IIAs was accurate as of January 2021. "International Investment Agreements Navigator."

plays the largest role in the WTO cases, while the renewable energy investor cases primarily claim violations of FET. Meanwhile, newer fossil fuel investor claims seem to be complaining of violations to the national treatment, FET and indirect expropriation standards. Furthermore, by including preestablishment investor protection, together with a broad definition of investment and the investor–state enforcement mechanism, these standards have an even wider reach.

New treaties negotiated with climate change in mind take three general approaches to addressing this challenge, ranging from general indirect statements to specific enforceable disciplines on policymaking. The most common approach focuses on the right to regulate preserved by the treaty parties, without any specific reference to language of renewable energy or climate change. The European Union, in particular, has begun incorporating provisions protecting that regulatory right, and even explicitly allowing treaty parties to withdraw subsidies or grants, or change the regulatory framework.[81] The USMCA recognizes the right of parties to regulate investment so that it is "undertaken in a manner sensitive to environmental" and other concerns.[82] Even within the chapter on environmental protection, the treaty only indirectly addresses the importance of climate change mitigation by generally encouraging "trade in legally harvested forests."[83]

A more direct approach, found in treaties like the Brazil–Chile Free Trade Agreement and the Ecuador–European Free Trade Area (EFTA) Comprehensive Economic Partnership, acknowledge the potential and actual impacts of trade on climate change and reaffirm the commitments of various multilateral climate change conventions and agreements.[84] The parties have committed to "effectively implement the Paris Agreement" and "promote the contribution of trade to the transition to a low-carbon, sustainable and climate resilient economy."[85] They also encourage collaboration in areas of climate finance and research and development in cost-effective technologies for lower emissions.[86] Nowhere, however, do the parties establish enforceable rules to address climate change.

---

81 EU-Viet Nam, "EU-Viet Nam IPA," 2.2; Canada-EU, "CETA," 8.9.

82 "USMCA," 14.16.

83 "USMCA," 24.23.

84 Chile-Brazil, "Chile-Brazil FTA"; EFTA-Ecuador, "EFTA-Ecuador FTA."

85 Chile-Brazil, "Chile-Brazil FTA," 17.14.2; EFTA-Ecuador, "EFTA-Ecuador FTA," 18.11.2.

86 In addition to the "Trade and Climate Change" provisions, EFTA–Ecuador protects the right of a state to regulate in accordance with other multilateral environmental agreements. EFTA-Ecuador, "EFTA-Ecuador FTA," 8.3.1. Brazil has begun to incorporate a provision on Corporate Social Responsibility in its IIAs, putting the onus on corporations to contribute to the sustainable development (including maintaining

A third approach is to tackle climate change challenges through enforceable trade and investment liberalization provisions that seek to *increase* economic activity in environmental goods and services. This is somewhat similar to the original goals of the EGA under the WTO. The EU–Japan Economic Partnership Agreement, for example, urges the parties to "strive to facilitate" trade and investment in environmental goods and services, especially those relevant to addressing climate change. At the same time, measures that facilitate such trade are bound by the basic standards of MFN and national treatment.[87] The European Union and Singapore ratcheted up this commitment with a specific chapter (chapter 7) on trade and investment in renewable energy, which focuses especially on prohibiting nontariff barriers in that sector (such as domestic regulations or investment performance requirements). Importantly, the agreement relies on lowering barriers as a way to promote the development of renewable energy industries globally, prohibiting local content, local hiring and joint venture requirements for foreign investors.

The three approaches also vary in their enforcement approach. In the first two examples, provisions allowing states to regulate in order to implement the Paris Agreement or contribute toward a low-carbon economy, to promote legally harvested forests, or to generally make sure investment is made with an eye toward the environmental impact are not enforced through the usual mechanisms of state–state or investor–state dispute resolution. Instead, these commitments are largely hortatory statements of priorities or future goals. The third approach, of facilitating trade and investment in EGS relies on traditional ISDS enforcement and doubles down on the existing investor treatment standards (national treatment, FET and the like), which can keep countries from responding agilely to the needs of constituents and domestic industry.

Treaty Text for Addressing Climate Change Mitigation and Meeting Domestic Needs

There needs to be a reimagining of treaty language—one that prioritizes the goals of avoiding or mitigating climate change impacts and gives deference to individual countries' implementation approaches. There is a rich literature of proposals for WTO reform, especially in the context of subsidies, which attempts to make space for a green-energy transition. These proposals include

---

high environmental standards) of their host state. Chile-Brazil, "Chile-Brazil FTA," 8.15.2; Brazil-India, "Brazil-India BIT," 11–12; Brazil-Guyana, "Brazil-Guyana BIT," 15.2; Brazil-Ethiopia, "Brazil Ethiopia BIT," 14.2.

87 EU-Japan, "EU-Japan EPA," 16.5.

drawing from a special subsidies rules—historical carve outs, and rules in the agriculture and fisheries contexts—to create analogous policy space for the transition to renewable energy. Each of these is a variation on a central theme—that subsidies which have the single-minded purpose or impact of encouraging the production and use of renewable energy are okay, and others are not.

The same sort of approach could work for other industrial policies with the same aim. Article 8 of the SCM agreement originally permitted WTO members to provide subsidies that provided assistance to adapt to new environmental regulations, to support research and development or those directed at disadvantaged regions, without the threat of a WTO dispute ("nonactionable" subsidies).[88] If the same method were used for industrial policies, new language might identify as "nonactionable" certain discriminatory policies, provided they are aimed at sustainably building a domestic renewable energy sector. The WTO's Agreement on Agriculture employ's a "box system" for agricultural subsidies. Using the box model, the most permissive box would include industrial policies that the WTO would most prefer countries to adopt—those that facilitate the renewable energy transition without distorting trade. The second box would include programs that have a significant benefit for the climate but have a dual purpose to build up industry, and the last box would include programs that only tangentially help the environment or disproportionately affect trade.[89] Another similar example, found in the CPTPP's fisheries subsidies rules, allows government support for fisheries that meet sustainability criteria and prohibits support for those that don't.[90] Along the same lines, governments could tailor provisions on national treatment, or those governing performance requirements for investors, to allow industrial policies, once more, provided they are primarily aimed at facilitating an energy transition away from traditional fuel sources.

Rationale-based rules of this sort, however, often have inequitable impacts and do not take into consideration the disparity between high-income and low- and middle-income countries, and the different hardships they face. Without specifying down to the letter what kinds of industrial policies are allowed and which are prohibited, these solutions largely serve to grant the sort of flexibilities desired by developed countries and not those pursued by countries in need of industrialization and economic diversification.

---

88 Van de Graaf and van Asselt, "Introduction to the Special Issue"; "Agreement on Subsidies and Countervailing Measures," 8.
89 Cosbey and Mavroidis, "A Turquoise Mess."
90 Young, "Energy Transitions and Trade Law."

It is important to note that critics argue that green industrial policies that serve the dual purpose of energy transition and economic development run the risk of increasing the costs of producing renewable energy, ultimately slowing the transition to that energy. Most economic models would find measures aimed at promoting domestic industry, at the expense of more efficient external players, welfare reducing and inefficient. There are other options, they argue—such as offering incentives for climate-friendly investment without requiring a direct link into the domestic economy.

Rodrik has suggested, however, that the future of industrial policy may look different from these more direct top-down government approaches. "[It may be more about] establishing a sustained collaboration between the public and private sectors around issues of productivity and social goals."[91] These collaborations, even more than traditional investment incentives will need to be "continuously monitored and revised in light of outcomes."[92] To undertake this requires policy space, and thus narrower and shallower trade integration.

We cannot underestimate the need for collective action that the climate crisis requires, however. By creating more enforceable climate commitments under trade agreements—a la the EU-Singapore treaty—countries demonstrate an admirable commitment to tackle the problem head-on. Unfortunately, by further limiting what countries can do to combine climate policy with other development goals, these treaties can undermine public support for energy transition efforts. Additionally, if incentive programs like those in Spain and the Czech Republic are left unbridled, without the flexibility to adjust incentives and policies, this can lead to other negative externalities like financial instability. Collective action for global crises should focus on building capacity to meet common challenges rather than punishing countries for violating treaty rules. As the final chapter shows, narrower and shallower multilateral economic integration that provides deference to national policy goals and institutions and encourages new national industrial capacities will ultimately be more successful in meeting domestic development challenges and tackling global crises.

---

91 Aiginger and Rodrik, "Rebirth of Industrial Policy and an Agenda for the Twenty-First Century."
92 Aiginger and Rodrik, "Rebirth of Industrial Policy and an Agenda for the Twenty-First Century."

Chapter 8

CONCLUSION: A WAY FORWARD

We have inherited a fractured system of global economic governance. Multilateral commitments at the WTO are undermined by preferential commitments in bilateral, regional and mega-regional free trade agreements that have broader and deeper commitments for treaty parties. Many of those treaties grant special privileges and rights to multinational corporations without demanding anything in return. Even commitments in nontrade areas of governance, such as public health and energy, are backed by trade rule enforcement mechanisms.

Narrower and Shallower: A Call to Scale Back International Trade and Investment Commitments

If we are to reform the system we must pull in the opposite direction. First, as has been noted in various parts of this volume: words matter. More specifically, treaty texts matter. The exact text of a treaty may make the difference between whether an exception applies[1] or whether the tribunal finds jurisdiction over the case at all.[2] Knowing what the existing texts say and, even more importantly, how they may be interpreted before an international tribunal is the first step toward making a change in the system.

The second, much more challenging, step is to guide the trajectory of new treaty texts toward a coherent and consistent goal—to resolve the tension in favor of individual state interests in making public policy. In order to meet that goal, new treaty texts must preserve and expand existing policy flexibilities. Negotiations should take place at a multilateral level where the playing field is more balanced. Treaties should give deference to state regulators and prefer domestic judicial processes and diplomatic methods of dispute settlement. New

---

1 Compare *Canada—Certain Measures Affecting the Renewable Energy Generation Sector*, wto.org; with Mesa Power Group, LLC. v. Government of Canada, www.italaw.com.
2 Compare Abaclat and others v. The Argentine Republic—Decision on Jurisdiction and Admissibility, www.italaw.com and Poštová banka, a.s. and ISTROKAPITAL SE v. Hellenic Republic, www.italaw.com.

commitments should focus on supporting "developing and least developed countries' integration into the global economy"[3] through capacity building and reinforcing special and differential treatment.

This volume acknowledges that not every national government has the altruistic aim to protect and preserve their citizens. In fact, in some cases, development and economic diversification goals can conflict with environmental or social sustainability.[4] Policies that benefit producers or consumers in one country may be bad for their trading partners or foreign investors.[5] Debt restructuring, while good for the economic stability of a country's constituents, necessarily involves losses for bondholders, both domestic and foreign. Even policies with good intentions may be misguided or poorly executed, as demonstrated by both Spain's and the Czech Republic's attempts to incentivize and manage the transition to renewable energy.[6]

Nevertheless, inasmuch as the mandate for national governments is to care for their citizens, we ought to preserve the policy flexibility for those measures. There is still much we do not know about the impact of policymaking. Pharmaceutical patenting and data protection is still relatively new in the majority world, and we do not yet fully know what the impacts will be in countries where the first patents have not yet expired.[7] We have not previously dealt with the public health, economic and environmental challenges posed by the current set of crises. We are still reeling from the initial year of the COVID-19 pandemic and facing the prospect of an even larger jump from new, more contagious, strains of the virus. The economic consequences of more than a year of battling a global pandemic are as yet unknown. And the climate crisis will still be there when we have a chance to look at it more directly once more.

Certainly, some of the challenges we're facing will need collective and cooperative solutions. Others will require individual experimentation. If all countries had uniformly adopted the ideas of neoliberalism (trade liberalization, deregulation, and privatization), we would not be able to look back and compare the industrialization outcomes in countries like South Korea, Chile, Argentina, Mexico and Indonesia.[8] The following proposes a plan for a scaled-back version of our trade and investment regime that

---

3 Taylor, "A Challenge to the Discourse of Development or Development Done Differently," 5.

4 Anon., " 'How They Tricked Us': Living with the Gibe Dam and Sugar Plantations in Southwestern Ethiopia."

5 Poštová banka, a.s. and ISTROKAPITAL SE v. Hellenic Republic, www.italaw.com.

6 Foresight Luxembourg Solar 1 S.A.R.L., et al. Claimants and The Kingdom of Spain Respondent, www.italaw.com.

7 Shadlen, Sampat and Kapczynski, "Patents, Trade and Medicines: Past, Present and Future."

8 Chang, *Bad Samaritans*.

prioritizes multilateral negotiation and rulemaking, phasing out investor-led enforcement mechanisms, and cooperation on global issues supported by capacity building rather than trade enforcement measures.

Multilateral negotiation and rulemaking

The current system of "trade and-" commitments is a result of the great success of tariff negotiations under the GATT. There was simply no further to go, and countries that desired more market access sought to introduce rules that would reach beyond tariff barriers to trade in goods. Technology had shifted during that time as well, and services were among the fastest growing sectors in the global economy.

Nevertheless, WTO negotiations have resulted in very little progress since the Uruguay Round. The Doha Round, initiated in 2001, has resulted in only one new multilateral agreement—the Trade Facilitation Agreement, adopted in 2013. In response to this deadlock, countries have pursued ever more bilaterl, regional and (now) mega-regional trade agreements to further deepen the cause of trade liberalization. As countries continuously seek more ways to gain access to international markets for their buyers and sellers, they simultaneously want to retain any existing competitive advantage over others. As a result, modern trade agreements are no longer about liberalizing trade but about constraining policymaking, or tightly directing it in order to harmonize regulations across borders.

Another approach countries have taken to overcome the multilateral deadlock is to create coalitions within the WTO of like-minded countries to pursue additional liberalization commitments. Current discussions are taking place within small, plurilateral, groups of countries to develop rules for electronic commerce, investment facilitation and even domestic regulation. These "plurilaterals," on the one hand, have the benefit of taking place within the multilateral forum and allowing all WTO members to join the agreement once they are negotiated.[9] Like agreements external to the WTO, however, these are attempting to add on to the current commitments—increase the depth and breadth of the current trade and investment regime.

An alternative, which is rarely discussed among WTO ministers and negotiators, is to simply back off. The GATT's comparatively "shallow" model of trade integration allowed much of the global gains from trade that countries enjoy today.[10] The formation of the WTO has deepened that integration, but

---

9 Hoekman and Sabel, "Open Plurilateral Agreements, International Regulatory Cooperation and the WTO."

10 Bagwell, Bown and Staiger, "Is the WTO Passé?"

members do retain important policy space in many areas of non-tariff barriers and behind-the-border measures.[11] The WTO has been relatively successful at monitoring trade policies worldwide, facilitating tariff reductions over time and, until recently, resolving trade disputes.

Certainly reforms are in order. In addition to the United States' vocal dissent and refusal to appoint new judges to the Appellate Body, other members are sufficiently unsatisfied with the process of Appellate Body review that changes have been proposed for more than a decade.[12] Negotiations around agricultural and fisheries subsidies have dragged on for more than two decades.[13] In addition to these agenda items, developing country members continue to pursue the realization of special and differential treatment within the WTO agreements, while other stakeholders push for a quicker resolution of the various plurilateral discussions.[14]

Nevertheless, the best way forward could be to take a step back. Multilateral negotiations involve many different interests and, as such, produce less comprehensive trade liberalization. However, "shallow" economic integration, that which does not attempt to unduly interfere with behind-the-border policies, has produced a functional trade regime. There is even evidence that the state of play in international integration under the GATT may have maximized economic efficiency.[15] Moreover, although not perfect, the balance of power in multilateral negotiations is arguably more inclusive and equitable than those at a bilateral or regional level.[16]

Phasing out investor-led enforcement mechanisms

The second piece of this call for a narrower and shallower trade and investment regime proposes countries move away from ISDS. Investor–state disputes have been criticized for a wide variety of shortcomings, including imbalances of power between investors and host states, as well as between developed and developing countries, special rights and protections for foreign investors that do not extend to domestic investors, and the excessively high

---

11 Hoekman and Nicita, "Non-Tariff Measures and Trade Facilitation: WTO Disciplines and Policy Space for Development"; Bagwell, Bown and Staiger, "Is the WTO Passé?"
12 Voon and Yanovich, "The Facts Aside: The Limitation of WTO Appeals to Issues of Law"; Hillman, "Three Approaches to Fixing the World Trade Organization's Appellate Body: The Good, the Bad and the Ugly?"
13 United Nations Environment Program (UNEP), *Fisheries Subsidies and Overfishing*.
14 Fiorini et al., "WTO Negotiation and Institutional Reform Priorities."
15 Bagwell, Bown and Staiger, "Is the WTO Passé?"
16 Kapstein, "Fairness Considerations in World Politics"; Shadlen, "Globalisation, Power and Integration."

costs of arbitration. From a legal and institutional perspective, ISDS falls short because it is not rooted in a common treaty nor does it have a common judicial body, and as such, can appear nontransparent and inconsistent.

There are three major solutions proposed to correct for these defects. The first is to introduce a multilateral investment court, akin to that introduced in the Comprehensive Economic Trade Agreement (CETA) between Canada and the European Union.[17] Under the CETA, foreign investors located in state parties to the treaty bring a claim to the Investment Court System, which is more judicial in nature than *ad hoc* arbitration. It incorporates both a Tribunal of First Instance for initial claims and an Appellate Mechanism, both of which are expected to maintain standing members to hear all cases.[18] Although this approach does address problems of inconsistency and transparency, it continues to provide investors with special rights without corresponding responsibilities under the treaties. Indeed, rather than correcting for the imbalances within the system, it may exacerbate them by creating a more permanent and well-established mechanism for investors to sue host states.

A second solution would be to demand that foreign investors are no longer simply third-party beneficiaries of these treaties, but that they be given real obligations under the treaties. This idea has been proposed both to incorporate negative investor responsibilities to *not* violate domestic and human rights laws or *not* cause environmental damage, as well as positive responsibilities to contribute to the development of the host state.[19] While this solution promises to rebalance the rights and responsibilities between investor and state, it faces both logistical and legal challenges. Investor accountability is an important but elusive aspect of international law.[20] Countries have been reluctant to introduce binding commitments on investors within investment treaties; they have even neglected to invoke violations of domestic law in their own defense in investor–state cases.[21] Although adopting investor obligations within treaties has begun to gain some traction, mostly in model BITs like South Africa's,[22] introducing obligations for private actors would be a fundamental departure from the current regime and its

---

17 Schacherer, "TPP, CETA and TTIP between Innovation and Consolidation—Resolving Investor–State Disputes under Mega-Regionals."
18 Fanou, "The Independence and Impartiality of the Hybrid CETA Investment Court System."
19 Southern African Development Community and Mann, "SADC Model BIT"; Sattorova, "Investor Responsibilities from a Host State Perspective."
20 Ho, "The Creation of Elusive Investor Responsibility."
21 Ho, "The Creation of Elusive Investor Responsibility"; Krajewski, "A Nightmare or a Noble Dream?"
22 Southern African Development Community and Mann, "SADC Model BIT."

objectives.[23] Moreover, reform that involves expanding the scope of existing commitments would conflict with the goal of scaling back global trade and investment rules. Although foreign investor obligations should not be ignored, investment treaties would not be effective in enforcing them.[24]

A better solution, and one more in keeping with historical customary international law,[25] would be to eliminate private investor–state arbitration in favor of a requirement to exhaust of local remedies prior to pursuing the option of a state–state dispute. In general, investor–state tribunals have interpreted investment treaties to not require the exhaustion, or even the pursuit, of local remedies.[26] The BITs and investment chapters were considered sufficient evidence of the consent of the state to be sued outside of its domestic courts and without an explicit reference to local remedies, the customary rule was dismissed.

Requiring the exhaustion of local remedies, however, places investor complaints squarely where they belong, in the jurisdiction of the host state. In that context, domestic laws would allow effective counterclaims and allow countries to introduce laws that protect their right to regulate. Of course, the trade and investment regime still contains thousands of investment agreements containing ISDS, but as countries modify, renegotiate and revoke these commitments, new treaties should eliminate ISDS and require the exhaustion of local remedies as a prerequisite to a state–state claim under the treaty.

Cooperation on global issues through capacity building

Even in areas where we need collective action—where allowing domestic political and legislative processes to have free reign could result in disastrous outcomes—narrower and shallower trade and investment rules will be more effective. On this point, we take a brief look at the Trade Facilitation Agreement (TFA), the most recent example of a multilateral negotiating success, and the only success since the formation of the WTO in 1995. The TFA, signed in Bali in 2013 and entered into force in 2017, is an agreement focused narrowly on the reform of border management processes. In response to extensive evidence that trade facilitation provides "a significant boost to

---

23 Sattorova, "Investor Responsibilities from a Host State Perspective."
24 Krajewski, "A Nightmare or a Noble Dream?"
25 Brauch, "Exhaustion of Local Remedies in International Investment Law."
26 Brauch, "Exhaustion of Local Remedies in International Investment Law"; Porterfield, "Exhaustion of Local Remedies in Investor-State Dispute Settlement: An Idea Whose Time Has Come?"

bilateral trade, supports diversification, and increases aggregate welfare,"[27] the goal of the agreement was to simply improve trade transactions through transparency, predictability and efficiency.[28]

The TFA is quite limited in scope, with few mandatory commitments and many statements about the parties' "best endeavors" to implement certain measures.[29] Its major contribution, however, and the primary reason it found consensus at the WTO, is the detailed set of provisions that allow developing and least developed countries to implement the agreement at their own pace and request funds to pay for technical expertise and capacity building. Developing countries are allowed to break down the TFA commitments into three categories: those they can implement immediately, those that will take some time, and those that they need both time and assistance to implement.[30] Alongside of the agreement, developing and least developed countries requested a TFA facility that has developed a needs assessment program as well as developing and delivering assistance through financing and technical expertise.[31]

Naturally, there are valid critiques. Some argue that this kind of agreement is a step away from the kind of "hard" international economic law that trade treaties have come to represent, while also creating perverse incentives for developing countries to demand "payment" for undertaking beneficial reforms.[32] Others argue that the actual benefits will be much lower than projected for developing countries because, on the one hand, they will not be willing or able to implement the reforms quickly enough, and on the other, export competitiveness constraints will keep them from exploiting the potential benefits.[33] Moreover, as one expert has pointed out, the TFA created commitments for LDCs (however modified), when the LDCs were supposed to be free of commitments entirely.[34]

---

27 Hoekman, "The Bali Trade Facilitation Agreement and Rulemaking in the WTO: Milestone, Mistake or Mirage?," 5.

28 Taylor, "A Challenge to the Discourse of Development or Development Done Differently"; Hoekman, "The Bali Trade Facilitation Agreement and Rulemaking in the WTO: Milestone, Mistake or Mirage?"

29 Hoekman, "The Bali Trade Facilitation Agreement and Rulemaking in the WTO: Milestone, Mistake or Mirage?"

30 Hoekman, "The Bali Trade Facilitation Agreement and Rulemaking in the WTO: Milestone, Mistake or Mirage?"

31 "About TFAF | TFAF—Trade Facilitation Agreement Facility."

32 Hoekman, "The Bali Trade Facilitation Agreement and Rulemaking in the WTO: Milestone, Mistake or Mirage?"

33 Hoekman, "The Bali Trade Facilitation Agreement and Rulemaking in the WTO: Milestone, Mistake or Mirage?"

34 Thrasher, "The Next Director-General and WTO Reform: An Interview with Rashmi Banga, UNCTAD."

Nevertheless, the successful negotiation of the TFA provides some opportunity to extrapolate what a narrower and shallower trade regime would look like, even for contexts where collective action is necessary. In the first place, with overwhelming evidence of both the problems of poor customs administration and the potential benefits of improvement, all countries could agree that collective action would benefit both individual countries and global commerce as a whole. Second, the narrow scope of the negotiations kept the commitment small and manageable. Countries did not have to research to find out how a wide range of new measures would impact their domestic laws. Third, the TFA represents a global commitment to a common goal supported by capacity building rather than by a trade enforcement mechanism—a carrot rather than a stick. This approach, and the acknowledgement that many countries will face insurmountable challenges in transitioning to renewable energy or managing a pandemic, could encourage state behavior with positive externalities without punitive measures aimed at countries already struggling under the weight of domestic and global crises.

As each chapter has shown, the overwhelming trend in international trade agreements is to expand and deepen. In an era of recognizing and pursuing sustainability goals, trade agreements are the instrument many countries turn to in order to enforce those standards. Good rules about climate change mitigation, the inclusion of vulnerable local community voices, and decreasing deforestation rates are beginning to be linked to trade-based enforcement—so that countries that do not comply with those rules will risk losing their much-needed access to the global markets. The trade and investment regime provides the most mandatory, most enforceable international system of rules, so it is natural to want to lean on it as a platform to increase state commitments in the areas that need collective action.

This approach, however, embodies severe shortcomings. In the first place, a country is not a singular entity. Punishment aimed at the government not adequately making and enforcing certain rules usually trickles down to the people laboring in the extractive, fossil fuel and other environmentally harmful sectors in the form of lower wages and lost jobs. These laborers are often as vulnerable as the communities they impact (if not coterminous with them). In the second place, since the producers of goods most directly connected with environmental degradation are almost all located in the Global South, trade rules *limiting* their access to global markets will also *limit* their ability to grow and diversify their economies, shifting away from these more harmful industries. New environmental obligations typified by the (urgent and necessary) climate commitments tend to be the hardest on the communities most impacted by climate change, and not demand as much from the communities and nations whose consumption drives the self-same change.

Trade and investment treaties are only one piece to a much larger puzzle of national and international policies making up global governance. Nevertheless, by shifting the way that countries integrate at an economic level toward a narrower and shallower agreement model, these treaties can preserve and expand policy space for sustainable development and increase global equity through capacity building.

REFERENCES

Abaclat and others v. The Argentine Republic—Consent Award. www.italaw.com (International Centre for the Settlement of Investment Disputes 2016).

Abaclat and others v. The Argentine Republic—Decision on Jurisdiction and Admissibility. www.italaw.com (International Centre for the Settlement of Investment Disputes 2011).

Abbott, Frederick M., and J. H. Reichman. "The Doha Round's Public Health Legacy: Strategies for the Production and Diffusion of Patented Medicines under the Amended TRIPS Provisions." *Journal of International Economic Law* 10, no. 4 (2007): 921–87. https://doi.org/10.1093/jiel/jgm040.

"About TFAF | TFAF—Trade Facilitation Agreement Facility." Accessed January 8, 2021. https://www.tfafacility.org/about-the-facility.

Ackerman, Frank, and Kevin P. Gallagher. "The Shrinking Gains from Global Trade Liberalization in Computable General Equilibrium Models: A Critical Assessment." *International Journal of Political Economy* 37, no. 1 (April 1, 2008): 50–77. https://doi.org/10.2753/IJP0891-1916370103.

ADF Group Inc. v. United States of America, No. ICSID Case No. ARB(AF)/00/1 (International Centre for the Settlement of Investment Disputes 2003).

African Union. "African Continental Free Trade Agreement—Protocol on Trade in Goods," 2019. https://www.tralac.org/documents/resources/african-union/2162-afcfta-agreement-legally-scrubbed-version-signed-16-may-2018/file.html.

"Agreement between the United States of America, the United Mexican States, and Canada." ustr.gov, December 13, 2019. https://ustr.gov/trade-agreements/free-trade-agreements/united-states-mexico-canada-agreement/agreement-between.

"Agreement on Subsidies and Countervailing Measures." World Trade Organization, 1994. https://www.wto.org/english/docs_e/legal_e/24-scm.pdf.

"Agreement on Trade-Related Investment Measures." World Trade Organization, 1994. https://www.wto.org/english/docs_e/legal_e/18-trims.pdf.

Aiginger, Karl, and Dani Rodrik. "Rebirth of Industrial Policy and an Agenda for the Twenty-First Century." *Journal of Industry, Competition and Trade* 20, no. 2 (June 1, 2020): 189–207. https://doi.org/10.1007/s10842-019-00322-3.

Alder, Simon, Lin Shao and Fabrizio Zilibotti. "Economic Reforms and Industrial Policy in a Panel of Chinese Cities." *Journal of Economic Growth* 21, no. 4 (2016): 305–49. https://doi.org/10.1007/s10887-016-9131-x.

Alfaro, Laura, Areendam Chanda, Sebnem Kalemli-Ozcan and Selin Sayek. "Does Foreign Direct Investment Promote Growth? Exploring the Role of Financial Markets on Linkages." *Journal of Development Economics* 91, no. 2 (2010): 242–56.

Amsden, Alice. *The Rise of "The Rest": Challenges to the West From Late-Industrializing Economies.* Oxford: Oxford University Press, 2001. https://www.oxfordscholarship.com/view/10.1093/0195139690.001.0001/acprof-9780195139693.

Anon. "'How They Tricked Us': Living with the Gibe Dam and Sugar Plantations in Southwestern Ethiopia." Oakland, CA: Oakland Institute, 2019. https://www.oaklandinstitute.org/sites/oaklandinstitute.org/files/ethiopia-tricked-gibe-dam-sugarcane-plantations.pdf.

Anseeuw, Ward, Liz Alden Wily, Lorenzo Cotula and Michael Taylor. "Land Rights and the Rush for Land: Findings of the Global Commercial Pressures on Land Research Project." Rome: IIED, CIRAD, International Land Coalition, 2012. https://www.cirad.fr/en/publications-resources/publishing/studies-and-documents/land-rights-and-the-rush-for-land.

Antaris GMBH and Dr. Michael Gode v. The Czech Republic—Award. www.italaw.com (Permanent Court of Arbitration 2018).

Antaris Solar GmbH and Dr. Michael Gode v. Czech Republic. www.italaw.com (Permanent Court of Arbitration 2018).

Antin Infrastructure Services Luxembourg S.A.R.L. and Antin Energia Termosolar B.V. v. Kingdom of Spain—Award. www.italaw.com (International Centre for the Settlement of Investment Disputes 2018).

APEC. "ANNEX C—APEC List of Environmental Goods." Accessed January 22, 2021. https://www.apec.org/Meeting-Papers/Leaders-Declarations/2012/2012_aelm/2012_aelm_annexC.

"Argentine Bonds Trade below Restructuring Level on Economic Woes." *Bloomberg.com*, August 7, 2020. https://www.bloomberg.com/news/articles/2020-08-07/argentina-bonds-are-trading-as-if-the-pandemic-never-happened.

Australia-Chile. "Australia-Chile Free Trade Agreement," 2009. https://wits.worldbank.org/GPTAD/PDF/archive/Australia-Chile.pdf.

Bagwell, Kyle, Chad P. Bown and Robert W. Staiger. "Is the WTO Passé?" *Journal of Economic Literature* 54, no. 4 (December 2016): 1125–231. https://doi.org/10.1257/jel.20151192.

Baker, Brook K. "Ending Drug Registration Apartheid: Taming Data Exclusivity and Patent/Registration Linkage." *American Journal of Law and Medicine* 34 (2008): 303–44. https://doi.org/10.1177/009885880803400209.

———. "The 'Lower Drug Costs Now Act of 2019': What's Good, What's Bad, and What Must Be Improved." *Health GAP (Global Access Project)* (blog), September 19, 2020. https://healthgap.org/the-lower-drug-costs-now-act-of-2019-whats-good-whats-bad-and-what-must-be-improved/.

———. "A Sliver of Hope: Analyzing Voluntary Licenses to Accelerate Affordable Access to Medicines." *Northeastern University Law Review* 10, no. 2 (2018): 226–315.

Baker, Brook K., and Katrina Geddes. "The Incredible Shrinking Victory: Eli Lilly v. Canada, Success, Judicial Reversal, and Continuing Threats from Pharmaceutical ISDS." *Loyola University Chicago Law Journal* 49, no. 2 (January 1, 2017): 479–513.

Baldwin, Richard, and Eiichi Tomiura. "Thinking Ahead about the Trade Impact of COVID-19." In *Economics in the Time of COVID-19*, edited by Richard Baldwin and Beatrice Weder di Mauro, 59–72. A VoxEU.Org Ebook. London: Center of Economic Policy Research Press, 2020.

Banga, Rashmi. "Growing Trade in Electronic Transmissions: Implications for the South." UNCTAD Research Paper. UNCTAD, 2019. https://unctad.org/en/PublicationsLibrary/ser-rp-2019d1_en.pdf.

Bialik, Kristen. "State of the Union 2019: How Americans See Major National Issues." *Pew Research Center* (blog), February 4, 2019. https://www.pewresearch.org/fact-tank/2019/02/04/state-of-the-union-2019-how-americans-see-major-national-issues/.

Blanchard, Emily. "The Role of Deep Agreements in a Post-COVID-19 World: Round Table and Q&A." Presented at the Trade Agreements in a Post-COVID-19 World, Washington, DC, July 28, 2020. https://www.worldbank.org/en/events/2020/07/28/trade-agreements-in-a-post-covid-19-world.

Blanchard, Emily J., Chad P. Bown and Robert C. Johnson. "Global Supply Chains and Trade Policy." Policy Research Working Papers. The World Bank, January 19, 2016. https://doi.org/10.1596/1813-9450-7536.

Borensztein, E., J. De Gregorio and J. -W. Lee. "How Does Foreign Direct Investment Affect Economic Growth?" *Journal of International Economics* 45 (1998): 115–35.

Borras Jr., Saturnino M., Ruth Hall, Ian Scoones, Ben White and Wendy Wolford. "Towards a Better Understanding of Global Land Grabbing: An Editorial Introduction." *Journal of Peasant Studies* 38, no. 2 (March 1, 2011): 209–16. https://doi.org/10.1080/03066150.2011.559005.

Brauch, Martin Dietrich. "Exhaustion of Local Remedies in International Investment Law." IISD Best Practices Series. Geneva: International Institute for Sustainable Development (IISD), 2017. https://www.iisd.org/system/files/publications/best-practices-exhaustion-local-remedies-law-investment-en.pdf.

Brazil-Ethiopia. "Agreement between the Federative Republic of Brazil and the Federal Democratic Republic of Ethiopia on Investment Cooperation and Facilitation," 2018. https://investmentpolicy.unctad.org/international-investment-agreements/treaty-files/5717/download.

Brazil-Guyana. "Cooperation and Investment Facilitation Agreement between the Federative Republic of Brazil and the Co-Operative Republic of Guyana," 2018. https://investmentpolicy.unctad.org/international-investment-agreements/treaty-files/5763/download.

Brazil-India. "Investment Cooperation and Facilitation Treaty between the Federative Republic of Brazil and the Republic of India," 2020. https://investmentpolicy.unctad.org/international-investment-agreements/treaty-files/5912/download.

Broadman, Harry G. "Protectionism Makes the Coronavirus Even More Lethal." *Forbes* (blog), March 31, 2020. https://www.forbes.com/sites/harrybroadman/2020/03/31/protectionism-makes-the-coronavirus-even-more-lethal/.

Broude, Tomer, Yoram Z. Haftel and Alexander Thompson. "The Trans-Pacific Partnership and Regulatory Space: A Comparison of Treaty Texts." *Journal of International Economic Law* 20, no. 2 (June 2017): 391–417. https://doi.org/10.1093/jiel/jgx016.

Brunei-Cambodia-Indonesia-Laos-Malaysia-Myanmar-Philippines-Singapore-Thailand-Vietnam. "ASEAN Trade in Goods Agreement," 2007. http://agreement.asean.org/media/download/20140119034633.pdf.

Buchheit, Lee C., and Augusto de la Torre. "Sovereign Debt Restructuring: From the Brady Plan to Ecuador 2020." Panel Discussion—Americas Society/Council of the Americas presented at the Sovereign Debt Restructuring: From the Brady Plan to Ecuador 2020, online, July 30, 2020. https://www.as-coa.org/events/sovereign-debt-restructuring-brady-plan-ecuador-2020#speakers.

Callaway, Ewen. "The Unequal Scramble for Coronavirus Vaccines—by the Numbers." *Nature* 584, no. 7822 (August 24, 2020): 506–07. https://doi.org/10.1038/d41586-020-02450-x.

Canada—Certain Measures Affecting the Renewable Energy Generation Sector—Report of the Appellate Body, wto.org (WTO Appellate Body 2013).

Canada-Australia-Brunei-Chile-Japan-Malaysia-Mexico-New Zealand-Peru-Singapore-Vietnam. "Comprehensive and Progressive Agreement for Trans-Pacific Partnership." Government of Canada, December 30, 2018. https://www.international.gc.ca/trade-commerce/trade-agreements-accords-commerciaux/agr-acc/tpp-ptp/text-texte/toc-tdm.aspx?lang=eng.

Canada-EU. "Comprehensive Economic Trade Agreement (CETA) between Canada, of the One Part, and the European Union and Its Member States, of the Other Part." *Official Journal of the European Union* L 11 (September 21, 2017): 23–1079.

"Canada-Panama Free Trade Agreement," 2013. https://www.international.gc.ca/trade-commerce/trade-agreements-accords-commerciaux/agr-acc/panama/fta-ale/index.aspx?lang=eng.

"Canada-Peru Free Trade Agreement," 2009. https://www.international.gc.ca/trade-commerce/trade-agreements-accords-commerciaux/agr-acc/peru-perou/fta-ale/index.aspx?lang=eng.

Carpenter, Theresa. "A Historical Perspective on Regionalism." In *Multilateralizing Regionalism: Challenges for the Global Trading System*, edited by Patrick Low and Richard Baldwin, 13–27. WTO Internal Only. Cambridge: Cambridge University Press, 2009. https://doi.org/10.1017/CBO9781139162111.003.

Caves, Richard, Ronald Jones and Jeffrey Frankel. *World Trade and Payments: An Introduction by Richard Caves, Ronald Jones and Jeffrey Frankel.* Boston: Addison Wesley Longman, 2007.

Chang, Ha-Joon. *Bad Samaritans: The Myth of Free Trade and the Secret History of Capitalism.* Reprint edition. New York: Bloomsbury, 2009.

———. *Kicking Away the Ladder: Development Strategy in Historical Perspective.* Business and Economics. London: Anthem Press, 2002. https://anthempress.com/kicking-away-the-ladder-pb.

Charanne and Construction Investments v. Kingdom of Spain—Final Award, italaw.com (Stockholm Chamber of Commerce 2016).

Chaudhuri, S., P. K. Goldberg and P. Jia. "Estimating the Effects of Global Patent Protection in Pharmaceuticals: A Case Study of Quinolones in India." *American Economic Review* 96, no. 5 (2006): 1477–514.

Chaurey, Ritam. "Location-Based Tax Incentives: Evidence from India." *Journal of Public Economics* 156 (December 1, 2017): 101–20. https://doi.org/10.1016/j.jpubeco.2016.08.013.

Chile—Taxes on Alcoholic Beverages: Report of the Appellate Body, World Trade Organization (Dispute Settlement Body: Appellate Body 1999).

Chile-Brazil. "Acuerdo de Libre Comercio entre la Republica de Chile y la Republica Federativa de Brasil," 2018. https://investmentpolicy.unctad.org/international-investment-agreements/treaty-files/5821/download.

China. "RCEP—Draft Investment Text: China (Based on Negotiating Draft of Oct 2015)." bilaterals.org, 2015. https://www.bilaterals.org/?rcep-draft-investment-text-china.

China-Georgia. "Free Trade Agreement between the Government of the People's Republic of China and the Government of Georgia," 2018. http://fta.mofcom.gov.cn/georgia/annex/xdzw_en.pdf.

Christian, Jeff, and Lana Shipley. "Electricity Regulation in Canada: Overview." Thomson Reuters: Practical Law, 2019. http://uk.practicallaw.thomsonreuters.com/5-632-4326?transitionType=Default&contextData=(sc.Default)&firstPage=true.

CME Czech Republic B.V. v. The Czech Republic (UNCITRAL 2003).

Coelho, Bruno, and Kevin P. Gallagher. "The Effectiveness of Capital Controls: Evidence from Colombia and Thailand." *International Review of Applied Economics* 27, no. 3 (May 1, 2013): 386–403. https://doi.org/10.1080/02692171.2012.734793.

Committee on Regional Trade Agreements. "Regional Trade Agreements Subject to Implementation Reports," WT/REG/W/140. Geneva: World Trade Organization, March 15, 2019.

Committee on World Food Security, and Food and Agriculture Organization. "Voluntary Guidelines on the Responsible Governance of Tenure of Land, Fisheries and Forests in the Context of National Food Security." Food and Agriculture Organization of the United Nations—Rome, 2012. http://www.fao.org/3/i2801e/i2801e.pdf.

"Communication from Albania; Argentina; Australia; Canada; Chile; Chin; Colombia; Costa Rica; The European Union; Hong Kong, China; Iceland; Israel; Japan; The Republic of Kazakhstan; The Republic of Korea; Liechtenstein; The Former Yugoslav Republic of Macedonia; Mexico; The Republic of Moldova; Montenegro; New Zealand; Norway; Peru; The Russian Federation; Switzerland; The Separate Customs Territory of Taiwan, Penghu, Kinmen and Matsu; Ukraine; and Uruguay: Disciplines on Domestic Regulation." Communication, WT/MIN(17)/7/Rev.2. Buenos Aires, Argentina: World Trade Organization, December 13, 2017.

Correa, Carlos. "Unfair Competitions under the TRIPS Agreement: Protection of Data Submitted for the Registration of Pharmaceuticals." *Chicago Journal of International Relations* 3, no. 1 (2002): 43–76.

Cosbey, Aaron, and Petros Mavroidis. "A Turquoise Mess: Green Subsidies, Blue Industrial Policy and Renewable Energy: The Case for Redrafting the Subsidies Agreement of the WTO." European University Institute, Robert Schuman Centre for Advanced Studies, Global Governance Programme Policy Paper No. RSCAS 2014/17; Columbia University School of Law, The Center for Law & Economic Studies Working Paper No. 473, January 1, 2014. https://scholarship.law.columbia.edu/faculty_scholarship/2374.

Cotula, Lorenzo. "Land Rights and Investment Treaties: Exploring the Interface." IIED Land, Investment and Rights Series. London: International Institute for Environment and Development, 2015. https://pubs.iied.org/pdfs/12578IIED.pdf.

Cotula, Lorenzo, and Thierry Berger. "Trends in Global Land Use Investment: Implications for Legal Empowerment." London: International Institute for Environment and Development, 2017. https://pubs.iied.org/pdfs/12606IIED.pdf.

Creskoff, Stephen, and Peter Walkenhorst. "Implications of WTO Disciplines for Special Economic Zones in Developing Countries." Policy Research Working Paper. The World Bank, Poverty Reduction and Economic Management Network, International Trade Department, April 2009. https://openknowledge.worldbank.org/bitstream/handle/10986/4089/WPS4892.pdf?sequence=1.

Cui, Shiliang, and Lauren Xiaoyuan Lu. "Optimizing Local Content Requirements under Technology Gaps." *Manufacturing & Service Operations Management* 21, no. 1 (June 27, 2018): 213–30. https://doi.org/10.1287/msom.2017.0698.

"Declaration on Global Electronic Commerce." Ministerial Conference: Second Session, WT/MIN(98)/DEC/2. Geneva: World Trade Organization, May 25, 1998. https://www.wto.org/english/tratop_e/ecom_e/mindec1_e.htm.

Defever, Fabrice, Jose-Daniel Reyes, Alejandro Riano and Miguel Eduardo Sanchez-Martin. "Does the Elimination of Export Requirements in Special Economic Zones Affect Export Performance?" Policy Research Working Paper. The World Bank Trade Competitiveness Global Practice Group, October 2016.

Delimatsis, Panagiotis. "Trade in Services and Regulatory Flexibility: 20 Years of GATS, 20 Years of Critique." In *2016 European Yearbook of International Economic Law.* Geneva: Springer International Publishing, 2016.

Devereaux, Charan, Robert Z. Lawrence and Michael D. Watkins. *Case Studies in US Trade Negotiation, Volume 1: Making the Rules.* Washington, DC: Peterson Institute for International Economics, 2006. http://ebookcentral.proquest.com/lib/bu/detail.action?docID=3385464.

Dominican Republic-Central America-United States. "The Dominican Republic–Central American–United States Free Trade Agreement." ustr.gov. Accessed August 20, 2020. https://ustr.gov/sites/default/files/uploads/agreements/cafta/asset_upload_file148_3916.pdf.

Dür, Andreas, Leonardo Baccini and Manfred Elsig. "The Design of International Trade Agreements: Introducing a New Dataset." *Review of International Organizations* 9, no. 3 (September 2014): 353–75.

Dutt, Devika, and Kevin P. Gallagher. "The Fiscal Impacts of Trade and Investment Treaties." GEGI Working Paper. Boston, MA: Global Development Policy Center, July 2020. http://www.bu.edu/gdp/files/2020/07/GEGI_WorkingPaper_040_Final.pdf.

Dutt, Devika, and Rachel D. Thrasher. "Growing Share of Online Trade Undercuts Government Ability to Pull in Revenue." GEGI Policy Brief. Global Development Policy Center, June 2020.

EDF International S.A., SAUR International S.A. and Leon Participaciones Argentinas S.A. v. Argentine Republic, No. ICSID Case No. ARB/03/23 (International Centre for the Settlement of Investment Disputes 2012).

Edsall, Rachel D. "Indirect Expropriation under NAFTA and DR-CAFTA: Potential Inconsistencies in the Treatment of State Public Welfare Regulations." *Boston University Law Review* 86 (2006): 931–62.

EFTA-Ecuador. "Comprehensive Economic Partnership Agreement between the EFTA States and the Republic of Ecuador," 2018. https://investmentpolicy.unctad.org/international-investment-agreements/treaty-files/5800/download.

Eichengreen, Barry, "Restructuring Sovereign Debt." *Journal of Economic Perspectives* 17(4) (2003): 75–98. doi: 10.1257/089533003772034907

Eiser Infrastructure Ltd. and Energia Solar Luxembourg S.A.R.L. v. Kingdom of Spain—Award, No. Case No. ARB/13/36 (International Centre for the Settlement of Investment Disputes May 4, 2017).

El Paso Energy International Company v. the Argentine Republic—the matter of the arbitration, www.italaw.com (International Centre for the Settlement of Investment Disputes 2010).

Emilio Agustín Maffezini v. The Kingdom of Spain, No. ICSID Case No. ARB/97/7 (International Centre for the Settlement of Investment Disputes 2000).

Emmott, Robin, and Ben Blanchard. "EU, China Resolve Solar Dispute—Their Biggest Trade Row by Far." *Reuters,* July 27, 2013. https://www.reuters.com/article/us-eu-china-solar-idUSBRE96Q03Z20130727.

EU-Japan. "Agreement between the European Union and Japan for an Economic Partnership." Brussels: European Commission, April 18, 2018. https://eur-lex.europa.eu/legal-content/EN/TXT/?uri=CELEX:52018PC0192#document2.

EU-Mexico. "Modernisation of the Trade Part of the EU-Mexico Global Agreement," 2018. https://trade.ec.europa.eu/doclib/docs/2018/april/tradoc_156795.pdf.

European Commission. "Declaration of the Member States of 15 January 2019 on the Legal Consequences of the Achmea Judgment and on Investment Protection in the European Union." European Commission, January 15, 2019. https://ec.europa.eu/info/sites/info/files/business_economy_euro/banking_and_finance/documents/190117-bilateral-investment-treaties_en.pdf.

———. "Directive 2009/28/EC of the European Parliament and of the Council of 23 April 2009 on the Promotion and the Use of Energy from Renewable Sources and Amending and Subsequently Repealing Directives 2001/77/EC and 2003/30/EC." (2009 Renewable Energy Directive). *Official Journal of the European Union* L 140 (2009): 16–62.

———. "Negotiations for a Plurilateral Agreement on Trade in Services." Text. European Commission Press Corner, February 15, 2013. https://ec.europa.eu/commission/presscorner/detail/en/MEMO_13_107.

European Union and Certain Member States—Certain Measures Affecting the Renewable Energy Generation Sector—Request for Consultations by China, wto.org (WTO Dispute Settlement Body 2012).

European Union and its Member States—Certain Measures Relating to the Energy Sector—Report of the Panel, wto.org (WTO Dispute Settlement Body 2018).

EU-Singapore. "Free Trade Agreement between the European Union and the Republic of Singapore." *Official Journal of the European Union*, no. L 294 (November 14, 2019). https://eur-lex.europa.eu/legal-content/EN/TXT/PDF/?uri=CELEX:22019A1114(01)&from=EN#page=1.

———. "Investment Protection Agreement between the European Union and Its Member States, of the One Part, and the Republic of Singapore, of the Other Part," October 19, 2018. https://eur-lex.europa.eu/resource.html?uri=cellar:55d54e18-42e0-11e8-b5fe-01aa75ed71a1.0002.02/DOC_2&format=PDF#page=2.

EU-South Africa. "Agreement on Trade, Development and Cooperation between the European Community and Its Member States, of the One Part, and the Republic of South Africa, of the Other Part." *Official Journal of the European Union* 1999, no. (L 311) 3 (December 1999). http://eur-lex.europa.eu/LexUriServ/LexUriServ.do?uri=OJ:L:1999:311:0003:0297:EN:PDF.

EU-Vietnam. "The European Union of One Part, and the Socialist Republic of Vietnam of the Other Part—Investment Protection Agreement." European Commission, September 2018. http://trade.ec.europa.eu/doclib/press/index.cfm?id=1437.

———. "Free Trade Agreement between the European Union and the Socialist Republic of Vietnam." *Official Journal of the European Union* 63, no. L 186 (June 12, 2020). https://eur-lex.europa.eu/legal-content/EN/TXT/PDF/?uri=OJ:L:2020:186:FULL&from=EN#page=46.

Evans, Peter B. *Embedded Autonomy: States & Industrial Transformation.* NJ: Princeton University Press, 1995. https://press.princeton.edu/books/paperback/9780691037363/embedded-autonomy.

Fan, Shenggen, Linxiu Zhang and Xiaobo Zhang. "Reforms, Investment, and Poverty in Rural China." *Economic Development and Cultural Change* 52, no. 2 (January 1, 2004): 395–421. https://doi.org/10.1086/380593.

Fanou, Maria. "The Independence and Impartiality of the Hybrid CETA Investment Court System: Reflections in the Aftermath of Opinion 1/17." *Europe and the World: A Law Review*, September 8, 2020. https://doi.org/10.14324/111.444.ewlj.2020.26.

Feibelman, Adam. "Ecuador's 2008–2009 Debt Restructuring." In *Sovereign Debt Crises: What Have We Learned?*, edited by Juan Pablo Bohoslavsky and Kunibert Raffer, 48–64. Cambridge: Cambridge University Press, 2017. https://doi.org/10.1017/9781108227001.004.

Finston, Susan. "India: A Cautionary Tale on the Critical Importance of Intellectual Property Protection." *Fordham Intellectual Property, Media & Entertainment Law Journal* 12 (2002, 2001): 887.

Fiorini, Matteo, Bernard Hoekman, Petros Mavroidis, Douglas Nelson and Robert Wolfe. "WTO Negotiation and Institutional Reform Priorities: Stakeholder Perspectives." *VoxEU.Org* (blog), July 9, 2020. https://voxeu.org/article/wto-negotiation-and-institutional-reform-priorities-stakeholder-perspectives.

Flores, Luis, and Anuradha Mittal. "Engineering Ethnic Conflict: The Toll of Ethiopia's Plantation Development on the Suri People." Oakland, CA: Oakland Institute, 2014. https://www.oaklandinstitute.org/sites/oaklandinstitute.org/files/Report_EngineeringEthnicConflict.pdf.

Fonseca, Elize M., Kenneth C. Shadlen and F. I. Bastos. "Integrating Science, Technology and Health Policies in Brazil: Incremental Change and Public Health Professionals as Agents of Reform." *Journal of Latin American Studies* 51, no. 2 (n.d.): 357–77. https://doi.org/10.1017/S0022216X18001050.

Foresight Luxembourg Solar 1 S.A.R.L., et al. Claimants v. The Kingdom of Spain Respondent—Final Award, italaw.com (Stockholm Chamber of Commerce 2018).

Gabble, R., and Jillian C. Kohler. "To Patent or Not to Patent? The Case of Novartis' Cancer Drug Glivec in India." *Globalization and Health* 10, no. 1 (2014). http://dx.doi.org/10.1186/1744-8603-10-3.

Gallagher, Kevin P. "Globalization and the Nation-State: Reasserting Policy Autonomy of Development." In *Putting Development First: The Importance of Policy Space in the WTO and International Financial Institutions*, edited by Kevin P Gallagher, 1–14. London: Zed Books, 2005.

———. "The New Vulture Culture: Sovereign Debt Restructuring and Trade and Investment Treaties." The IDEAs Working Paper Series. Accessed August 11, 2020. http://www.networkideas.org/working/jul2011/02_2011.pdf.

———, ed. *Putting Development First*, 2005. https://press.uchicago.edu/ucp/books/book/distributed/P/bo20851652.html.

———. *Ruling Capital: Emerging Markets and the Reregulation of Cross-Border Finance*. 1st edition. Ithaca, NY: Cornell University Press, 2014.

Gallagher, Kevin P., and Richard Kozul-Wright. "Breaking Out of the Double Squeeze: The Need for Fiscal and Policy Space during the COVID-19 Crises." Global Policy Journal: GP Opinion, June 26, 2020. https://www.globalpolicyjournal.com/blog/26/06/2020/breaking-out-double-squeeze-need-fiscal-and-policy-space-during-covid-19-crises.

———. "A New Multilateralism for Shared Prosperity: Geneva Principles for a Global Green New Deal." Boston, MA: Global Development Policy Center & United Nations

Conference on Trade and Development, 2019. http://www.bu.edu/gdp/files/2019/05/Updated-New-Graphics-New-Multilateralism-May-8-2019.pdf.

Gallagher, Kevin P., and Yuan Tian. "Regulating Capital Flows in Emerging Markets: The IMF and the Global Financial Crisis." *Review of Development Finance* 7, no. 2 (December 1, 2017): 95–106. https://doi.org/10.1016/j.rdf.2017.05.002.

Gallagher, Kevin P., Sarah Sklar and Rachel D. Thrasher. "Quantifying the Policy Space for Regulating Capital Flows in Trade and Investment Treaties: A G24 Working Paper." Intergovernmental Group of Twenty-Four, 2019. https://www.g24.org/wp-content/uploads/2019/03/Gallagher_Capital_Flows_and_Treaties.pdf.

Gallup, Inc. "Most Important Problem." Gallup.com, October 12, 2007. https://news.gallup.com/poll/1675/Most-Important-Problem.aspx.

Gas Natural SDG, S. A. v. Argentine Republic, No. ICSID Case No. ARB/03/10 (International Centre for the Settlement of Investment Disputes 2005).

GATT. "Differential and More Favourable Treatment Reciprocity and Fuller Participation of Developing Countries." Tokyo: General Agreement on Tariffs and Trade, November 28, 1979. https://www.wto.org/english/docs_e/legal_e/enabling_e.pdf.

Gelpern, Anna. "Sovereign Debt: Now What?" *Yale Journal of International Law*, Special Edition on Sovereign Debt, 41, no. 2 (2016): 45–95.

"General Agreement on Tariffs and Trade (GATT)." *U.N.T.S.* 55 (1947): 194.

Gertz, Geoffrey. "Reopening the World: Coordinating the International Distribution of Medical Goods." *Brookings* (blog), June 30, 2020. https://www.brookings.edu/blog/up-front/2020/06/30/reopening-the-world-coordinating-the-international-distribution-of-medical-goods/.

Gleeson, Deborah H., Kyla S. Tienhaara and Thomas A. Faunce. "Challenges to Australia's National Health Policy from Trade and Investment Agreements." *Medical Journal of Australia* 196, no. 5 (2012): 354–56. https://doi.org/10.5694/mja11.11635.

Gleeson, Deborah, Joel Lexthin, Ronald Labonte, Belinda Townsend, Marc-Andre Gagnon, Jillian Kohler, Lisa Forman and Kenneth C. Shadlen. "Analyzing the Impact of Trade and Investment Agreements on Pharmaceutical Policy: Provisions, Pathways and Potential Impacts." *Globalization and Health* 15, no. 78 (2019). https://doi.org/10.1186/s12992-019-0518-2.

Gleeson, Deborah, Joel Lexthin, Ruth Lopert and Burcu Kilic. "The Trans Pacific Partnership Agreement, Intellectual Property and Medicines: Differential Outcomes for Developed and Developing Countries." *Global Social Policy* 18, no. 1 (2017): 7–27. https://doi.org/10.1177/1468018117734153.

Glinavos, Ioannis. "Haircut Undone? The Greek Drama and Prospects for Investment Arbitration." *Journal of International Dispute Settlement* 5, no. 3 (November 1, 2014): 475–97. https://doi.org/10.1093/jnlids/idu008.

Gore, Timothy. "Extreme Carbon Inequality: Why the Paris Climate Deal Must Put the Poorest, Lowest Emitting and Most Vulnerable People First." Oxfam International, 2015. https://doi.org/10.1163/2210-7975_HRD-9824-2015053.

Grabel, Ilene, and Kevin P. Gallagher. "'Capital Controls and the Global Financial Crisis: An Introduction.'" *Review of International Political Economy* 22, no. 1 (January 2, 2015): 1–6. https://doi.org/10.1080/09692290.2014.931873.

Grant, Matthew. "Why Special Economic Zones? Using Trade Policy to Discriminate across Importers." *American Economic Review* 110, no. 5 (May 1, 2020): 1540–71. https://doi.org/10.1257/aer.20180384.

Greentech Energy Systems A/S, Novenergia II Energy & Environment SICAR and Novenergia II Italian Portfolio S. A. v. The Italian Republic—Final Award, italaw.com (Stockholm Chamber of Commerce 2018).

Grossman, Sanford J., and Joseph E. Stiglitz. "On the Impossibility of Informationally Efficient Markets." *American Economic Review* 70, no. 3 (1980): 393–408.

Grover Goswami, Arti, Denis Medvedev and Ellen Olafsen. *High-Growth Firms: Facts, Fiction, and Policy Options for Emerging Economies*. The World Bank, 2019. https://doi.org/10.1596/978-1-4648-1368-9.

Guzman, Martin, José Antonio Ocampo and Joseph E. Stiglitz, eds. *Too Little, Too Late: The Quest to Resolve Sovereign Debt Crises*. NY: Columbia University Press, 2016.

Guzman, Martin, and Joseph E. Stiglitz. "Creating a Framework for Sovereign Debt Restructuring That Works." In *Too Little, Too Late: The Quest to Resolve Sovereign Debt Crises*, 3–32. NY: Columbia University Press, 2016.

———. "A Soft Law Mechanism for Sovereign Debt Restructuring Based on the UN Principles." International Policy Analysis. Friedrich Ebert Stiftung, October 2016. https://doi.org/10.7916/d8-96mp-7a59.

Hagan, Sean. *Transfer of Funds*, edited by United Nations Conference on Trade and Development. UNCTAD Series on Issues in International Investment Agreements. NY: United Nations, 2000. https://doi.org/10.1017/CBO9781139162111.003.

Handley, Kyle, Fariha Kamal and Ryan Monarch. "Rising Import Tariffs, Falling Export Growth: When Modern Supply Chains Meet Old-Style Protectionism." National Bureau of Economic Research, January 6, 2020. https://doi.org/10.3386/w26611.

Hantman, Ronald D. "Experimental Use as an Exception to Patent Infringement." *Journal of the Patent and Trademark Office Society* 67 (1985): 617.

Harrison, Ann, John McLaren and Margaret McMillan. *Recent Perspectives on Trade and Inequality*. Policy Research Working Papers. The World Bank, 2011. https://doi.org/10.1596/1813-9450-5754.

Hillman, Jennifer. "Three Approaches to Fixing the World Trade Organization's Appellate Body: The Good, the Bad and the Ugly?" Washington, DC: Institute of International Economic Law, Georgetown University Law Center, 2018. https://www.law.georgetown.edu/wp-content/uploads/2018/12/Hillman-Good-Bad-Ugly-Fix-to-WTO-AB.pdf.

Ho, Jean. "The Creation of Elusive Investor Responsibility." *American Journal of International Law* 113 (2019): 10–15. https://doi.org/10.1017/aju.2018.91.

Hoadley, Stephen, and Jian Yang. "China's Cross-Regional FTA Initiatives: Towards Comprehensive National Power." *Pacific Affairs* 80, no. 2 (June 1, 2007): 327–48. https://doi.org/10.5509/2007802327.

Hoekman, Bernard. "The Bali Trade Facilitation Agreement and Rulemaking in the WTO: Milestone, Mistake or Mirage?" In *The World Trade System: Trends and Challenges*. Cambridge, MA: MIT Press, 2016. https://cadmus.eui.eu/bitstream/handle/1814/33031/RSCAS_2014_102.pdf.

Hoekman, Bernard, and Alessandro Nicita. "Non-Tariff Measures and Trade Facilitiation: WTO Disciplines and Policy Space for Development." In *Non-Tariff Measures: Economic Assessment and Policy Options for Development*. UNCTAD/DITC/TAB/2017/2. Geneva: UNCTAD, 2019. https://unctad.org/system/files/official-document/ditctab2018d3_en.pdf.

Hoekman, Bernard, and Charles Sabel. "Open Plurilateral Agreements, International Regulatory Cooperation and the WTO." *Global Policy* 10, no. 3 (2019): 297–312. https://doi.org/10.1111/1758-5899.12694.

Hoen, Ellen 't. *The Global Politics of Pharmaceutical Monopoly Power: Drug Patents, Access, Innovation and the Application of the WTO Doha Declaration on TRIPS and Public Health.* The Netherlands: AMB publishers, 2009.

Hofmann, Claudia, Alberto Osnago and Michele Ruta. "Horizontal Depth: A New Database on the Content of Preferential Trade Agreements." World Bank Group Working Paper Series. Washington, DC: World Bank Group, February 22, 2017. https://doi.org/10.1596/1813-9450-7981.

Hornbeck, J. F. "Argentina's Defaulted Sovereign Debt: Dealing with the 'Holdouts'." Congressional Research Service Report for Congress. Washington, DC: Congressional Research Service, January 21, 2010. https://www.everycrsreport.com/files/20100121_R41029_c22890f77ee92c0115ec6aa0e9bd85cc7468f0a8.pdf.

Houston, Adam R., and Reed F. Beall. "Could the Paragraph 6 Compulsory License System Be Revised to Increase Participation by the Generics Industry: Lessons Learned from a Unheralded and Unsuccessful Attempt to Use Canada." *McGill Journal of Law and Health* 12 (2018): 227–46.

Howse, Robert. "Towards a Framework for Sovereign Debt Restructuring: What Can Public International Law Contribute." In *Too Little, Too Late: The Quest to Resolve Sovereign Debt Crises*, 241–52. NY: Columbia University Press, 2016.

Ikenson, Daniel. "A Compromise to Advance the Trade Agenda: Purge Negotiations of Investor-State Dispute Settlement." *Cato Institute: Free Trade Bulletin*, March 4, 2014. https://www.cato.org/publications/free-trade-bulletin/compromise-advance-trade-agenda-purge-negotiations-investor-state.

India—Certain Measure Relating to Solar Cells and Solar Modules—Appellate Body Report, wto.org (WTO Appellate Body 2016).

India—Patent Protection for Pharmaceutical and Agricultural Chemical Products—Appellate Body Report, wto.org (WTO Appellate Body 1997).

India—Quantitative Restrictions on Imports of Agricultural, Textile and Industrial Products—Report of the Appellate Body, World Trade Organization (Dispute Settlement Body, Appellate Body 1999).

Indonesia—Certain Measures Affecting the Automobile Industry—Report of the Panel, World Trade Organization (Dispute Settlement Body–Panel 1998).

International Criminal Court. "ICC Tackling Global Challenges: Environmental Destruction and Land-Grabbing." Coalition for the International Criminal Court, 2020. http://www.coalitionfortheicc.org/global-challenges-ICC-environmental-destruction-landgrabbing.

International Monetary Fund. "IMF Data Coordinated Direct Investment Survey." IMF Data Access to Macroeconomic and Financial Data, 2018. https://data.imf.org/?sk=40313609-F037-48C1-84B1-E1F1CE54D6D5.

———. "The Liberalization and Management of Capital Flows: An Institutional View." *Policy Papers*, 2012. https://doi.org/10.5089/9781498339612.007.

Islam, Deen, Warren A. Kaplan, Veronika J. Wirtz and Kevin P. Gallagher. "The Social Costs of Graduating from Least Developed Country Status: Analyzing the Impact of Increased Protection on Insulin Prices in Bangladesh." GEGI Working Paper. Boston, MA: Global Development Policy Center, May 2020.

Ismail, Yasmin. "E-Commerce in the World Trade Organization: History and Latest Developments in the Negotiations under the Joint Statement." Geneva: International Institute for Sustainable Development (IISD) and CUTS International, January 2020. https://www.iisd.org/sites/default/files/publications/e-commerce-world-trade-organization-.pdf.

Isolux Infrastructure Netherlands v. Kingdom of Spain—Award, italaw.com (Stockholm Chamber of Commerce 2016).

Janeba, Eckhard. "Regulatory Chill and the Effect of Investor State Dispute Settlements." *Annual Conference 2017 (Vienna): Alternative Structures for Money and Banking.* Annual Conference 2017 (Vienna): Alternative Structures for Money and Banking. Verein für Socialpolitik/German Economic Association, 2017. https://ideas.repec.org/p/zbw/vfsc17/168255.html.

Janetos, Anthony C. "Why Trade Matters to a Climate Agreement." In *Trade in the Balance: Reconciling Trade and Climate Policy: Report of the Working Group on Trade, Investment and Climate Policy,* 14–19. Boston, MA: Global Development Policy Center, Boston University, 2016. https://open.bu.edu/bitstream/handle/2144/22909/Pardee_TradeClimate_110316final.pdf?sequence=1&isAllowed=y.

Japan-Mongolia. "Agreement between Japan and Mongolia for an Economic Partnership." Ministry of Foreign Affairs of Japan, March 10, 2015. https://www.mofa.go.jp/a_o/c_m2/mn/page3e_000298.html.

Jayaraman, T., and Baljeet Singh. "Foreign Direct Investment and Employment Creation in Pacific Island Countries: An Empirical Study of Fiji." Working Paper Series. Asia-Pacific Research and Training Network on Trade, June 1, 2007. https://www.researchgate.net/publication/5017456_Foreign_Direct_Investment_and_Employment_Creation_in_Pacific_Island_Countries_An_Empirical_Study_of_Fiji.

Johnson, Lise. "Ripe for Refinement: The State's Role in Interpretation of FET, MFN, and Shareholder Rights." *Global Economic Governance Programme, University of Oxford,* Global Economic Governance Working Paper, 2015/101 (2015): 40.

"Joint Ministerial Statement on Investment Facilitation for Development." World Trade Organization, December 13, 2017. https://docs.wto.org/dol2fe/Pages/FE_Search/FE_S_S009-DP.aspx?language=E&CatalogueIdList=240870.

"Joint Statement between the United States and Kenya on the Launch of Negotiations towards a Free Trade Agreement | United States Trade Representative," July 8, 2020. https://ustr.gov/about-us/policy-offices/press-office/press-releases/2020/july/joint-statement-between-united-states-and-kenya-launch-negotiations-towards-free-trade-agreement.

Judge Griesa. NML Capital LTD., and others v. Republic of Argentina, No. Case 1:08-cv-06978 (U.S. Dist. Ct., S. Dist. N.Y. March 12, 2015).

Kapstein, Ethan B. "Fairness Considerations in World Politics: Lessons from International Trade Negotiations." *Political Science Quarterly* 123, no. 2 (2008): 229–45.

Kelsey, Jane. "From GATS to TiSA: Pushing the Trade in Services Regime beyond the Limits." In *2016 European Yearbook of International Economic Law.* Geneva: Springer International Publishing, 2016.

Keynes, Soumaya, and Chad P. Bown. "What's in the New EU-UK Trade Deal? Brexperts Explain." Trade Talks. Accessed January 15, 2021. https://www.tradetalkspodcast.com/podcast/147-whats-in-the-new-eu-uk-trade-deal-brexperts-explain/.

Korea. "RCEP—Draft Investment Text: Korea (Based on Negotiating Draft of Oct 2015)." bilaterals.org, 2015. https://www.bilaterals.org/?rcep-draft-investment-text-korea.

Korinek, Anton. "The New Economics of Prudential Capital Controls: A Research Agenda." *IMF Economic Review* 59, no. 3 (August 2011): 523–61. https://doi.org/10.1057/imfer.2011.19.

Krajewski, Markus. "A Nightmare or a Noble Dream? Establishing Investor Obligations through Treaty-Making and Treaty-Application." *Business and Human Rights Journal* 5, no. 1 (January 2020): 105–29. https://doi.org/10.1017/bhj.2019.29.

Kremer, M., and E. Maskin. "Globalization and Inequality," 2006. http://piketty.pse.ens.fr/fichiers/KremerMaskin2003.pdf.

Krikorian, Gaëlle P., and Dorota M. Szymkowiak. "Intellectual Property Rights in the Making: The Evolution of Intellectual Property Provisions in US Free Trade Agreements and Access to Medicine." *Journal of World Intellectual Property* 10, no. 5 (2007): 388–418. https://doi.org/10.1111/j.1747-1796.2007.00328.x.

Krugman, Paul. *Development, Geography and Economic Theory*. Cambridge, MA: MIT Press, 1995.

Kuhlik, Bruce N. "The Assault on Pharmaceutical Intellectual Property." *The University of Chicago Law Review* 71, no. 1 (2004): 93–109.

Kumar, Nagesh, and Kevin P. Gallagher. "Relevance of 'Policy Space' for Development: Implications for Multilateral Trade Negotiations." Discussion Paper. Research and Information System For Developing Countries, 2007. https://www.ris.org.in/relevance-%E2%80%98policy-space%E2%80%99-development-implications-multilateral-trade-negotiations.

Lall, Sanjaya. "Rethinking Industrial Strategy: The Role of the State in the Face of Globalization." In *Putting Development First: The Importance of Policy Space in the WTO and International Financial Institutions*, edited by Kevin P Gallagher, 33–68. London: Zed Books, 2005.

Landmatrix.org. "Data: All Deals." Database. Land Matrix, 2020. https://landmatrix.org/data/.

Larik, Joris. "Brexit, the EU-UK Withdrawal Agreement, and Global Treaty (Re-) Negotiations." *American Journal of International Law* 114, no. 3 (July 2020): 443–62. https://doi.org/10.1017/ajil.2020.29.

Lassen, David Dreyer, and Soren Serritzlew. "Jurisdiction Size and Local Democracy: Evidence on Internal Political Efficacy from Large-Scale Municipal Reform." *American Political Science Review* 105, no. 2 (May 2011): 238–58.

Lavers, Tom. "Patterns of Agrarian Transformation in Ethiopia: State-Mediated Commercialisation and the 'Land Grab.'" *Journal of Peasant Studies* 39, no. 3–4 (2012): 795–822. https://doi.org/10.1080/03066150.2012.660147.

Lietzan, Erika, Aaron S. Kesselheim and David S. Olson. Antitrust Concerns and the FDA Approval Process, § House Committee on the Judiciary (2017). https://www.youtube.com/watch?v=5QPUYZT7v5c.

Loudenback, Tanza, and Abby Jackson. "The 10 Most Critical Problems in the World, According to Millennials." Business Insider, February 26, 2018. https://www.businessinsider.com/world-economic-forum-world-biggest-problems-concerning-millennials-2016-8.

Lucas, Robert E. "On the Mechanics of Economic Development." *Journal of Monetary Economics* 22 (1988): 3–42.

Lybecker, Kristina M. "Intellectual Property Protection for Biologics: Why the Trans-Pacific Partnership (TPP) Trade Agreement Fails to Deliver." *Journal of Commercial Biotechnology; London* 22, no. 1 (January 2016). http://dx.doi.org/10.5912/jcb731.

Magud, Nicolas E., Carmen M. Reinhart and Kenneth S. Rogoff. "Capital Controls: Myth and Reality." *Annals of Economics and Finance* 19, no. 1 (2018): 3.

"Mapping of IIA Content | International Investment Agreements Navigator | UNCTAD Investment Policy Hub." Accessed August 14, 2020. https://investmentpolicy.unctad.org/international-investment-agreements/iia-mapping.

Marchetti, Juan A., and Petros C. Mavroidis. "The Genesis of the GATS (General Agreement on Trade in Services)." *European Journal of International Law* 22, no. 3 (August 1, 2011): 689–721. https://doi.org/10.1093/ejil/chr051.

Masdar Solar & Wind Cooperatief U.A. v. Kingdom of Spain—Award, italaw.com (International Centre for the Settlement of Investment Disputes 2018).

McCall, Angelique, and Gene Quinn. "The FDA Process, Patents and Market Exclusivity." *IPWatchdog.Com | Patents & Patent Law* (blog), March 12, 2017. https://www.ipwatchdog.com/2017/03/12/fda-process-patents-market-exclusivity/id=79305/.

Melo, Jaime de, and Jean-Marc Solleder. "The EGA Negotiations: Why They Are Important, Why They Are Stalled, and Challenges Ahead." *Post-Print*. Post-Print. HAL, October 29, 2018. https://ideas.repec.org/p/hal/journl/hal-01907634.html.

Mesa Power Group, LLC. v. Government of Canada, Award—Arbitration under Chapter 11 of the NAFTA and the UNCITRAL Arbitration Rules, 1976, italaw.com (Permanent Court of Arbitration 2016).

Metalclad Corporation v. The United Mexican States—Award, italaw.com (International Centre for the Settlement of Investment Disputes 2000).

Methanex Corporation v. the United States of America—the matter of an international arbitration under Chapter 11 of the North American Free Trade Agreement and the UNCITRAL arbitration rules—Final Award of the Tribunal on Jurisdiction and Merits, 44 International Legal Materials 1345 (UNCITRAL 2005).

Meyer, Timothy. "How Local Discrimination Can Promote Global Public Goods." *Boston University Law Review* 95 (2015): 1939–2025.

Mittal, Anuradha. "Nicaragua's Failed Revolution: The Indigenous Struggle for Saneamiento." Oakland, CA: Oakland Institute, 2020. https://www.oaklandinstitute.org/sites/oaklandinstitute.org/files/nicaraguas-failed-revolution.pdf.

Montes, Manuel. "Policy Space for Fiscal Revenue Mobilization under FTAs and BITs." In *Domestic Resource Mobilization and the Trade and Investment Regime: The Need for Policy Coherence*, 39–44. Boston, MA: Global Development Policy Center, Boston University, 2020. http://www.bu.edu/gdp/files/2020/07/GDP_Fiscal-Stability-Report_Final.pdf.

Mousseau, Frederic. "Herakles Exposed: The Truth behind Herakles Farms: False Promises in Cameroon." Oakland, CA: Oakland Institute and Greenpeace International, 2013. https://www.oaklandinstitute.org/sites/oaklandinstitute.org/files/OI_Report_Herakles_Exposed.pdf.

Mousseau, Frederic, and Anuradha Mittal. "Country Report: Mozambique." Country Report. Understanding Land Investment Deals in Africa. Oakland, CA: Oakland Institute, 2011. https://www.oaklandinstitute.org/sites/oaklandinstitute.org/files/OI_country_report_mozambique_0.pdf.

———. "Country Report: Tanzania." Country Report. Understanding Land Investment Deals in Africa. Oakland, CA: Oakland Institute, 2011. https://www.oaklandinstitute.org/sites/oaklandinstitute.org/files/OI_country_report_tanzania.pdf.

Mousseau, Frederic, and Granate Sosnoff. "Country Report: Ethiopia." Country Report. Understanding Land Investment Deals in Africa. Oakland, CA: The Oakland Institute, 2011. https://www.oaklandinstitute.org/sites/oaklandinstitute.org/files/OI_Ethiopa_Land_Investment_report.pdf.

MTD Equity Sdn. Bhd. and MTD Chile S.A. v. Republic of Chile, No. ICSID Case No. ARB/01/7 (International Centre for the Settlement of Investment Disputes 2004).

Murphy, Kevin, Andrei Shleifer and Robert Vishny. "Industrialization and the Big Push." *Journal of Political Economy* 97, no. 5 (1989): 1003–26.

Netherlands-Indonesia. "Netherlands and Indonesia Agreement on Economic Cooperation (with Protocol and Exchanges of Letters Dated on 17 June 1968)," July 7, 1968. https://investmentpolicy.unctad.org/international-investment-agreements/treaty-files/3329/download.

New, William. "WTO Members Celebrate Treaty Amendment On Medicines Access, Look Ahead." *Intellectual Property Watch* (blog), January 30, 2017. https://www.ip-watch.org/2017/01/30/wto-members-celebrate-treaty-amendment-medicines-access-look-ahead/.

Nicaragua-Chinese Taipei. "Free Trade Agreement between the Republic of China (Taiwan) and the Republic of Nicaragua" (Nicaragua-Taiwan FTA), 2008. http://www.sice.oas.org/Trade/NIC_TWN/NIC_TWN_e/index_e.asp.

Nichols, Robert. *Theft Is Property: Dispossession and Critical Theory*. Durham, NC: Duke University Press, 2020.

Nicholson, Francis J. "The Protection of Foreign Property under Customary International Law." *Boston College Industrial and Commercial Law Review* 6, no. 3 (1965): 391–415.

Niemelä, Dr. Pekka, Harro van Asselt, Kati Kulovesi and Dr. Mikko Rajavuori. "Risky Business: Uniper's Potential Investor-State Dispute against the Dutch Coal Ban." *EJIL: Talk!* (blog), March 18, 2020. https://www.ejiltalk.org/risky-business-unipers-potential-investor-state-dispute-against-the-dutch-coal-ban/.

Nikièma, Suzy H. "Performance Requirements in Investment Treaties." Best Practices Series. Winnipeg, Manitoba: International Institute for Sustainable Development (IISD), December 2014. https://www.iisd.org/sites/default/files/publications/best-practices-performance-requirements-investment-treaties-en.pdf.

NML Capital, LTD., and others v. Republic of Argentina (2d Cir. 2012).

Novenergia II–Energy & Environment, SICAR v. Kingdom of Spain—Final Arbitration Award, italaw.com (Stockholm Chamber of Commerce 2018).

NPR.org. "What Will It Take To End The COVID-19 Pandemic?" Accessed January 28, 2021. https://www.npr.org/sections/goatsandsoda/2021/01/05/953653373/some-experts-say-temporary-halt-on-drug-patents-is-needed-to-stop-pandemic-world.

"Oakland Institute. Reframing the Debate Inspiring Action." Accessed August 25, 2020. https://www.oaklandinstitute.org/.

Ocampo, José Antonio. "A Brief History of Sovereign Debt Resolution and a Proposal for a Multilateral Instrument." In *Too Little, Too Late: The Quest to Resolve Sovereign Debt Crises*, 189–205. NY: Columbia University Press, 2016.

Ohlin, Bertil. *Interregional and International Trade*. Revised edition. Cambridge: Harvard University Press, 1967.

Olivet, Cecilia. "Why Did Ecuador Terminate All Its Bilateral Investment Treaties?" Transnational Institute, May 25, 2017. https://www.tni.org/en/article/why-did-ecuador-terminate-all-its-bilateral-investment-treaties.

Ostry, Jonathan, Atish Ghosh, Karl Habermeier, Marcos Chamon, Mahvash S. Qureshi and Dennis B. S. Reinhardt. "Capital Inflows: The Role of Controls." *IMF Staff Position Notes* 2010, no. 04 (2010). https://doi.org/10.5089/9781462347513.004.

Palmer, Doug, and Leonora Walet. "China Agrees to Halt Subsidies to Wind Power Firms." *Reuters*, June 7, 2011. https://www.reuters.com/article/us-china-windpower-idUSTRE7561B920110607.

Perera, Oshani. "The Globalisation of Services and Its Implications for Sustainable Development: A Preliminary Discussion Document." Geneva: International Institute for Sustainable Development (IISD), December 2007. http://test.iisd.org/pdf/2008/globalisation_services_sd.pdf.

Pope & Talbot, Inc. v. Canada (NAFTA Chapter 11 Arbitration April 10, 2001).

Porterfield, Matthew C. "Exhaustion of Local Remedies in Investor-State Dispute Settlement: An Idea Whose Time Has Come?" *The Yale Journal of International Law Online* 41 (2015): 1–12.

———. "State Practice and the (Purported) Obligation under Customary International Law to Provide Compensation for Regulatory Expropriations." *North Carolina Journal of International Law and Commercial Regulation* 37 (2012, 2011): 159.

Poštová banka, a.s. and ISTROKAPITAL SE v. Hellenic Republic, www.italaw.com (International Centre for Settlement of Investment Disputes 2015).

Poulsen, Lauge N. Skovgaard. "British Foreign Investment Policy Post-Brexit: Treaty Obligations vs. Bottom-Up Reforms." University College of London. European Institute Working Paper. Rochester, NY: Social Science Research Network, July 2017. https://doi.org/10.2139/ssrn.3001782.

Power, Richard. "Novenergia v. Kingdom of Spain, the ECT and the ECJ: Where to Now for Intra-EU ECT Claims?" *Kluwer Arbitration Blog* (blog), March 20, 2018. http://arbitrationblog.kluwerarbitration.com/2018/03/20/novenergia-v-kingdom-of-spain/.

Rajan, Ramkishen S., and Rahul Sen. "The New Wave of FTAs in Asia: With Particular Reference to ASEAN, China, and India," June 2004. https://www.researchgate.net/publication/228364705_The_New_Wave_of_FTAs_in_Asia_with_particular_reference_to_ASEAN_China_and_India

"Regional Comprehensive Economic Partnership Agreement" (RCEP), 2021. https://rcepsec.org/legal-text/

Ricardo, David. *On the Principles of Political Economy, and Taxation*. London: John Murray, 1821.

Roche Product, Inc. v. Bolar Pharmaceutical Co., 733 Federal Second 858 (Court of Appeals for the Federal Circuit 1984).

Rodrik, Dani. "The Global Governance of Trade as If Development Really Mattered." UNDP, 2001. https://drodrik.scholar.harvard.edu/files/dani-rodrik/files/global-governance-of-trade.pdf.

———. *The Globalization Paradox: Democracy and the Future of the World Economy*. Reprint edition. NY: W. W. Norton, 2012.

———. *One Economics, Many Recipes: Globalization, Institutions and Economic Growth*. NJ: Princeton University Press, 2009. https://press.princeton.edu/books/paperback/9780691141176/one-economics-many-recipes.

———. *Straight Talk on Trade: Ideas for a Sane World Economy*. Princeton, NJ: Princeton University Press, 2017.

———. "What Do Trade Agreements Really Do?" *Journal of Economic Perspectives* 32, no. 2 (May 2018): 73–90. https://doi.org/10.1257/jep.32.2.73.

Rogers, Richard J., and FIDH. "Questions & Answers: Crimes against Humanity in Cambodia from July 2002 until Present." London and Paris: International Federation for Human Rights (FIDH), July 10, 2014. https://www.fidh.org/IMG/pdf/qanda_ cambodia_icc-2.pdf.

Rolland, Sonia. "The Impact of Trade and Investment Treaties on Mobilization of Taxation in Developing Countries." GEGI Working Paper. Boston, MA: Global Development Policy Center, October 2019. http://www.bu.edu/gdp/files/2019/11/ Rolland-22Impact-of-Trade-and-Investment-Treaties...22.pdf.

———. "The WTO and Tax Mobilization for Developing Countries." In *Domestic Resource Mobilization and the Trade and Investment Regime: The Need for Policy Coherence*, 28–33. Boston, MA: Global Development Policy Center, Boston University, 2020. http://www.bu.edu/ gdp/files/2020/07/GDP_Fiscal-Stability-Report_Final.pdf.

RosInvestCo. UK, Ltd. v. The Russian Federation, No. SCC Arbitration V (079/2005) (Stockholm Chamber of Commerce 2010).

Ross, Alison. "India's Termination of BITs to Begin." *Global Arbitration Review*, March 22, 2017. https://globalarbitrationreview.com/article/1138510/ indias-termination-of-bits-to-begin.

Roy, Martin, Juan Marchetti and Hoe Lim. "Services Liberalization in the New Generation of Preferential Trade Agreements (PTAs): How Much Further than the GATS?" Staff Working Paper, Economic Research and Statistics Division. Geneva: World Trade Organization, September 2006.

Sachs, Lisa E., and Karl P. Sauvant. "BITs, DTTs and FDI Flows: An Overview." In *The Effect of Treaties on Foreign Direct Investment: Bilateral Investment Treaties, Double Taxation Treaties and Investment Flows*, xxvii–lvii. Oxford: Oxford University Press, 2009.

Sachs, Lisa E., Ella Merrill and Lise J. Johnson. "Environmental Injustice: How Treaties Undermine the Right to a Healthy Environment." *Kluwer Arbitration Blog* (blog), November 13, 2019. http://arbitrationblog.kluwerarbitration.com/2019/11/13/ environmental-injustice-how-treaties-undermine-the-right-to-a-healthy-environment/.

Salini Costruttori S.P.A. and Italstrade S.P.A. v. Kingdom of Morocco, 42 International Legal Materials 609 (International Centre for the Settlement of Investment Disputes 2001).

Salini Costruttori S.P.A. and Italstrade S.P.A. v. The Hashemite Kingdom of Jordan, No. ICSID Case No. ARB/02/13 (International Centre for the Settlement of Investment Disputes 2002).

Sattorova, Mavluda. "Investor Responsibilities from a Host State Perspective: Qualitative Data and Proposals for Treaty Reform." *American Journal of International Law* 113 (2019): 22–27. https://doi.org/10.1017/aju.2018.93.

Schacherer, Stefanie. "TPP, CETA and TTIP between Innovation and Consolidation— Resolving Investor–State Disputes under Mega-Regionals." *Journal of International Dispute Settlement* 7, no. 3 (November 1, 2016): 628–53. https://doi.org/10.1093/jnlids/ idw022.

Schill, Stephan W. *The Multilateralization of International Investment Law*. Reprint edition. Cambridge, NY: Cambridge University Press, 2014.

Schultz, Thomas, and Cédric Dupont. "Investment Arbitration: Promoting the Rule of Law or Over-Empowering Investors? A Quantitative Empirical Study." *European Journal of International Law* 25, no. 4 (November 2014): 1147–68. https://doi.org/10.1093/ejil/ chu075.

Schwebel, Stephen M. "In Defense of Bilateral Investment Treaties." *Columbia FDI Perspectives: Perspectives on Topical Foreign Direct Investment Issues* (blog), November 24, 2014. https://doi.org/10.1093/arbint/aiv017.

Sell, Susan K. "TRIPs Was Never Enough: Vertical Forum Shifting, FTAS, ACTA, and TPP." *Journal of Intellectual Property Law* 18 (2011 2010): 447.

Serrichio, Sergio. "Kevin Gallagher, el profesor de la Universidad de Boston que defiende al país y ataca a los bonistas: 'El mundo está mirando a la Argentina.'" infobae Economico, July 25, 2020. https://www.infobae.com/economia/2020/07/25/kevin-gallagher-el-profesor-de-la-universidad-de-boston-que-defiende-al-pais-y-ataca-a-los-bonistas-el-mundo-esta-mirando-a-la-argentina/

Shadlen, Kenneth C. *Coalitions and Compliance: The Political Economy of Pharmaceutical Patents in Latin America*. Oxford, UK: Oxford University Press, 2017.

———. "Policy Space for Development in the WTO and Beyond: The Case of Intellectual Property Rights." Working Paper. Global Development and Environment Institute, Tufts University, November 2005. https://core.ac.uk/reader/7051868.

Shadlen, Kenneth C., Bhaven N. Sampat and Amy Kapczynski. "Patents, Trade and Medicines: Past, Present and Future." Edited by Susan K. Sell and Owain D. Williams. *Review of International Political Economy*, Special Issue on Political Economies of Global Health, 27, no. 1 (2019): 75–97. https://doi.org/10.1080/09692290.2019.1624295.

Shellenberger, Michael. "Why Apocalyptic Claims about Climate Change Are Wrong." *Forbes*, November 19, 2019, online edition, sec. Energy. https://www.forbes.com/sites/michaelshellenberger/2019/11/25/why-everything-they-say-about-climate-change-is-wrong/.

Siegel, Deborah E. "Capital Account Restrictions, Trade Agreements and the IMF." In *Capital Account Regulations and the Trading System: A Compatibility Review*, edited by Kevin Gallagher and Leonardo E Stanley, 13. Boston, MA: Frederick S. Pardee Center for the Study of the Longer-Range Future, Boston University, 2013. http://www.networkideas.org/wp-content/uploads/2016/08/CAR_Trading_System.pdf.

———. "Using Free Trade Agreements to Control Capital Account Restrictions: Summary of Remarks on the Relationship to the Mandate of the IMF." *ILSA Journal of International and Comparative Law* 10 (2004): 297–304.

Siegel, Deborah E., Kevin P. Gallagher and Rachel D. Thrasher. "Movement of Capital." In *Handbook of Deep Trade Agreements*, edited by Aaditya Mattoo, Nadia Rocha and Michele Ruta. Washington, DC: World Bank Group, 2020. https://openknowledge.worldbank.org/bitstream/handle/10986/34055/9781464815393.pdf?sequence=2.

Sikor, Thomas. "Tree Plantations, Politics of Possession and the Absence of Land Grabs in Vietnam." *Journal of Peasant Studies* 39, no. 3–4 (2012): 1077–1101. https://doi.org/10.1080/03066150.2012.674943.

Sircar, Neil. "Public Health Emergencies: Reconciling TRIPS and IHR (2005)." *Houston Journal of International Law*, no. 2018 (2018): 101–21.

Slovak Republic v. Achmea B.V.—Judgment of the Court, italaw.com (European Court of Justice 2018).

Smaller, Carin, and Howard Mann. "A Thirst for Distant Lands: Foreign Investment in Agricultural Land and Water." Foreign Investment for Sustainable Development Program. Geneva: International Institute for Sustainable Development (IISD), May 2009. https://www.iisd.org/sites/default/files/publications/thirst_for_distant_lands.pdf.

Smarzynska Javorcik, Beata. "Does Foreign Direct Investment Increase the Productivity of Domestic Firms? In Search of Spillovers through Backward Linkages." *American Economic Review* 94, no. 3 (June 2004): 605–27. https://doi.org/10.1257/0002828041464605.

Smith, Colby, Benedict Mander and Robin Wigglesworth. "Argentina Strikes Debt Agreement after Restructuring Breakthrough." *Financial Times*. August 4, 2020, sec. Argentina. https://www.ft.com/content/ecb81529-7853-4403-95a9-577ee1ebc4b8.

Son, Kyung-Bok, Ruth Lopert, Deborah Gleeson and Tae-Jin Lee. "Moderating the Impact of Patent Linkage on Access to Medicines: Lessons from Variations in South Korea, Australia, Canada, and the United States." *Globalization and Health* 14, no. 1 (October 24, 2018): 101. https://doi.org/10.1186/s12992-018-0423-0.

South Africa. "Intellectual Property and Public Interest: Beyond Access to Medicines and Medical Technologies towards a More Holistic Approach to TRIPS Flexibilities." Council for Trade-Related Aspects of Intellectual Property Rights. Geneva: World Trade Organization, July 17, 2020. https://www.keionline.org/wp-content/uploads/W666.pdf.

Southern African Development Community and Howard Mann. "SADC Model Bilateral Investment Treaty Template with Commentary." Gaborone, Botswana: Southern African Development Community, July 2012. https://www.iisd.org/itn/wp-content/uploads/2012/10/sadc-model-bit-template-final.pdf.

Stephenson, Sherry. "Addressing Local Content Requirements in a Sustainable Energy Trade Agreement." Geneva: International Centre for Trade and Sustainable Development, 2013. https://pdfs.semanticscholar.org/8d6e/3864668d88c93f1218eab0c1174b5436e64e.pdf.

Stiglitz, Joseph E. "Development Policies in a World of Globalization." In *Putting Development First: The Importance of Policy Space in the WTO and International Financial Institutions*, edited by Kevin P Gallagher, 15–32. London: Zed Books, 2005.

———. *Globalization and Its Discontents*. 1 edition. NY: W. W. Norton & Company, 2003.

Stiglitz, Joseph E., Andrew Shoyer and Robert Howse. "Climate Change, China and the WTO." Presented at the Climate Change, China and the WTO, Sabin Center for Climate Change Law, Columbia University, 2011. http://columbiaclimatelaw.com/news-events/events/2011-2/climate-change-china-and-the-wto/.

Sweet, Alec Stone, Michael Yunsuck Chung and Adam Saltzman. "Arbitral Lawmaking and State Power: An Empirical Analysis of Investor–State Arbitration." *Journal of International Dispute Settlement* 8, no. 4 (December 1, 2017): 579–609. https://doi.org/10.1093/jnlids/idx009.

Taylor, John B. "Testimony before the Subcommittee on Domestic and International Monetary Policy, Trade and Technology." Department of the Treasury, Committee on Financial Services, US House of Representatives, April 1, 2002. https://ia601306.us.archive.org/6/items/gov.gpo.fdsys.CHRG-108hhrg89081/CHRG-108hhrg89081.pdf.

Taylor, Nathan L. "A Challenge to the Discourse of Development or Development Done Differently: The Discourse of Experts in the WTO Agreement on Trade Facilitation." Text, Carleton University, 2018. https://curve.carleton.ca/25b40a3f-4987-4022-b8c0-f69022f6c5c4.

Técnicas Medioambientales Tecmed, S.A. v. The United Mexican States, No. ICSID Case No. ARB(AF)/00/2 (International Centre for the Settlement of Investment Disputes 2003).

Thompson, Alexander, Tomer Broude and Yoram Z. Haftel. "Once Bitten, Twice Shy? Investment Disputes, State Sovereignty, and Change in Treaty Design." *International Organization* 73, no. 4 (2019): 859–80. https://doi.org/10.1017/S0020818319000195.

Thrasher, Rachel D. "The Next Director-General and WTO Reform: An Interview with Rashmi Banga, UNCTAD." *Global Development Policy Center Blog* (blog), November 23, 2020. https://www.bu.edu/gdp/2020/11/23/the-next-director-general-and-wto-reform-an-interview-with-rashmi-banga-unctad/.

———. "Policy Space for Jobs and Clean Energy: Trade, Investment Rules and Local Content Requirements in Renewable Energy Policies." In *Yearbook on International Investment Law and Policy 2018*, 414–31. Yearbook on International Investment Lawy and Policy. Oxford, UK: Oxford University Press, 2019.Thrasher, Rachel Denae, and Kevin P. Gallagher. "21st Century Trade Agreements: Implications for Development Sovereignty." *Denver Journal of International Law and Policy* 38, no. 2 (March 22, 2010): 313.

———. "Defending Development Sovereignty: The Case for Industrial Policy and Financial Regulation in the Trading Regime." In *Rethinking Development Strategies After the Financial Crisis: Volume I: Making the Case for Policy Space*, edited by Alfredo Calcagno, Sebastian Dullien, Alejandro Marquez-Velazquez, Nicolas Maystre, and Jan Priewe, 93–104. New York and Geneva: United Nations Conference on Trade and Development, 2014.

———. "Mission Creep: The Emerging Role of International Investment Agreements in Sovereign Debt Restructuring." *Journal of Globalization and Development* 6, no. 2 (December 1, 2015): 257–85. https://doi.org/10.1515/jgd-2015-0018.

Tienhaara, Kyla. "Regulatory Chill and the Threat of Arbitration: A View from Political Science." In *Evolution in Investment Treaty Law and Arbitration*, edited by Chester Brown and Kate Miles, 28. Cambridge, NY: Cambridge University Press, 2011.

Tienhaara, Kyla, and Christian Downie. "Risky Business? The Energy Charter Treaty, Renewable Energy, and Investor-State Disputes." *Global Governance* 24, no. 3 (September 12, 2018): 451–71. https://doi.org/10.1163/19426720-02403009.

Timperley, Jocelyn. "Explainer: The Challenge of Defining Fossil Fuel Subsidies." Carbon Brief, June 12, 2017. https://www.carbonbrief.org/explainer-the-challenge-of-defining-fossil-fuel-subsidies.

Trachtenberg, Danielle, Warren A. Kaplan, Veronika J. Wirtz and Kevin P. Gallagher. "Trade Treaties & Access to Medicines: What Does the Evidence Tell Us? | Global Development Policy Center." GEGI Policy Brief. Boston, MA: Global Development Policy Center, Boston University, May 2019. http://www.bu.edu/gdp/2019/06/07/trade-treaties-access-to-medicines-what-does-the-evidence-tell-us/.

Trade Policy Review Body. "Report of the TPRB from the Director-General on Trade-Related Developments," WT/TPR/OV/23/Corr.1. World Trade Organization, July 10, 2020.

TransCanada Corporation and TransCanada Pipelines Limited v. United States of America, italaw.com (International Centre for the Settlement of Investment Disputes 2017).

Trebilcock, M. J., Robert Howse and Antonia Eliason. *The Regulation of International Trade*. Routledge, 2013.

Tucker, Todd N. *Judge Knot: Politics and Development in International Investment Law*. Illustrated edition. London: Anthem Press, 2018.

———. "The Looming GATS Conflict with Capital Controls." In *Capital Account Regulations and the Trading System: A Compatibility Review*, 10. Frederick S. Pardee Center for the Study of the Longer-Range Future, Boston University, 2013. http://www.networkideas.org/wp-content/uploads/2016/08/CAR_Trading_System.pdf.

———. "Mind-Maps for Market Failure, Perfect Competition, and Government Failure." *Medium* (blog), November 3, 2018. https://medium.com/@toddntucker/mind-maps-for-market-failure-perfect-competition-and-government-failure-aa3bdec20a69.

———. "RIP, World Trade Organization?," December 9, 2019. https://www.thenation.com/article/archive/wto-trade-tariff-trump/.

Twohey, Megan, Keith Collins and Katie Thomas. "With First Dibs on Vaccines, Rich Countries Have 'Cleared the Shelves.'" *The New York Times*, December 15, 2020, sec. U.S. https://www.nytimes.com/2020/12/15/us/coronavirus-vaccine-doses-reserved.html.

UN Secretary-General. "Report of the United Nations Secretary-General's High-Level Panel on Access to Medicines: Promoting Innovation and Access to Health Technologies." United Nations Development Programme, September 2016. http://www.unsgaccessmeds.org/resources-documents/2017/7/19/report-of-the-united-nations-secretary-generals-high-level-panel-on-access-to-medicines.

UNCTAD. "The Changing IIA Landscape: New Treaties and Recent Policy Developments." *IIA Issues Note*, IIA Issues Note: International Investment Agreements, no. 1 (July 2020). https://unctad.org/en/PublicationsLibrary/diaepcbinf2020d4.pdf.

———. "Investor-State Dispute Settlement Cases Pass the 1,000 Mark: Cases and Outcomes in 2019." *IIA Issues Note*, IIA Issues Note: International Investment Agreements, no. 2 (July 2020). https://unctad.org/en/PublicationsLibrary/diaepcbinf2020d6.pdf.

UNCTAD Investment Policy Hub. "International Investment Agreements Navigator." Accessed July 17, 2020. https://investmentpolicy.unctad.org/international-investment-agreements.

UNCTAD Investment Policy Hub. "Investment Dispute Settlement Navigator." Accessed August 25, 2020. https://investmentpolicy.unctad.org/investment-dispute-settlement.

United Nations. "Paris Agreement." United Nations, 2015. https://unfccc.int/files/essential_background/convention/application/pdf/english_paris_agreement.pdf.

UNDESA Statistics Division: National Accounts. "United Nations National Accounts Analysis of Main Aggregates," 2018. https://unstats.un.org/unsd/snaama/index.

United Nations Environment Program (UNEP). *Fisheries Subsidies and Overfishing: Towards a Structured Discussion*. UNEP/Earthprint, 2003.

United States—Certain Measures Relating to the Renewable Energy Sector—Report of the Panel, wto.org (WTO Panel 2019).

United States—Measures Affecting the Cross-Border Supply of Gambling and Betting Services, www.wto.org (Dispute Settlement Body–World Trade Organization 2005).

United States-Chile. "United States-Chile Free Trade Agreement." *International Legal Materials* 42 (June 2003): 1026.

United States-Mexico-Canada. "North American Free Trade Agreement (NAFTA)." *International Legal Materials* 32 (May 1993): 605.

United States-Mexico-Canada. "Agreement between the United States of America, the United Mexican States and Canada (USMCA)." ustr.gov, July 2020. https://ustr.gov/trade-agreements/free-trade-agreements/united-states-mexico-canada-agreement/agreement-between.

United States-Colombia. "United States-Colombia Free Trade Agreement." ustr.gov, November 2006. https://ustr.gov/trade-agreements/free-trade-agreements/colombia-tpa/final-text.

United States-Israel. "Agreement on the Establishment of a Free Trade Area between the Government of Israel and the Government of the United States of America." ustr.gov, 1985. https://ustr.gov/sites/default/files/files/agreements/FTA/israel/Israel%20FTA.pdf.

United States-Korea. "Free Trade Agreement between the United States of America and the Republic of Korea" (KORUS). United States Trade Representative, January 2019. https://ustr.gov/trade-agreements/free-trade-agreements/korus-fta/final-text.

United States-Peru. "United States-Peru Free Trade Agreement" (United States-Peru FTA). United States Trade Representative, 2009. https://ustr.gov/trade-agreements/free-trade-agreements/peru-tpa/final-text.

Van de Graaf, Thijs, and Harro van Asselt. "Introduction to the Special Issue: Energy Subsidies at the Intersection of Climate, Energy, and Trade Governance." *International Environmental Agreements: Politics, Law and Economics* 17, no. 3 (June 1, 2017): 313–26. https://doi.org/10.1007/s10784-017-9359-8.

Vaughan, Adam. "Earth Day: Leading Scientists Say 75% of Known Fossil Fuels Must Stay Underground." *The Guardian,* April 22, 2015, sec. Environment. https://www.theguardian.com/environment/2015/apr/22/earth-day-scientists-warning-fossil-fuels-.

Vawda, Yousuf, and Brook Baker. "COVID-19: The Time for Procrastination over Patents Is Over." *Spotlight* (blog), April 20, 2020. https://www.spotlightnsp.co.za/2020/04/20/covid-19-the-time-for-procrastination-over-patents-is-over/.

Viterbo, Annamaria. *International Economic Law and Monetary Measures.* Elgar International Economic Law Series. UK: Edward Elgar, 2012. https://www.e-elgar.com/shop/usd/international-economic-law-and-monetary-measures-9781848446342.html.

Voon, Tania. "Balancing Regulatory Autonomy with Liberalisation of Trade in Services: An Analytical Assessment of Australia's Obligations under Preferential Trade Agreements." *Melbourne Journal of International Law* 18, no. 2 (December 2017): 373.

Voon, Tania, and Alan Yanovich. "The Facts Aside: The Limitation of WTO Appeals to Issues of Law." *Journal of World Trade* 40, no. 2 (2006): 239–58.

Wade, Robert Hunter. "What Strategies Are Viable for Developing Countries Today? The World Trade Organization and the Shrinking of 'Development Space.'" In *Putting Development First: The Importance of Policy Space in the WTO and International Financial Institutions,* edited by Kevin P. Gallagher. London: Zed Books, 2005.

Waibel, Michael. "Opening Pandora's Box: Sovereign Bonds in International Arbitration." *American Journal of International Law* 101, no. 4 (October 2007): 711–59. https://doi.org/10.1017/S0002930000037702.

———. *Sovereign Defaults before International Courts and Tribunals.* Cambridge Studies in International and Comparative Law. Cambridge, NY: Cambridge University Press, 2011. https://doi.org/10.1017/CBO9780511974922.

Wang, Katherine. "The China Drug Administration Proposes a Working Procedure for Pharmaceutical Study Data Protection." Ropes&Gray Newsroom Alert, May 8, 2018. http://www.ropesgray.com/en/newsroom/alerts/2018/05/The-China-Drug-Administration-Proposes-a-Working-Procedure-for-Pharmaceutical-Study-Data-Protection.

Weiss, John. "Export Growth and Industrial Policy: Lessons from the East Asian Miracle Experience." In *LAEBA 2005 Second Annual Meeting.* Buenos Aires, Argentina, 2005. https://publications.iadb.org/publications/english/document/Export-Growth-and-Industrial-Policy-Lessons-from-the-East-Asian-Miracle-Experience.pdf.

Wellhausen, Rachel L. "Recent Trends in Investor–State Dispute Settlement." *Journal of International Dispute Settlement* 7, no. 1 (March 1, 2016): 117–35. https://doi.org/10.1093/jnlids/idv038.

Westmoreland Mining Holdings LLC v. Government of Canada—Canada's Statement of Defense, italaw.com (International Centre for the Settlement of Investment Disputes 2020).

White Industries Australia Ltd. v. The Republic of India (UNCITRAL 2011).

Whitley, Shelagh, and Laurie van der Burg. "Fossil Fuel Subsidy Reform: From Rhetoric to Reality." Working Paper. London: New Climate Economy, 2015.

Wiedenbrüg, Anahi Elisabeth. "What Is Really Owed: Structural Injustice, Responsibility, and Sovereign Debt." D Phil, London School of Economics, 2018. http://etheses.lse.ac.uk/3793/1/Wiedenbru%CC%88g__what-is-really-owed.pdf.

Williams, Heidi L. "Intellectual Property Rights and Innovation: Evidence from Health Care Markets." *Innovation Policy and the Economy* 16 (2016): 53–87. https://doi.org/10.1086/684986.

Wolff, Alan Wm. "COVID-19 and the Future of World Trade." Remarks by Deputy Director General Wolff presented at the Webinar—Korean International Trade Association, Geneva, May 27, 2020. https://www.wto.org/english/news_e/news20_e/ddgaw_27may20_e.htm.

Working Group on Trade, Investment Treaties and Access to Medicines. "Rethinking Trade Treaties and Access to Medicines: Toward a Policy Oriented Research Agenda." Workshop Report. Global Development Policy Center, October 2019. http://www.bu.edu/gdp/files/2019/11/Trade-Report-2019-GDP-Center-3.pdf.

World Bank. "Content of Deep Trade Agreements," 2017. https://datacatalog.worldbank.org/dataset/content-deep-trade-agreements.

World Bank. "World Development Indicators." World Bank Data Catalogue, 2018. https://datacatalog.worldbank.org/dataset/world-development-indicators.

World Health Organization, World Intellectual Property Organization, and World Trade Organization, eds. *Promoting Access to Medical Technologies and Innovation: Intersections between Public Health, Intellectual Property and Trade.* 2nd edition. Geneva: WHO, WIPO & WTO, 2020. https://www.who.int/publications-detail-redirect/9789240008267.

World Trade Organization. "Agreement on Trade-Related Aspects of Intellectual Property Rights." Marrakesh Agreement Establishing the World Trade Organization, Annex 1C, Legal Instruments—Results of the Uruguay Round, *International Legal Materials* 33 (April 15, 1994): 1197.

———. "Declaration on the TRIPS Agreement and Public Health." Doha, Qatar: World Trade Organization, November 20, 2001. https://www.wto.org/english/thewto_e/minist_e/min01_e/mindecl_trips_e.htm.

———. "General Agreement on Trade in Services (GATS)." Marrakesh Agreement Establishing the World Trade Organization, Annex 1B, Legal Instruments—Results of the Uruguay Round, *International Legal Materials*, 33 (April 15, 1994): 1125.

———. "International Trade and Tariff Data," 2019. https://www.wto.org/english/res_e/statis_e/statis_e.htm.

———. "WTO Contribution to the United Nations 2020 High Level Political Forum." Geneva: United Nations, 2020. https://sustainabledevelopment.un.org/content/documents/26126WTO_HLPF_Input_2020.pdf.

———. "WTO Legal Texts," 1994. http://www.wto.org/english/docs_e/legal_e/legal_e.htm.

Wouters, Jan, and Dominic Coppens. "Gats and Domestic Regulation: Balancing the Right to Regulate and Trade Liberalization." In *The World Trade Organization and*

Trade in Services, 205–64. Brill/Nijhoff, 2008. https://brill.com/view/book/edcoll/9789047431404/Bej.9789004162440.1-1024_007.xml.

Wu, Mark. "Intellectual Property Rights." In *Handbook of Deep Trade Agreements*, edited by Aaditya Mattoo, Nadia Rocha and Michele Ruta. Washington, DC: World Bank Group, 2020.

Young, Margaret A. "Energy Transitions and Trade Law: Lessons from the Reform of Fisheries Subsidies." *International Environmental Agreements: Politics, Law and Economics* 17 (March 9, 2017): 371–90. https://doi.org/10.1007/s10784-017-9360-2.

Yu, Peter K. "TRIPS and Its Discontents." *Marquette Intellectual Property Law Review* 10 (2006): 369.

Zettelmeyer, Jeromin, Christoph Trebesch and Mitu Gulati. "The Greek Debt Restructuring: An Autopsy." *Economic Policy* 28 (January 1, 2013): 513–63. https://doi.org/10.1111/1468-0327.12014.

Zucman, Gabriel. "Global Wealth Inequality." *Annual Review of Economics* 11, no. 1 (2019): 109–38. https://doi.org/10.1146/annurev-economics-080218-025852.

INDEX

African Continental Free Trade Agreement
(AfCFTA) 21, 30, 79, 101
Agreement on Subsidies and
Countervailing Measures (SCM
Agreement) (WTO) 25, 132, 142
Andean Community trade agreement
21, 92
Arbitration, Investor–State 36, 80–1,
112–13, 120, 150
Argentina 2, 5, 26, 108–9
debt restructuring 9, 103, 115
flexibility in TRIPS 48
industrialization outcomes 146
investor–state disputes 110–12
Italy–Argentina BIT 111

balance of trade 11
bilateral investment treaties (BITs) 1,
6, 32, 54, 77–8, 104–5
framework for measuring 85
Brazil 15, 48, 77–78, 107
Brazil–Chile Free Trade Agreement 140
local content requirements 131
opposition to reducing protections of
service sectors 26
Secretariat of Health, Science,
Technology and Strategic Inputs 46
Bretton Woods meetings 17
Brexit 117

Cameroon 76
BITs w/ 76
Canada 12, 30, 59, 131, 137
export-based license 53
domestic regulation 30
local content requirements 131

Canada-FIT 132–34
Canada–United States Free Trade
Agreement 4
capacity building 7–10, 146–7, 150–53
capital flow
liberalization 86
regulation 83
Chile 146
trade liberalization 5
China 58
as emerging market 107
economy 24
FTAs
–Georgia free trade agreement 30
local content requirements 131
policy, industrial and trade 14
RCEP 21, 80–81, 117, 118t6.4, 119
renewable energy industry 128, 132
trade war 6
climate change 6, 9, 38, 60, 125–41
Climate Leadership Plan, Alberta 137
Colombia 59
2007 regulations 84
Committee on Regional Trade
Agreements 16
Comprehensive Economic Trade Agreement
(CETA, Canada-EU) 70, 149
Comprehensive and Progressive Trans-
Pacific Partnership (CPTPP) 20, 30–
31, 69, 72, 79, 101, 117, 122, 142
concession agreements 65, 68–70, 74,
76, 80–81
Councils on Trade in Goods and Trade in
Services 38
COVID-19 pandemic 8, 38, 41–45, 53,
81–82, 103, 125, 146

Czech Republic 143, 146
 ECT 134–36

Deep Trade Agreements project 87
diversification and development 1, 7, 9,
 12–13, 27, 38, 61, 64, 126–30, 142,
 146, 151
Doha Declaration 46, 51
Doha Round (2001) 147
domestic regulation 25, 29–33, 66, 86,
 138, 147
duty drawback, example of WTO-
 compliant policy 24–25

East Asia
 industrial policy 5, 24
 states 61
Ecuador 108
Ecuador–European Free Trade Area
 (EFTA) 140
Egypt 99
emerging markets 14, 83, 107
Ethiopia 75
 bilateral investment w/ 76
Europe 42, 44, 61, 133
European Union 8, 12, 26, 70, 111
 economic partnership agreements 21,
  79, 101, 141
 Energy Charter Treaty (ECT) 134
 new service rules 27–29
 renewable energy directive 133
 treaties w/ 17, 35
 Environmental Goods Agreement (EGA)
  139, 141
 Free Trade Association 54
 intra-EU investment treaties 67, 136
European Commission 111, 136
European Court of Justice (2018) 136
European Union (EU) treaties
 EU–Japan Economic Partnership
  Agreement 141
 EU–Mexico tariff elimination
  schedule 21
 EU–Morocco treaty 99
 EU–Singapore treaty 143
 EU–Vietnam treaty 79
expropriation, indirect and direct 80, 105,
 110, 114, 123, 138–40

fair and equitable treatment (FET) 32, 35,
 69–72, 76, 78, 105, 110, 115, 133–37
financial crisis
 2008 5, 9, 62, 81, 84, 101, 110
 East Asia 5
foreign direct investment (FDI) 31–32, 61,
 64–65, 94, 96, 100, 102
fossil fuels 2, 127–29
 subsidies 129–30
 subsidy challenges WTO dispute
  settlement body 130
full protection and security 72, 76

General Agreement on Tariffs and Trade
 (GATT) 3–5, 132–33, 148
 3 pillars 17
 Article XXIV 4, 16
 decision on "differential and more
  favorable treatment" 16
 negotiations 126
 quantitative restriction policies
  18, 22, 32
General Agreement on Trade in Services
 (GATS) 16, 25–31, 44
 Article V 16
 Article VI 86
GATS+ commitments 27
Georgia (country of) 30
Germany–Czech bilateral investment
 treaty 135
Global South ii, 26, 93, 100
global trading system 1
Greece 2, 9, 110–11
 Economy 112
Greece–Slovakia bilateral investment
 treaty 111
Greek Bondholder Act 111
green economy 6
green industrial policies 9, 126–27, 143
group of 7 (G-7) 107

Hong Kong multilateral accord for service
 suppliers 26
hyper-globalization 6–7

India 24, 46, 48, 77, 119, 128, 131, 133
 opposition to reducing protections of
  service sectors 26

Indonesia 15, 146
  Netherlands–Indonesia BIT 36
International Monetary Fund (IMF) 8, 17,
      83–87, 102, 107, 111
International Investment Agreements
      (IIAs) 9, 32–33, 67, 103
International Law Commission 104
International Trade Organization 17
intellectual property (IP) 4, 8, 16, 47
  as form of investment 41
  law 2
  protection 5, 54, 67
  rights 4, 6, 12
  rules 45, 67
  standards 3
investor–state concession
      agreements 68–69
investor–state dispute settlement (ISDS)
      6, 10, 31, 33–34, 36, 58, 60, 66–67,
      76, 78, 80, 88, 91, 98, 110, 117–22,
      136–38, 141, 148
investor–state tribunals 59, 70–71, 90,
      110–12, 115, 122–23, 134–37,
      145, 149
Italy–Argentine bilateral investment
      treaty 110

Japan 30–31, 35, 72, 77–78, 132
  EU–Japan Economic Partnership
      Agreement 141
  right of establishment to foreign
      investors 78
Joint Initiative in Services Domestic
      Regulation, improvements to GATS
      rules 30

Kenya 117
Keynes, John Maynard 84
Keystone Pipeline, TransCanada/USA 137
KORUS 117

labor rights 8, 65–66
land
  conflicts 73–74, 77
  governance 68, 74
  investment 66, 68–70, 74, 77–78, 80–82
  laws 72
  rights 68, 75

Latin American debt crisis (1980s)
      103, 106
least developed countries (LDCs) 47,
      146, 151
list schedules, Positive and Negative
      26, 28, 31
local content 23, 38, 130–33, 141

Malaysia
  and Asian Financial Crisis 84
  BIT 76
market failures 12–15, 83, 128
Medecins Sans Frontieres 46
mega-regional trade agreements 145, 147
MERCOSUR, Southern Common
      Market 21
Mexico 5, 107, 146
  EU–Mexico tariff elimination
      schedule 21
  Financial Crisis (1994) 107
Morocco 99, 112
most favored nation (MFN) clause 16, 93–
      94, 97–99
  MFN treatment standard 17, 19, 28, 69,
      79, 86, 117, 139
  MFN violations 118
Mozambique 77–78
  BITs w/ 77
multilateral accord 26
multilateral climate change
      conventions 140
multilateral commitments/cooperation 4,
      60, 145
multilateral institutions 120
multilateral investment court 149
multilateral level 7, 67
multilateral negotiations 96, 148, 150
multilateral trade agreements 1, 147
multilateral rules 17, 19, 30
multilateral trade system 16, 47, 143

national treatment provisions 114
neoclassical trade theory 12, 114
neoliberalism 11, 146
Netherlands 138
  Netherlands–Indonesia Bilateral
      Investment Treaty (1968) 36
Nicaragua 75

Nigeria 15
North American Free Trade Agreement
      (NAFTA) 4–5, 34, 69, 133, 137

Oxfam 46

patent protection 2, 42, 44, 47, 57, 59
pharmaceutical
   MNCs 46, 58
   patents 47, 53, 59, 146
preestablishment rights 69, 78–79
price volatility 13
public health 44, 46, 53, 58, 60, 72, 82
   crisis 41, 51, 73
   impacts 43

quantitative restrictions 18, 22, 32

Regional Comprehensive Economic
      Partnership (RCEP) 21, 69, 80, 101,
      117, 119
renewable energy 2, 9, 126, 127–34,
      140–43, 152
   market 127
Ricardo, David 12
right of establishment to foreign investors
      32, 35, 105, 113, 118
Rodrik, Dani 6, 143
Rwanda 53

Salini v. Morocco 112
service sector, modes of supply 26, 27
Siegel, Deborah, former. senior
      council, IMF 87
Singapore 67, 141
   EU–Singapore treaty 143
   multilateral accord for service
      suppliers 26
South Africa 46, 131
   BIT/w Ethiopia 76
   WTO 53
Southern African Development
      Community (SADC) 79–81
South America 5, 61, 95
Southeast Asia 61
South Korea 14, 21, 146
South–South trade agreements 12,
      17, 21

sovereignty 2, 6, 10, 11, 81, 90, 120
sovereign debt restructuring (SDR) 7, 9,
      103, 106–7, 109, 123
Spain 131, 134–36, 138, 143
special economic zones 23–25
   and preferential tariff treatment 23
Stiglitz, Joseph 127
Sub-Saharan Africa 61

Taiwan 5, 14
Tariffs (bound and applied rates) 20
trade rules 1, 3–4, 7, 15, 17, 25, 38, 60
TRIMs Agreement, WTO Agreement on
      Trade-Related Investment Measures
      31–34, 132
TRIPS Agreement, WTO Agreement
      on Trade-Related Aspects of
      Intellectual Property Rights 44,
      46–47, 51–53
   Article 27, 48
   Article 30, 56–57
   Article 31, 101
   Article 39, 52
   TRIPS-plus 54

United Kingdom 6, 11
Ukraine 59
United States 27, 30–31, 35, 44, 54, 59,
      61, 70, 87, 90, 103, 107,
      132–33, 148
   BIT w/ Cameroon 76
   BIT w/ Mozambique 77
   Brady Plan 106
   COVID-19 42
   dissent to WTO reform 131
   Green New Deal 125
   Keystone XL 137
   multilateral accord for service
      suppliers 26
   withdraw from TPP 101
United States–Mexico–Canada Agreement
      (USMCA) 11, 30–31, 69, 111,
      117–18, 140
Uruguay Round 3–4, 147

Vietnam 67
   Bank for Social Policies 78
   BIT w/ EU 79

import substitution industrialization
    policies 78
Voluntary Guidelines on the Responsible
    Governance of Tenure of Land,
    Fisheries and Forests 68

World Bank 17, 36, 84, 87, 102, 126
World Trade Organization (WTO) 2, 3,
    4, 16, 19, 23, 28, 34, 43, 47, 51, 53,
    104, 126, 130, 138, 141, 145, 147
  agreements 42, 148
  dispute settlement body 6, 27, 86, 142

extra-WTO treaties 34–35, 54
Moratorium on Customs Duties on
    Electronic Transmissions 37
nondiscrimination cases 131
reform 67, 141
Regional Trade Agreements database 87
'single undertaking' 16, 44
subsidies rules 24–25
tariff commitments 2–4, 17–20, 37, 139
Trade Facilitation Agreement (Bali,
    2013) 150
World War II 5